AF600586

WRITING BELOVEDS

Humanist Petrarchism and the Politics of Gender

AILEEN A. FENG

Writing Beloveds

Humanist Petrarchism and the Politics of Gender

UNIVERSITY OF TORONTO PRESS
Toronto Buffalo London

Toronto Buffalo London
www.utppublishing.com

ISBN 978-1-4875-0077-1

Toronto Italian Studies

Library and Archives Canada Cataloguing in Publication

Feng Aileen A., author
Writing beloveds : humanist Petrarchism and the politics of gender / Aileen A. Feng.

(Toronto Italian studies)
Includes bibliographical references and index.
ISBN 978-1-4875-0077-1 (cloth)

1. Petrarca, Francesco, 1304–1374 – Influence. 2. Italian poetry – 16th century – History and criticism. 3. Petrarchism. 4. Humanism in literature. 5. Politics in literature. 6. Sex roles in literature. I. Title II. Series: Toronto Italian studies

PQ4103.F45 2016 851'409 C2016-904897-7

This book has been published with the financial assistance of The Provost's Author Support Fund at the University of Arizona, and a Book Subvention Award from the Medieval Academy of America.

University of Toronto Press acknowledges the financial assistance to its publishing program of the Canada Council for the Arts and the Ontario Arts Council, an agency of the Government of Ontario.

Canada Council for the Arts Conseil des Arts du Canada

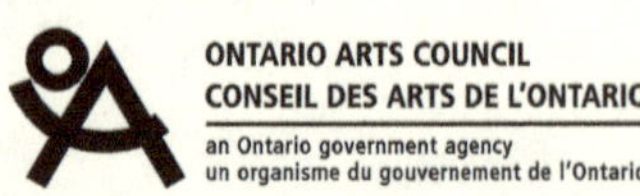

Funded by the Government of Canada Financé par le gouvernement du Canada

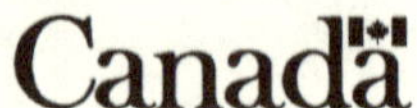

For Paul

Contents

Abbreviations

EpGr	Poliziano, *Angeli Politiani liber epigrammatum Graecorum*
Fam.	Petrarca, *Familiares* (*Rerum familiarium libri*)
RVF	Petrarca, *Rerum vulgarium fragmenta*
Rime	Bembo, *Rime* (1530)

Acknowledgments

It gives me great pleasure to thank and acknowledge all of the people and various communities who have supported me in the writing of this book. First, I must thank those who have supported me from the earliest stages of my career. Daniela Bini first introduced me to Petrarch's poetry as an undergraduate, igniting a passion in me that would forever change the course of my professional career. JoAnn DellaNeva opened my eyes to the richness of the Pléiade poets and to Petrarch's influence beyond the Italian borders. I am indebted to Albert Ascoli, Steven Botterill, Tim Hampton, and Barbara Spackman for their guidance and all manner of advice during my doctoral studies and beyond. Likewise, my fellow Berkeley *italianisti* were a source of continual intellectual stimulation, while providing much-needed social diversion and support at just the right moments: Andre Barashkov, Angela Matilde Capodivacca, Jonathan Combs-Schilling, Susan Gaylard, Amyrose Gill, Janaya Lasker-Ferretti, Tony Martire, Scott Millspaugh, Tamao Nakahara, Jessica Otey, Marco Ruffini, Nora Stoppino, Silvia Valisa, Maurizio Vito, Karina Xavier, and Irene Zanini-Cordi. A special *grazie del cuore* to Stephanie Malia Hom, Rhiannon Welch, and Rebecca Falkoff – my *muliebris respublica* and partners in crime. My studies at Berkeley were enhanced by other close friends and colleagues whom I still hold dear: Mark and Kimberly Allison, Penelope Anderson, Craig Davidson, Alan Drosdick, Sarah Engel, Mia Fuller, Stephanie Green, Kristine Ha, Slavica Naumovska, and Rob Schipano.

While writing a monograph is a solitary and often isolating experience, I greatly benefited from the many conversations I had about this project with trusted friends and colleagues alike. I would like to thank Susan Gaylard and Nora Stoppino, who provided invaluable critiques of my book project in the early stages of the writing process. Unn Falkeid, Faith Harden, Paul Hurh, Silvia Valisa, and Gur Zak read and meticulously commented on chapter drafts. The two anonymous readers for the University of Toronto Press gave generous and thoughtful feedback that helped me to see more clearly the project from an external perspective. Their insights have undoubtedly made this book better. I am also grateful to Beppe Cavatorta, David Lummus, and Maurizio Vito for their help with my translations, though any errors remain my own. My Hellenist colleague and friend John Bauschatz provided the English translations of Poliziano's and Alessandra Scala's Greek epigrams, which are part of our current collaboration on an English translation and edition of Poliziano's Greek poetry. Finally, working with the University of Toronto Press has been one of the best editorial experiences I could imagine, thanks to the expert guidance of Suzanne Rancourt. She has been a great supporter of this project from the beginning, an indispensable interlocutor during the revisions process, and a steadying hand throughout. Special thanks go to Anne Laughlin, who shepherded this book through production, Margaret Allen for her keen eye and invaluable revisions during copy-editing, and TextFormations for building the index to this book.

I could not have survived the Arizona summers and the so-called "dry heat" without the support of my earliest Tucson friends and colleagues – Megan Campbell, Andrea Dallas, Juan Diaz, Allison Dushane, Mike and Laura Lippman, Clint McCall, Ander Monson, Manuel Muñoz, and Jonathon Reinhardt – who share in my every success. My colleagues in the Department of French and Italian at the University of Arizona have been a continual source of support for me. I want to especially thank Lise Leibacher – senior faculty mentor *par excellence*, cherished colleague, and friend – who has had my back from the first day I stepped onto campus and whose own professional successes inspire me. *Je te remercie du fond du cœur.*

I would like to thank my family for their immeasurable support and love: my parents, David and Liana Astorga Feng, who instilled in me a passion for reading and other cultures; and my brother and sister-in-law, Nick and Meredith Feng, and twin nieces, Harper and Hayden, for keeping me grounded and constantly entertained. Rob and Tracy Hurh Prescott have been my strongest supporters from among my in-laws, and for that I thank them.

Finally, Paul Hurh has been on this journey with me since we first met on the steps of Dwinelle Hall in the summer of 2002. He read more of this manuscript than should ever be asked of an academic spouse, without giving it a second thought. I will never be able to fully express my gratitude for his unwavering support, optimism, and love. He is my North Star, in more ways than one.

WRITING BELOVEDS

Humanist Petrarchism and the Politics of Gender

Introduction

Itaque tibi spondeo fide Athica … tibi iuro me tuam dulcem memoriam inter arcana pectoris servare.

I promise you, therefore, with Attic faith – in the event you would not believe me without this vow – by wind and earth I swear to you that I preserve your sweet memory within the secret places of my heart.[1]

Lauro Quirini to Isotta Nogarola, mid-1400s

Sollicitata precibus tuis, non potui non obtemperare tibi, Germana, cujus ad amatum vultu[m], atque ordinatos mores ante animu[m] semper fero.

While I have worried about your request, I could not refuse to oblige you, sister, whose dear face and orderly ways I always carry with me in my heart.[2]

Laura Cereta to Nazaria Olympica, 1486

La vostra immagine, come che io l'abbia sempre nel cuore, pure ho io carissima sopra quanti doni ebbi giammai.

Your image, despite my always carrying it in my heart, I truly cherish more than any other gift I have ever received.[3]

Pietro Bembo to Maria Savorgnan, 1500

I carry your image in my heart. In three very different letters of early modern Italy, one to an intellectual peer, another to a friend, and the third to a lover, this singular conceit emerges as a point of intersection and intertextual resonance, pursuing different aims through a single model: Italian poet laureate Francesco Petrarca's lyrical model of unrequited love. When Petrarch described his beloved Laura as "'l bel viso leggiadro che depinto / porto nel petto, e veggio ove ch'io miri" ("that lovely smiling face, which I carry painted in my breast and see wherever I look"),[4] he turned the figure of the unattainable beloved into the ubiquitous source of poetic inspiration. This conversion – turning person to image, image to possession, and possession to projection – underlies Petrarch's tremendous influence on Renaissance poetics throughout Europe. Thus when these three letters invoke that trope, they also elicit other defining characteristics of Petrarch's love poetry: the silent, chaste beloved's war against the wounded poet-lover, the tension between sacred and profane love, the paradoxical state of inner turmoil that can only be expressed through oxymora, and idealized female beauty and virtue. *I carry your image in my heart* is a declaration of Petrarchan love and all that it entails.

In each of the three epistolary excerpts above, the imitation of this iconic Petrarchan trope is uniquely unexpected. The fifteenth-century humanists Lauro Quirini (1420–75) and Laura Cereta (1469–99) translate vernacular lyric verses into Ciceronian Latin and apply them to their respective social realities. Yet the humanist epistle, a genre formed to showcase the author's command of classical studies and Latin composition, is an unconventional place to find lyrical professions of devotion that stem from the vernacular tradition. The original intent of Quirini's letter was to praise Isotta Nogarola's humanistic accomplishments and the female intellect and to establish an intellectual correspondence with the learned woman. Yet, in doing so he portrays a humanist Nogarola alongside a lyrical Petrarchan one, describing a curious hybrid figure who can both inspire love and letters and also speak back to him as an intellectual peer. She becomes his "interactive muse," a speaking, reasoning, and intellectually attainable beloved.[5] Quirini portrays her as such despite the fact that the social context of Latin humanism – intellectual exchange between educated men and women – is completely foreign to the Petrarchan original, which reifies the one-way relationship between the sexes: Petrarch speaks; Laura is silent. Such surprising adaptation may show the flexibility of the Petrarchan conceit, but it also opens new questions. To what degree can the figure of the Petrarchan beloved be lifted from its context without bringing along with it all of the associated connotations? How could Latin humanism incorporate Petrarch's vernacular lyricism, and furthermore, why would it want to?

Similar questions might be raised by Laura Cereta's repurposing of the trope, although to a much different end. Cereta's letter is an autobiographical account of how she became a learned woman. She holds dear not just the image of her friend – Nazaria Olympica, a nun – but also her "orderly ways." Like Petrarch and Quirini before her, she draws on the theme of inspiration but transforms Olympica's face into a symbol of exemplary work ethic, rather than a symbol of desire or classical female virtues. Cereta's use of "germana" (sister) in her address to Olympica plays with the notion of sisterhood in two ways. First, taken as a title, it refers to Olympica's vocation as a nun, which includes a vow of chastity – a classical female virtue present in the figure of Petrarch's Laura. Second, taken as a term of sorority, it creates an intellectual kinship between the two women. This sense of female kinship replaces the paradigm of unrequited love, but the Petrarchan trope still communicates a strong feeling of admiration and devotion. For both Quirini and Cereta, then, Petrarch's lyric offered a linguistic and tropic model that could be adapted to fit their needs. Yet, in such adaptation, both also become sites of tension between the male-centred logic internal to the Petrarchan lyric and the early attempts to exemplify the intellectual woman in the humanist tradition.

At the turn of the century Pietro Bembo (1470–1547) – widely considered to be the "father of Petrarchism" – radically adapts the trope by applying it to his lover, Maria Griffoni Savorgnan. First, he discards the one-way nature of Petrarchan love by depicting requited love. The "immagine" (image) he describes in his letter has a double referent: Savorgnan had sent him a portrait of herself, which replicated the image he already carried in his heart. The "dono" (gift) that he holds above all others is thus both her love (symbolized by the image in his heart) and the physical portrait she has sent. Such reciprocal exchange voids the Petrarchan trope of the fundamentally unidirectional paradigm of Petrarchan love and desire founded in the *Rerum vulgarium fragmenta.* Furthermore, Bembo's allusion to Petrarch broaches a new form of proto-nationalist literary imitation. While Bembo's imitation of Petrarch's poetry in a private prose letter belies the staunchly Ciceronian position he will take in his argument against cross-genre imitation in the 1512–13 Ciceronian Quarrel, it looks forward to the most ambitious linguistic project of his career: the 1525 *Prose della volgar lingua.*[6] There he publicly called for new Italian models of imitation, replacing Vergil with Petrarch in poetry, and Cicero with Boccaccio in prose. Bembo's codification of Italian grammar and orthography based on the writings of Petrarch and Boccaccio was an attempt to politically unite Italy under a Petrarch-inspired "national" language. In the Savorgnan letters, we see that in the early stages of his career he had been privately experimenting with the real-world applicability of Petrarchan rhetoric in his epistolary correspondence with his lover.

While the letters by Quirini, Cereta, and Bembo all share a common Petrarchan trope, the more striking connection is the efficacy with which each writer adapts Petrarchan rhetoric to diverse social – rather than exclusively poetic – discourses. These early examples occur during a historical sea-change within Italian letters. With the advent of neo-Latin female humanists in the fifteenth century, classical erudition and oratory were no longer restricted to the male, elite sphere. The female humanist letterbooks display a level of erudition that places them among those of the leading male intellectuals of the century. However, there were no classical models for male-female or female-female intellectual correspondence. Thus, the frequency with which Petrarchan tropes are translated into humanist Latin leads us to several fundamental questions: How is Petrarchan imitation in real correspondence different from its poetic counterpart? How does this unconventional use of Petrarchan imitation change the contours of the later poetic movement? In what ways did the language of Petrarch mediate gendered dialogues, and what can that mediation tell us about identity politics and early modern cultural discourses? This book answers these questions by identifying and analysing what I call humanist Petrarchism: the appropriation and translation of Petrarchan poetry into Latin humanist prose during the fifteenth century.

The influence of Petrarch's poetry in sixteenth-century Europe has been widely accepted. Petrarchism – the poetic imitation of Petrarch's lyric poetry – swept across the continent and even across the ocean to the Americas, gaining a cultural capital never before seen in Western literature. The sonnet form, topos of unrequited love, and other Petrarchan conventions were adopted by poets like Shakespeare, John Donne, Pierre de Ronsard, and Garcilaso de Vega. While most studies of Petrarchism focus on vernacular poetic or other literary imitations, *Writing Beloveds* recovers the influentially gendered inflections of the earliest form of Petrarchan imitation – humanist Petrarchism in Latin – by recovering texts not normally associated with the conventions of poetic Petrarchism. This includes men's prose works *to* and *about* women, women's responses to them, and women's writing to each other. The chapters within this study thus consider not only poetry but linguistic treatises, debates on imitation, prose representations of gender, and epistolary correspondence in Latin and Italian. By discovering the literary motifs that span the gaps between women's and men's writing about gender, we can map how certain figures in Petrarch's writing transmitted gendered ideas of power that signalled an anxiety concerning the rising place of women as intellectual interlocutors, public figures, and, eventually, patrons of the arts. By focusing on fifteenth-century humanist Petrarchism, and the poetic framework through which men and women learned to engage with each other intellectually (and otherwise), this book reveals how humanist Petrarchism transmitted and reinforced prescriptive ideals about gendered identities and performance,[7] while at the same time contesting these very ideals.

Writing Beloveds concentrates on the age of neo-Latin humanism between Petrarch and the Renaissance – a period that just precedes the conventional periodization of Petrarchism. It thus expands the linguistic range, historical chronology, and social functions of Petrarchan imitation that begins in the century after Petrarch's death and then takes off as a global phenomenon in the high Renaissance. One primary objective is to reconstruct the political influence of writing on gender as Petrarchan rhetoric was deployed in real correspondence between educated men and women in the fifteenth century. In telling the story of how humanist Petrarchism emerges as a model for male-female interaction that is at hand for male humanists seeking to frame their new relation to learned women, this book focuses attention on the complex struggle to determine the significance of gender in the full range of writing within that period. It shows how Petrarchan poetic conventions were part of a social discourse that played a fundamental role in prescribing gendered identities in relation to power and agency. The socio-political consequences of humanist Petrarchism profoundly influenced Pietro Bembo's own Petrarchan poetry and linguistic treatises, placing him in the middle, rather than at the beginning, of the history of Petrarchism, broadly conceived.

This book engages with three distinct fields – Petrarchism, the intellectual history of early modern women, and gender and women's studies – yet bridges them in a new way by revealing how humanist Petrarchism mediates gendered interactions. It reveals a long history of Petrarchism that is founded on its role as a cultural rather than exclusively poetic discourse, with real consequences for emerging proto-nationalistic identities in the Italian Renaissance. Within the field of Petrarchism studies, two distinct bodies of scholarship have attempted to answer similar questions regarding the politics of gender: the poetic movement's role in the growth of early modern women's writing, and the political uses of the Petrarchan sonnet. In the first approach, scholars have investigated *how* women adapted the Petrarchan form to the female voice. Ann Rosalind Jones's groundbreaking study, *The Currency of Eros*, highlights the ways in which women's writing between 1540 and 1620 contested gender ideologies and male-authored literary conventions in England, France, and Italy.[8] She credits Petrarchism with liberating female voices and with levelling the playing field for women. *Writing Beloveds* expands and builds upon the work of Jones by accounting for gender in greater context and widening the gendered view of Petrarchism to include not only lyric works by women writers but also the considerable correspondence between men and women. In doing so, it tells the story of how humanist Petrarchism emerges as a model for male-female interaction, and how these writings constructed and reinforced prescriptive ideals about women's behaviour. The conclusions of this book are in dialogue with the research of Deanna Shemek, who has studied the ways in which issues of femininity and the threat of women's "wayward" behaviour for male identity and social order reached far beyond the border of didactic and prescriptive treatises to popular and canonical literature, the visual arts, public festivals, and actual legal proceedings.[9] This study seeks to explore the boundaries between prescriptive literature and canonical literature by investigating how, just as Renaissance Petrarchism became a transnational poetic discourse, humanist Petrarchism initially provided the framework within which men and women could define a new intellectual relationship that did not ignore the longer literary tradition that had defined the sexes in binary terms, but rather adapted it to the new social reality of women writers confronting early modern Europe.

Writing Beloveds also engages with a second critical trend in Petrarchism studies: the concern over how Petrarchan poetry could be adapted to address – directly or indirectly – social and political concerns. The ground for this question is explored primarily in Roland Greene's *Unrequited Conquests*, which exposed the use of Petrarchism in the colonialist project of exploring the Americas.[10] William J. Kennedy's more wide-reaching study of the role of the Petrarchan sonnet in expressing national sentiments uses a poststructuralist frame to show how the Petrarchan sonnet was adapted to express national sentiments while defining social class, political power, and national identity in Italy, France, England, Spain, and Germany.[11] More recently, Konrad Eisenbichler has examined how Sienese female poets in the 1530s to 1550s used the Petrarchan sonnet to express their political opinions at a tumultuous time in Siena's history.[12] The women examined by Eisenbichler discussed political events in the safe, discursive space of the lyric, divorced from Italian courtly culture, unlike their male courtier counterparts. In this light, his study both expands the work of Greene and Kennedy while also providing an interesting, gendered counterpart to the work being done in the Italian academy on the political role of Petrarchism in various court cultures. Recent work by Domenico Chiodo has shown how courtiers, advisers, and secretaries used the Petrarchan sonnet to record less-than-flattering accounts of the political nemeses of their patrons, such as Francesco Maria Molza's poem about Charles V's public humiliation at the hand of Ippolito de'Medici.[13] Stefano Cremonini has also recently focused on the role of Petrarchism in paying homage to one's patron in the funerary verses written in honour of members of such notable families as the Medici and the Sforza.[14] He has noted the contamination of the archetypical "donna-angelicata" figure made famous by Petrarch (and Dante before him) and the deceased patrons, although he does not extend his analysis to gender politics.

While closing the gap between poetry and politics broadens the field of Petrarchism, all of these studies' focus on overtly political poetry still reinforces an often-held distinction between two categories of Petrarch's poetry: amorous, apolitical poems devoted to his beloved Laura and political poems addressing patronage, Italian politics, and the church. *Writing Beloveds* contributes to this rich body of scholarship by showing how even, and indeed especially, the amorous tradition of Petrarchan rhetoric was always already political from the perspective of agency. One cannot hold apart the amorous and the political poems when, as this book shows, Petrarch's poetry often conflated the figures of his patrons with that of the beloved. Thus, the legacy of Petrarchism illuminates and extends the politics of gender that can already be found in the *RVF*. By tracing the history of Petrarch's construction of gender – power associated with men, and a lack of agency with women – through its imitation in correspondence between intellectual men and women in the fifteenth and sixteenth centuries, this book uncovers another kind of political work of the poetic tradition.

Considering the deep historical relations of gender and politics in Petrarchism may reframe questions about the intellectual history of women and feminism, identity politics, and gendered power structures. Recently, there has been a renewed interest in re-evaluating the networks of men who helped women enter into humanist intellectual circles and the publishing world – an attempt to correct earlier theories about men's roles in marginalizing women. Diana Robin was the first to look at the simultaneous emergence of female-led literary salons and "virtual" salons of women writers created by male editors of anthologies, exposing the complex network of men and women involved in publishing women.[15] Sarah G. Ross has taken a similar approach to the broader field of early modern feminism by examining the role of the "intellectual family" that enabled women to publish their work and emerge publicly as learned women under the protection of their father's households.[16] Although traditionally the history of women's writing had been seen through the lens of an exclusionary division – the intellectual woman existed either because she rebelled against men, or because of men's support – both Robin and Ross collapse the two accounts to show how the larger cultural rebellion was enabled by complex networks of men working in conjunction with women. Robin and Ross show how feminism, the female intellectual tradition, and the conception of femininity itself emerge from historically specific institutional collaborations between men and women. My work builds upon this by showing not only how Petrarchism allowed women to write but moreover how the political dimensions of its gendered poetics determined what "woman" and "women's writing" would mean, providing a crucial textured account of the origins of early modern conceptions of gender. The outcome of this study is thus a more fraught account of feminist politics and the intellectual history of women's writing, one that complicates the narrative of the birth of feminism by showing how female empowerment was from the start bound up in questions of male identity.

Scholarship in Italian studies has generally treated masculinity studies and women's studies as separate trajectories within the larger field of gender studies, with each methodology following the gender of the author under examination. Women writers are examined as having distinctly "feminine" voices and issues separate from those confronted by their male peers who, even when taking a proto-feminist stance in their writing, are understood always to be working within a masculine, patriarchal system. Traditionally, Italian gender studies as a field has thus been defined by a fractured methodology, one that accounts for only half of the problem of identity politics at any given time. Only recently have Italian studies scholars attempted to bridge the gap, a move best exemplified by the recent volume of criticism *Verso una storia di genere della letteratura italiana,* co-edited by Virginia Cox and Chiara Ferrari.[17] In the editors' introduction, Cox and Ferrari challenge the categorization of women's writing as separate from that of men, calling on scholars to account for gender in all its aspects: language use, how texts are circulated, how the relationship between the author and his/her readership is construed, and how gender is constructed in different genres of literature. Only then, when the issue of gender is viewed as a whole, rather than as a male-female binary, will we be able to understand the ways in which both men and women contributed to the formation of a history of Italian literature. Courtney Quaintance has done just that in her recent book on the Venetian dialect poetry of Domenico Venier's literary salon, where she examines their highly formalized (public) poetry against the pornographic and often violent dialect poetry circulated within their circle.[18] For Quaintance, both public and private poems work towards preserving both female virtues and male homosociality and access to power. *Writing Beloveds* responds to Cox and Ferrari's call by providing a gendered history of Petrarchism that studies the different ways in which male and female humanists engaged with Petrarchan rhetoric and tropes when forging new and unprecedented intellectual relationships with each other. This puts us in a better position to understand how Petrarchism is much more involved in the political and social world than has usually been seen. When used outside the confines of the contemplative, lyric space, Petrarchism becomes a language of mastery and power that mediates both gendered dialogues and identities in early modern Italy.

This study is split into two parts, between Petrarch and Latin humanist Petrarchism, and Bembo's inauguration of vernacular Petrarchism. The division is meant to distinguish between two distinct phases of Petrarchan imitation, both steeped in very different cultural contexts and enacted in different languages. The first part (chapters 1–3) provides a pre-history of Renaissance Petrarchism by concentrating on Petrarch and his neo-Latin humanist imitators in the fifteenth century. Chapter 1 focuses on the struggle between poetic and political agency in Petrarch's Latin works and in his vernacular lyrics, and the effect of that struggle on the construction of the gendered identities that his later imitators would recall. Petrarch's grappling with these issues of agency culminates in what I term Petrarch's "intellectual masculinity": the masculine intellect defined against powerless women and feminized men. The ramifications of Petrarch's gendered constructions inform the remaining chapters of *Writing Beloveds* by revealing how this gendered hierarchy of power is drawn out from Petrarchan tropes and rhetoric by his imitators in the fifteenth and sixteenth centuries.

The construction of gendered identities in relation to power, including the use of Petrarch's poetic language to reify these gendered constructions, is the central issue of the second chapter's analysis of the earliest examples of humanist Petrarchism: the imitation of Petrarch's vernacular poetic tropes and language in neo-Latin humanist writing. In letters addressed to Italy's first generations of women writers, male humanists translated Petrarchan amatory tropes from Italian into Latin and adapted them to praise the female intellect. These adapted translations release the latent political issues of agency and power examined in chapter 1. By recalling Petrarchan amatory tropes in their letters, male humanists echo the paradigm emerging from the previous chapter whereby the "masculine intellect" aligns learned men with power while disempowering a feminine intellectuality. These earliest examples of humanist Petrarchism broaden both the chronological and the contextual understanding of the later Renaissance poetic movement and expose it as a social discourse that mediated gendered dialogues between intellectual men and women. Turning from the question of how male humanists deployed Petrarchan rhetoric to both praise and limit the political power of women's writing, the third chapter examines women's responses to the general imitative practice. While the female recipients of Petrarch-inspired letters never replied in like manner, they did engage in a distinct form of humanist Petrarchism to establish models of female sociality, political *amicitia* between women, and marital love. These women writers adopted Petrarchan rhetoric to mount a complicated defence, accepting the praise but not the consequences. They thus challenged social, moral, and religious expectations by overturning prescriptive ideals about women, extracting the political undertones of Petrarch's poetry to carve out a space for women and women's issues in the male-dominated world of humanism.

The second part of the book moves from fifteenth-century humanist Petrarchism to its broader consequences for Renaissance humanism. Where Part I focused on the gendered politics of Petrarch's lyrics, and its appropriation by both male and female neo-Latin humanists in the fifteenth century, Part II looks ahead to the high Renaissance of the sixteenth century and Pietro Bembo – the founder of the poetic movement now known as Petrarchism. This book's fourth chapter turns to the epistolary exchange between Bembo and Gianfrancesco Pico della Mirandola during the Ciceronian Quarrel – the most influential example of the debate on neo-Latin language and imitation. Although their debate is not explicitly concerned with gender, their theorizations about Latin imitation focus on female mythology and nation building and thus offer an idealized portrait of the political uses of educated women and their place in humanist projects. This connection between women, language, and nation building looks forward to Bembo's literary friendships with female vernacular poets and his attempt to politically unite the Italian peninsula under a common, Petrarch-inspired vernacular language. The final chapter examines the two sides of Pietro Bembo's Petrarchism: the private poet-lover of his Petrarchist epistolary exchanges with his lovers, and the public poet and founder of poetic Petrarchism. His letters and poetry present a major historical innovation: the two roles Petrarch kept separate – patron and beloved – are now conflated in a single, female person. Bembo's working out of the patron-poet relationship, grounded in the question of agency, highlights that gender and politics are inherent to the Petrarchan aesthetic. The afterword explores the broader socio-political and literary ramifications of a gendered history of Petrarchism, one that includes non-poetic texts, private and public correspondence, and language treatises, and that expands the chronology of the movement.

Taken together, the chapters in this study show a long tradition of using Petrarchan rhetoric both to forge and negotiate an intellectual relationship between men and women, and to establish a new linguistic norm linked to political power and hegemony. The expansion of Petrarchism to include humanist Petrarchism nuances and problematizes our understanding of both gender politics in early modern Europe and the expansive role of poetry in determining gendered identities.

The letters that opened this book pose a fundamental question about the effect of lyric Petrarchism in the humanist period before proto-nationalism. Humanist Petrarchism shows how gender enters into politics through fundamental language use. The implementation of a new linguistic norm rooted in Petrarch's vernacular lyric poetry defines female intellectuality against masculine identity in an unsettling way. In the same way that Ciceronian Latin and its model of male *amicitia* defined homosocial relations for centuries, humanist Petrarchism became a social discourse that mediated gendered dialogues. The continuum between this early phenomenon of Latin Petrarchan imitations and Bembo's founding of the vernacular poetic movement places the politics of gender at the heart of proto-nationalist discourse. The longer history of Petrarchism is thus a gendered history. The poetic tropes that gave a voice to women in the publishing world of sixteenth-century Italy were the same ones that men had used to render women's voices ineffectual in the previous century. The social uses of Petrarchism would continue to influence not only the development of the courtly love tradition in Italy but also the broader shape of early modern poetics for which it was vital. In the end, we gain a new understanding of this crucial story in the formation of Renaissance poetics and politics, and a new measure of the reach of Petrarch's influence on early modern Italy.

PART I

Intellectual Masculinity and the Female Intellect in Humanist Petrarchism

1 Women of Stone: Gender and Politics in the Petrarchan World[1]

After the death of his brother Gherardo's beloved, Petrarch sends him a sonnet consoling him on his loss.[2] What we expect is a poem in homage to the deceased beloved and words of consolation for Gherardo's loss, yet what we encounter is something quite unexpected – a Dantean discourse on patronage and agency:

La bella donna che cotanto amavi
subitamente s'è da noi partita,
et per quel ch'io ne speri al ciel salita,
sì furon gli atti suoi dolci soavi.

Tempo è da ricovrare ambo le chiavi
del tuo cor, ch'ella possedeva in vita,
et seguir lei per via dritta expedita:
peso terren non sia più che t'aggravi. (*RVF* 91, 1–8)[3]

The beautiful lady whom you so much loved has suddenly departed from us and, I hope, has risen to Heaven, so sweet and gentle were her deeds. // It is time to recover both the keys of your heart, which she possessed while she lived, and to follow her by a straight and unimpeded road: let there be no further earthly weight to hold you down.

The first quatrain describes the death of Gherardo's beloved in a way that recalls the figure of Petrarch's own beloved, Laura: this pure soul has now taken her place among the blessed.[4] Yet the tone of the poem changes in the second quatrain, where the discourse abruptly turns to one of a political nature. Petrarch evokes Dante when he tells his brother:

"Tempo è da ricovrare ambo le chiavi del tuo cor" (5–6). These are not the words of a poet-lover lamenting the death of his beloved; rather, they belong to Pier delle Vigne (ca 1190–1240), poet of the Scuola siciliana, confidant of Frederick II, and suicide immortalized in *Inferno* XIII. The episode Petrarch cites is the one in which the damned soul uses periphrasis to present himself to Dante-pilgrim.[5] Pier delle Vigne states,

> Io son colui che tenni ambo le chiavi
> del cor di Federigo e che le volsi,
> serrando e diserrando, sì soavi
>
> che del segreto suo quasi ogn'uom tolsi;
> fede portai al gloriïoso offizio,
> tanto ch'i' ne perde' li sonni e' polsi. (*Inf.* XIII.58–63)[6]

> I am he who held both the keys to the heart of
> Frederick and turned them, locking and unlocking, so gently
>
> that I excluded almost everyone else from his
> intimacy; I kept faith with my glorious office, so
> much that because of it I lost sleep and vigor.

Pier delle Vigne does not have to tell Dante-pilgrim his name, for his identity is known through the description of his *political* role in life: he was the man who held the keys to the heart of Frederick II, the possession of which he claims gave him power over the most powerful ruling monarch during the *Duecento*. Furthermore, Pier delle Vigne's emphasis on *fede* in this passage – "cor di *Fede*rigo" (v. 59) and "*fede* portai al gloriïoso offizio" (v. 62) – attempts to recuperate his name by reiterating the faith and loyalty with which he served both his patron and his office as chancellor and secretary. He leaves out the crucial details that would explain his presence in the wood of the suicides – the accusation that he betrayed the confidence of Frederick II, his subsequent imprisonment, and his ultimate suicide – and instead focuses on his earlier political identity. Ironically, although he claims to have controlled the two keys to Frederick's heart, if we follow the metaphor to its conclusion, Frederick ultimately took back the keys to his heart, leading to Pier delle Vigne's demise.

Petrarch's citation of this politically charged episode in his advice to his brother carries with it a political dimension that raises the larger issue of power and agency. Here, love is presented as a system of patronage starkly different from the courtly love model both Dante and Petrarch had inherited: the Lady is stripped of her power over the lover when Petrarch tells his brother to take back the power over his destiny, as presumably Frederick II did in a political context. The emphasis on *fede* that we find in the Dantean passage is missing in Petrarch's advice to Gherardo – the beloved is dead, as should be Gherardo's *fede* and loyalty to her. What is implied in Petrarch's advice to his brother is that the poet himself has retaken possession of the keys to his heart and speaks from a place of wisdom, placing the poet in the position of the patron (Frederick II), rather than the poet (Pier delle Vigne), in this analogy. By likening the paradigm of love and desire to a system of patronage in such a manner, Petrarch reveals that both systems of power could be controlled by the poet-lover – not the beloved or patron – if the poet-lover were to take control away from them. Pier delle Vigne's lack of agency is a vivid and more recent reminder of the dangers of patronage than the case of Seneca, for example, whose forced suicide by Nero Petrarch laments and criticizes in *Familiares* 24.5. The figure of Frederick II, then, presents an interesting dilemma for Petrarch. On the one hand, Petrarch lauds him in *Seniles* 2.1 for having patronized the first fathers of Italian literature.[7] On the other hand, the king set in motion the events leading to the suicide of one his poets, in a manner too reminiscent of the relationship between Seneca and the tyrant Nero for Petrarch to ignore. The intertwining of the poetic and the political in Petrarch's consolation poem to Gherardo presents a counter example to the cases of Seneca and Nero. The poet is figured as more powerful than the patron, and this new hierarchy of power is co-opted to love.

The struggle between poetic and political agency that we see in *RVF* 91 plays out in myriad ways throughout Petrarch's vernacular poetry, as well as his Latin works. He presents himself as a "rosigniuol" singing under the shadow of the Colonna (*RVF* 10), a poet indebted to Robert d'Anjou, a king not yet worthy of his own epic poem (*Africa*, dedication), and an ambassador for the Visconti who is not implicated in their tyranny, despite what Boccaccio might think.[8] Petrarch's often complicated relationship to his various patrons is well documented in his works, and has been the subject of much criticism.[9] What has not been examined is the subject of this chapter: the effect of that struggle on the construction of gendered identities and their relationship to power and agency, which the poet's humanist imitators will recall in their letters to educated women in the following century.

When, as in the poem to Gherardo, Petrarch strips the beloved and the patron of the power they presumably hold over him, he creates an analogy between powerless women and male patrons, essentially feminizing the latter. This is emblematized in Petrarch's figure of Laura-Medusa in his vernacular poetry. By recovering the political origins of the Medusa myth, where the gorgon's disembodied head is used as a weapon by Perseus against his political enemies, Petrarch creates a complicated theory of poetic inspiration that reaches beyond the relationship between poet-lover and Laura-Medusa to encompass the fraught paradigm of power between poet and patron. By discursively harnessing the petrifying gaze of Medusa, Petrarch aligns himself with Perseus after the slaying, thereby denying his female beloved the petrifying agency with which Medusa is normally associated. This connection between femininity and impotence frames Petrarch's writings about patronage. Discursively feminized in his writing, Petrarch's patrons are exposed as being subject to the author's pen. Using Medusa as a figure for the poet-patron relationship not only stages the difficult relation between writing and power, but does so through a significantly gendered frame. By comparing the Medusa myth through the figures of Laura in the lyric collection and Sofonisba in the Latin epic *Africa* to the representation of his patrons in both collections, we encounter the unwitting ramifications of Petrarch's gendered constructions of political agency. This comparison pits what I term Petrarch's "intellectual masculinity" against powerless women and feminized men. As the remaining chapters of this book show, this notion of Petrarchan intellectual masculinity will later be appropriated by his male imitators in the fifteenth and sixteenth centuries.

The Politics of Medusa's Gaze and Petrarch's "Intellectual Masculinity"

In 1962, Kenelm Foster published one of the first and most often cited articles on the figure of Medusa in Petrarch's *Rerum vulgarium fragmenta*, one which continues to influence scholarship on the subject.[10] By investigating whether or not Petrarch's Laura functioned as a Dantean *beatrice* (conduit to God), or as a Medusa (obstacle to God), Foster argued for a binary opposition between the figures of Beatrice and Laura that would have the former guide Dante towards the Beatific Vision while the latter's beauty competed with it and put Petrarch's soul in danger. For Foster, Laura-as-Medusa represents Petrarch's moral arrest, particularly in the three so-called Medusa poems[11] wherein the beloved is a "mere image of the lover-obsession, almost without moral overtones" (52–3). He reads these three poems as the obstacle that Petrarch finally overcomes in the Hymn to Madonna at the end of the lyric collection (*RVF* 366). In other words, Petrarch's final turn towards the Virgin, his proclamation "Medusa et l'error mio m'àn fatto un sasso" (v. 111; "Medusa and my error have made me a stone"),[12] signifies his repentance and overcoming of Laura-Medusa, the final obstacle in his salvation. In the end, for Foster, the figure of Laura-Medusa represents the crux of a penitential theme that primarily characterizes the latter half of the lyric collection, and that permeates the *Secretum* and *Triumphi*.

In the almost half a century since the publication of Foster's article, Italian scholarship has witnessed several theoretical approaches to the figure of Medusa within Petrarch's poetics, all of which ultimately come back to the same penitential theme highlighted in 1962, and almost always in comparison to Dante's beloved, Beatrice. From theological and Dantean-inspired readings of the letter versus the spirit, to the psychosexual approach in Freudian studies and feminist critiques of the silent – yet menacing – beloved, scholars have tended to emphasize a singular episode involving the gorgon – her ability to turn men into stone and deprive them of life, like the fallen warriors Perseus encounters in her cave.[13] The fixation on Medusa's gaze and emphasis on its arresting qualities have, in part, been due to our taking Petrarch's fiction at face value: when in *RVF* 129 Petrarch refers to himself as a "pietra morta in pietra viva" (v. 51), he creates a pun on his name (*Petra-*, rock), applying the Dantean maxim "nomina sunt consequentia rerum" (*Vita nova* XIII, 4) to create a (super)natural relationship between himself and Laura-Medusa.[14] We have generally linked the pun to its logical counterpart in the figure of the beloved, since the notion that Petrarch's name identifies him as rock legitimizes his relationship to the beloved by presenting her as uniquely destined to be his beloved.[15] Yet this brings up a host of issues that are not easily resolved. If Petrarch's name is already associated with rock, then it would seem that Laura-Medusa's petrifying powers would be at best redundant. What is his fear of being turned into stone when he is already a rock? In order to assess the paradigm of power between Petrarch and Laura-Medusa, we must go to Petrarch's source for the Medusa myth, Ovid's *Metamorphoses*, and consider closely how Petrarch adopts and deviates from it.

Critics have long privileged the encounter between Perseus and Medusa as the primary source of Petrarch's figure of Laura-Medusa, overlooking details in his poems that would indicate otherwise. When, in poem 197, Petrarch claims that Laura's eyes "ànno vertú di farne un marmo" (v. 14; "have the power to turn it to marble"),[16] he describes a power that is only associated with Medusa after the slaying: while alive, Medusa has the power to turn men into stone, but it is Medusa's disembodied head, in the hands of Perseus, that has the ability to turn men into marble. The material difference between stone and marble is perhaps less important than the way the semantic difference hints at a change in Medusa's power when it is appropriated by Perseus. That is, if Medusa-as-Medusa turns men to stone, and later Medusa-as-wielded-by-Perseus turns men to marble, then the difference between stone and marble signals an alteration in Medusa's power itself by the fact of its appropriation. The implications thus lead us to an examination of Medusa's agency, intact during life, and appropriated by Perseus in death. A closer look at Petrarch's Medusa poems reveals a repetition of the detail concerning the beloved's gaze and marble and Petrarch's understanding of the difference appropriation makes in Ovid's Medusa. Readers of Petrarch vis-à-vis Ovid rarely distinguish between the scenes of Medusa's power in the myth: the encounter between Perseus and Medusa in her cave, the Perseus and Atlas episode, or the battle in Cepheus's palace. They have all traditionally been interpreted as different means towards the same end: petrification and death. While acknowledging that Petrarch knew his Ovidian subtext well, scholarship has not accounted for the multiple ways in which he engages with the differences between the Medusa myths that are recounted over the course of the *Metamorphoses*. In other words, where both Ovid and Petrarch see a multifaceted Medusa, we, as modern scholars, have seen a one-dimensional character: a morally damning figure, the idol in Foster's "cult of Laura-laurel" that Petrarch ultimately rejects for a Christian salvation.

The distinction between Medusa's agency in turning men to stone and Perseus's agency in using her head to turn men into marble is most explicit in the description of Perseus's political exploits in Cepheus's palace. There, Medusa's disembodied head is used as a weapon to immortalize Perseus's opponents as cowards in the form of marble statues. By turning his opponents into statues, Perseus creates dual-purpose monuments: they are a warning to others who might challenge him (from the Latin *moneo, monere*), and they are reminders of Perseus's victories, visual markers of his self-aggrandizement. This second point plays an important role in Petrarch's poetics, not only in the *Rerum vulgarium fragmenta* but also in the Latin *Familiares*. As shall be explored in this section, attributing to Laura-Medusa the power to monumentalize the poet in marble denies the beloved agency and power over the poet-lover, since she becomes, like Medusa, a tool in the hands of the poet. As Perseus did before him, Petrarch defeats Laura-Medusa and appropriates her agency in a move towards his own self-aggrandizement. In turn, she serves as a simultaneous source of spiritual doom for Petrarch – as we also see in the *Secretum* – and a tool towards his own exaltation.

Particularly in the opening poems of the *Rerum vulgarium fragmenta,* the Petrarchan persona that emerges from vernacular poetry is one that speaks with a distinctly different tone than the one encountered in the Latin works. The authoritative *ego* of the Latin epistles and epic is virtually forgotten in the naive, wounded, fragile, and admittedly fragmented *io* of the lyric.[17] Much like Dante's Beatrice in the *Vita nova,* Laura is often presented throughout the poetic collection as haughty and cruel. Yet her cruelty takes on many forms depending on her association with mythological figures. As Daphne, her cruelty is in her refusal to return love – a refusal for which she pays dearly when she is metamorphosed into a tree.[18] As the Medusa, she has the power to turn men into stone with her gaze. Through her association with the gorgon, Laura appears to wield and enact power over the poet-lover: she has power over his fate. When the two myths are presented together, as in *RVF* 197, "L'aura celeste che 'n quel verde lauro" ("The heavenly breeze that breathes in that green laurel"), the power of Laura's gaze becomes more powerful in its comparison to the submissiveness of Daphne:[19]

L'aura celeste che 'n quel verde lauro
spira, ov'Amor ferì nel fianco Apollo,
et a me pose un dolce giogo al collo,
tal che mia libertà tardi restauro,

pò quello in me che nel gran vecchio mauro
Medusa quando in selce transformollo;
né posso dal bel nodo omai dar crollo,
là 've il sol perde, non pur l'ambra, o l'auro: (1–8)

The heavenly breeze that breathes in that green laurel, where Love smote Apollo in the side and on my neck placed a sweet yoke so that I restore my liberty only late, // has the power over me that Medusa had over the old Moorish giant, when she turned him into flint; nor can I shake loose that lovely knot by which the sun is surpassed, not to say amber or gold.[20]

The series of Ovidian self-identifications in the quatrains presents a conflicting portrait of the relationship between Petrarch and Laura. The initial reference to Apollo in the first quatrain recalls the theme of unrequited love that has come to define the poetic collection as a whole. The appropriation of the Daphne-Apollo myth is directly linked to the poetic process through the laurel and paronomastic play on the beloved's name: "l'aura" (wind/Laura) constantly "spira" (breathes/emanates from) the "verde lauro" (green laurel). Laura, like Daphne, is figured as a living, breathing laurel tree, but in this case, the power of the beloved is analogous to a constant wind of poetic inspiration. In both readings the beloved is deprived of agency. Although the poet suffers from unrequited love, as does his Apollonian counterpart, he is not figured as being harmed; rather, he is deified.

The transition to the second quatrain, however, recalls a second Ovidian myth, which seemingly reverses the consequences that emerge from the analogy to the Apollo-Daphne myth: as Medusa, Laura is given the power to petrify Petrarch and deprive him of life, as she did to Atlas. The reference to the gorgon Medusa portrays Laura in a much different light than did the veiled association with Daphne. Petrarch aligns himself with Atlas, the strongest mortal turned to stone by Medusa in Book 4 of the *Metamorphoses*:

> viribus inferior (quis enim par esset Atlantis
> viribus?) 'at, quoniam parvi tibi gratia nostra est,
> accipe munus!' ait laevaque a parte Medusae
> ipse retro versus squalentia protulit ora.
> quantus erat, mons factus Atlas: nam barba comaeque
> in silvas abeunt, iuga sunt umerique manusque,
> quod caput ante fuit, summo est in monte cacumen,
> ossa lapis fiunt (4.653–60)

> At length, finding himself unequal in strength – for who would be a match in strength for Atlas? – he [Perseus] said: "Well, since so small a favor you will not grant to me, let me give you a boon"; and, himself turning his back, he held out from his left hand the ghastly Medusa-head. Straightaway Atlas became a mountain huge as the giant had been; his beard and hair were changed to trees, his shoulders and arms to spreading ridges; what had been his head was now the mountain's top, and his bones were changed to stones.[21]

Petrarch apparently models his relationship with his beloved on that between Atlas and Medusa: both Atlas and Petrarch are mortals subject to the supernatural powers of mythic women. Thus, in recalling this second myth, Petrarch bestows upon Laura the ability to control his fate and to transform him into something unrecognizable. Yet the parallel is not quite as clear as it first appears. The Ovidian episode Petrarch recalls in the second quatrain comes after Perseus has slain Medusa, when the gorgon has lost her own agency. In fact, Atlas is the first man to be turned to stone by the sight of the disembodied head of Medusa in Book 4 of Ovid's *Metamorphoses,* when he refuses to offer Perseus hospitality in his kingdom. In this episode, Medusa's head is used as a weapon by her slayer, whose physical strength is no match for that of Atlas, a detail that significantly alters our understanding of Petrarch's appropriation of this Ovidian scene. At first, it would appear that Petrarch is aligning himself with Atlas, the one who is turned to stone by Medusa. But when we recall that it is not Medusa herself who petrifies Atlas, but rather Perseus bearing Medusa's head, then it would seem that the compliment is backhanded. For if Laura's power is like Medusa's in this episode, then it is like that of her disembodied head: powerful, certainly, but ultimately directed and appropriated by another.

Petrarch's Medusa is less a living, threatening, powerful female agent and more a manipulated and severed head of a prior conquest. When Petrarch returns to the Medusa myth in the tercets, he figures her in the same terms that Ovid does after she is killed and her power appropriated by Perseus. So when Petrarch rhapsodizes about Laura-Medusa's petrifying gaze, we should pause when we notice that it turns him to marble rather than stone:

dico le chiome bionde, e 'l crespo laccio,
che sì soavemente lega et stringe
l'alma che d'umiltate e non d'altr'armo.

L'ombra sua sola fa 'l mio cor un ghiaccio,
et di bianca paura il viso tinge;
ma li occhi ànno vertù di farne un marmo. (9–14)

I mean the blond locks and the curling snare that so softly bind tight my soul, which I arm with humility and nothing else. // Her very shadow turns my heart to ice and tinges my face with white fear, but her eyes have the power to turn it to marble.[22]

Laura's "chiome bionde" (blond locks) are in stark contrast to the classical image of Medusa with her frightful, serpentine hair. Although at first the use of "vertú" (virtue) to describe the power of her eyes to deprive men of life through a transformation into marble seems misplaced, perhaps even ironic, it clarifies, through Ovidian intertext, that the episodes Petrarch recalls in this sonnet concern Medusa after the slaying.

By figuring Laura as Medusa after the slaying, Petrarch seems to be reserving a measure of control over her influence and her power. The change in her power's effects, from stone to marble, furthermore draws attention to the reversal of what her power represents – from the history-less void of her cave from which no man ever returns to the monumentalized fame of Cepheus's banquet. When Perseus describes the fallen warriors he sees in the gorgon's cave as he proceeds to his encounter with her – "passimque per agros / perque vias vidisse hominum simulacra ferarumque / in silicem ex ipsis visa conversa Medusa" (vv 779–81; "On all sides through the fields and along the ways he saw the forms of men and beasts changed into stone by one look at Medusa's face")[23] – the implication is that the names of the men, linked directly to fame, die with them since the only one to learn of their fate is himself about to die. It is only in Perseus's hands that the Medusa becomes a tool of immortality, as illustrated by the wedding banquet scene in Cepheus's palace in Book 5 of the *Metamorphoses*, where petrification into marble is explicitly linked to fame and exemplarity in the case of Phineus.[24] Perseus's encounter with Phineus is particularly relevant because it is the first time that Medusan petrification is linked explicitly to fame. Before Phineus turns to marble, Perseus tells him,

[...] "quod" ait, "timidissime Phineu,
et possum tribuisse et magnum est munus inerti, —
pone metum! — tribuam: nullo violabere ferro.
quin etiam mansura dabo monimenta per aevum,
inque domo soceri semper spectabere nostri,
ut mea se sponsi soletur imagine coniunx."
dixit et in partem Phorcynida transtulit illam,
ad quam se trepido Phineus obverterat ore. (5.224–31)

"Most craven Phineus, dismiss your fears; what I can give (and 'tis a great boon for your coward soul), I will grant: you shall not suffer by the sword. Nay, but I will make of you a monument that shall endure for ages; and in the house of my father-in-law you shall always stand on view, so that my wife [Andromeda] may find solace in the statue of her promised lord!" So saying, he bore the Gorgon-head where Phineus had turned his fear-struck face.[25]

Perseus promises him immortality through monumentalization, yet to an unexpected end: Phineus will be immortalized as a most timid and submissive warrior, as an example for others to see:

[…] saxoque oculorum induruit umor,
sed tamen os timidum vultusque in marmore supplex
submissaeque manus faciesque obnoxia mansit. (5.233–5)

[…] the very tears upon his cheeks were changed to stone. And now in marble was fixed the cowardly face, the suppliant look, the pleading hands, the whole cringing attitude.[26]

Even though Phineus is the last warrior standing, so to speak, implying that he was the most courageous and talented of his cohort, he will forever be remembered as a coward, and will serve as a reminder of Perseus's victory over him. The public nature of this scene is important. Medusa's lair was hidden, and the stone statuary within the cave stood as a silent testimony to the various warriors' failure to defeat the female monster. Here, however, the wedding banquet is public, and Phineus is turned into a public monument of Perseus's victory for Andromeda's significantly female gaze. By defeating Medusa, Perseus turns her passive power into an active one, turns her power to erase men by turning them into earth (stone) into his power to immortalize men by turning them into public sculpture (marble).

Petrarch's reference to this specific episode has far-reaching discursive consequences for it echoes Petrarch's writings on poetic immortality in the Latin *Familiares* 24.10, the famous Ode to Horace. In this letter Petrarch privileges the poetic plume over the tools of a sculptor:

Sculpunt que rigido marmore durius
Heroas veteres sique firent, novos,

Eternam meritis et memorem notam
Affixam calamo, nequa premat dies. (30–3)

Your pen carves ancient heroes in something
harder than marble, and, if there be any, new heroes as well
in words of everlasting and eternal praise
such as time cannot erase.[27]

By telling Horace that his pen carves ancient heroes into something harder than marble, Petrarch compares military power and poetic power. This is similar to what we witness in the Ovidian scene: military power (Phineus) confronts and loses to the power of art (Perseus with Medusa's head). In his final moments of life, Phineus is immortalized as a coward; his past military accomplishments cease to define him, and no longer carry meaning. At the heart of the Ovidian episode, including Petrarch's use of it, is exemplarity: both Perseus and Petrarch are given the power to confer immortality and create monuments. The key to *Familiares* 24.10 is recognizing that Petrarch does not make an equal analogy between writing poetry and sculpting. Instead, poetry, the written word and the page upon which it is written, is more immortal than even a sculpture.

The privileging of poetry over sculpting as an artistic medium and the power of Medusa's head recur in *RVF* 104, a sonnet addressed to Pandolfo Malatesta:

L'aspectata vertù, che 'n voi fioriva
quando Amor cominciò darvi bataglia,
produce or frutto, che quel fiore aguaglia,
et che mia speme fa venire a riva.

Però mi dice il cor ch'io in carte scriva
cosa, onde 'l vostro nome in pregio saglia,
ché 'n nulla parte sì saldo s'intaglia
per far di marmo una persona viva. (1–8)

The hoped-for virtue that was flowering in you at the age when Love first gave you battle, now produces fruits that are worthy of the flower and make my hope come true. // Therefore my heart tells me I should write on paper something to increase your fame, for nowhere can sculpture be solid enough to give a person life through marble.[28]

In this sonnet, Petrarch assumes the power he initially seemed to grant Laura through her association with Medusa by explicitly telling Pandolfo that he will honour him in verse. His power is to grant everlasting life since in the second quatrain he claims that nowhere other than "in carta" (on paper) can a sculpture be hard enough to give someone life through marble. Sculptures proper are frail in comparison to the poetic word, as he explains in the tercets:

> Credete voi che Cesare o Marcello
> o Paolo od Affrican fossin cotali
> per incude già mai né per martello?
>
> Pandolfo mio, quest'opere son frali
> al lungo andar, ma 'l nostro studio è quello
> che fa per fama gli uomini immortali. (9–14)

> Do you believe that Caesar or Marcellus or Paulus or Africanus ever became so famous because of any hammer or anvil? // My Pandolfo, those works are frail in the long run, but our study is the one that makes men immortal through fame.

Again, military power (represented by the sequence of great rulers, beginning with Caesar) is given significance only by way of the poet's pen, not the sculptor's tools. The distinction made between the two arts elevates poetry as a living monument. That is, before the slaying, Medusa purveyed a pure mortality: her gaze turned men into stone, returning them to an elemental earthiness. Her severed head, used as a tool by Perseus, allowed Perseus to fulfil the role of sculptor, yet even marble is not as durable as the poetry written by Petrarch using Laura (under the guise of Medusa's head) as a tool.

Through a series of Ovidian references, Petrarch undermines the power of Laura as Medusa by figuring her as Medusa's severed head, and presenting her as a tool used in his own poetic process. Leonard Barkan has noted that, "the Medusa, like the Daphne myth in Petrarch's hands, becomes an emblem of poetry,"[29] yet it is the nuances of the myth that have gone unnoticed by scholars; nuances, moreover, that are central to Petrarch's concerns about the power of poetic agency in fixing and altering a reputation for history. That is, Laura's role in the so-called Medusa sonnets is as her severed head – a disembodied body part that lacks agency and becomes a tool in the hands of the poet. It is not Medusa's power of petrification that characterizes Petrarch's appropriation of the myth, it is his ability to harness and wield her power.

If Petrarch is comparing himself to Perseus, then the traditional view of Petrarch as primarily being threatened by the power of the female beloved needs to be reconsidered. While he certainly presents himself as a victim to Laura-Medusa's gaze, with his salvation in jeopardy, he simultaneously harnesses her gaze to his own poetic end. To understand how Petrarch figures his conquest, like Perseus, by appropriating and instrumentalizing the power of the beloved, I turn now to Petrarch's *tenzone* with Geri Gianfigliazzi.[30] Again employing Ovid's Medusa myth, and turning on the distinction between Medusa as agent and Medusa as instrument, Petrarch's advice to Gianfigliazzi lays out the strategy for the poet's conquest of the beloved's agency through a matter of reflection. In the first sonnet of the *tenzone*, Gianfigliazzi seeks advice on how to survive the battle of love – a war he claims Petrarch has already won:

Messer Francesco, chi d'amor sospira
per donna ch'esser pur vuolgli guerrera,
et com più merzé grida, et più gli è fera,
calendogli i duo sol' che più desira, (1–4)

Messer Francesco, he who sighs in love for a lady who still wills to be his enemy, and the more he cries mercy the crueler she is to him, hiding from him the two suns that he most desires.[31]

Gianfigliazzi begins with a description of unrequited love that summarizes the power dynamic of Petrarch's entire poetic collection: Petrarch is inspired by the love of a woman who wages war on him, yet the more he is spurned, the more he desires her. Gianfigliazzi claims he is unable to win his love battle and attributes his defeat to his inability to "ragionare" like Petrarch. As we see in the tercets, Petrarch is figured as an intellectual rather than a love-sick poet:

Voi ragionate con Amor sovente
et nulla sua condition so v'è chiusa
per l'alto ingegno de la vostra mente;

la mia, che sempre mai co llui è usa,
et men ch'al primo il conosce al presente,
consigliate, et ciò fia sua vera scusa. (9–14)

> You reason often with Love, and I know that no condition of his is hidden from you, thanks to the high wit of your mind. // My mind, which has always been with him and understands him less now than at the beginning, do you counsel; and that will be my true excuse. (translation amended)[32]

Petrarch's habit of reasoning with Love seemingly protects him from perishing. The intellect is figured as Petrarch's weapon against the beloved in the war of love – a detail that recalls Perseus and Minerva's shield. Indeed, Gianfigliazzi says it is Petrarch's "alto ingegno" (high wit; 11) that distinguishes him as a poet-lover and sets him up as an exemplar for other love poets.

Petrarch's response in *RVF* 179, "Geri, quando talor meco s'adira" ("Geri, when from time to time [my sweet enemy] becomes angry with me"), continues the thread concerning wisdom ("alto ingegno"; high wit). In this poem, Petrarch recognizes the power of his beloved, under the guise of Medusa, only to then strip her of that which has heretofore defined her. In response to the question of how Petrarch manages the cruelty of his beloved, Petrarch replies:

> Ovunque ella sdegnando li occhi gira
> (che di luce privar mia vita spera)
> le mostro i miei pien' d'umiltà sì vera,
> ch'a forza ogni suo sdegno indietro tira.
>
> E cciò non fusse, andrei non altramente
> a veder lei, che 'l volto di Medusa,
> che facea marmo diventar la gente. (9–11)

> wherever she angrily turns her eyes, who hopes to deprive my life of light, I show her mine full of such true humility that she necessarily draws back all her anger. // And if that were not so, I would not go to see her otherwise than to see the face of Medusa, which made people become marble.[33]

Petrarch's eyes serve the same purpose as Perseus's shield: they deflect the harm of the gorgon's gaze. At the end of Book 4 of the *Metamorphoses*, Perseus uses the shield of Minerva – symbol of wisdom – to avoid looking at Medusa directly.[34] Thus wisdom is understood to mediate Perseus's sight during the fateful scene: his ability to look beyond Medusa deflects the gorgon's power long enough for him to slay her. Yet, in Petrarch's response, the detail concerning marble in the tercet ("'l volto di Medusa, / che facea marmo diventar la gente"; "the face of Medusa, which made people become marble") suggests he is speaking of Medusa's severed head, when she lacks her own agency. Furthermore, what is striking here is the implied repetition of the scene – he would not otherwise go to see her face if he were not certain that he was immune to her gaze – which suggests that Petrarch's power, and his immortality, rest in his ability to look at her and remain alive. He figures himself as a living marble monument, the Perseus who slays Medusa and can look at her. The consequence of this for Laura's representation as Medusa is one of agency, since Petrarch can choose when to look at Laura-Medusa. At the root of this statement is a conflicting view of poetic inspiration: despite Laura's paranomastic presence throughout the landscape, and her portrait which Petrarch carries in his heart (*RVF* 96),[35] the poet figures himself as able to seek out and refute poetic inspiration. Thus, Laura becomes the means through which Petrarch monumentalizes himself only when he sees fit.[36]

Petrarch finalizes his self-aggrandizement in the closing tercet of the sonnet, where we encounter his explicit advice to the lovelorn Gianfigliazzi:

> Così dunque fa' tu: ch'i' veggio exclusa
> ogni altra aita, e 'l fuggir val nïente
> dinanzi a l'ali che 'l signor nostro usa. (12–14)

> You therefore do the same; for I see all other help cut off, and flight avails nothing against the wings that our lord uses.[37]

Petrarch sets himself up as an example to be followed. He urges his friend not to flee, as has presumably been his custom, but instead to confront and slay the beloved-Medusa. The implication is that Gianfigliazzi's own "ingegno," like Minerva's shield, can protect him and allow him to gaze upon the Medusa without the fear of death. As a result, the figure of the beloved no longer possesses the petrifying and threatening power she seemed to have as Medusa. Laura is stripped of her agency, and Petrarch's conquest over her, through wisdom, becomes the example he provides Gianfigliazzi in the final tercet.

Petrarch's advice to Gianfigliazzi imparts the knowledge of how to harness the negative power of the beloved-Medusa into poetic productivity. Here, we confront the authoritative voice of a mature poet who has finally come to the realization that his "ingegno" could conquer the beloved and grant him the power to confer and deny immortality, much like Perseus. This is what Petrarch's later humanist imitators will draw upon – a construction I am calling Petrarch's "intellectual masculinity," wherein the male intellect compensates for the poet's vulnerability and feminization in the battle of love. As we see in *RVF* 2, Petrarch is penetrated by Amor's arrows, and figured as passive and lacking in power and agency, much like Laura throughout the poetic collection. In the Ovidian myths favoured by Petrarch, we see a clear pattern emerge: men who flee, like Actaeon, are ultimately destroyed, while those who exert agency against women are deified (Apollo) or held up as paragons of masculinity (Perseus). For poets, like Petrarch and Gianfigliazzi, intellectual masculinity combines the exempla of Apollo and Perseus into one model, rather than pitting the sword against the pen. The sonnets about Medusa, thus, become the monuments of the poet's conquest, resulting in a gendered binary that reveals the female lacking the agency that the male intellect grants to men. This sense of authority is a parody of Dante's distinction between the letter and the spirit in the Medusa episode of *Inferno* IX, since Petrarch's lesson to Gianfigliazzi (and, presumably, to the reader) is, essentially, to look behind the veil. Whereas Dante needed Vergil to cover his eyes to protect him from the vision of the Medusa, Petrarch looked at her, emerged victorious, and continued to look at her. Petrarch's use of Medusa points to a deliberate rejection of Dante's eschatological concerns embodied by the Medusa of the *Commedia,* passing directly to that other kind of immortality sought after by both poets: self-monumentality and poetic immortality.

"Il mio doppio thesauro": The Feminization of the Colonna Patrons

The previous section has shown us the way in which Petrarch undercuts and appropriates the very power that he would grant to the beloved by relying on his greatest virtue: his intellect. This strategy of reflection and instrumentalization, of turning the passive and captive beauty of poetry into an active tool of immortalization and political statement, suggests Petrarch's conception of the potential political power of poetry. We should not be surprised, then, when we discover the same strategy of appropriation and reversal in Petrarch's vernacular and Latin works dedicated to and about his patrons. Mastering that which he would appear to be mastered by, Petrarch turns to his own masters, the moneyed and powerful patrons, and enacts a Perseus-like critique and reversal of their power.

Petrarch's relationship to political figures and his involvement in a system of patronage involving families viewed by several of his contemporaries as tyrants were a concern even in his lifetime. Boccaccio famously criticized his decision in 1351 to remain under the patronage of Giovanni Visconti instead of returning to Florence where he could have officially established himself and, perhaps most importantly, received the patrimony confiscated from Petrarch's father upon his and his family's exile.[38] For Boccaccio, Petrarch's decision to remain with the Visconti implicated him in their political tyranny. The discomfort Boccaccio felt over Petrarch's political ties has been echoed in modern scholarship as well. Victoria Kirkham's recent examination of the five speeches (ca 1353–73) to "promote the politics of ruling despots" takes as its subject something that Petrarch scholars have usually ignored, since these speeches sharply contradict the carefully constructed image of the apolitical poet.[39] Scholars have preferred to take Petrarch at his word, believing in the separation between his public and private personae, as well as that between his politics and his poetry. But as Kirkham notes, "Although they [the speeches] contradict our mythic picture of Petrarch, they reflect a system of courtly patronage that would flourish in the Renaissance. 'Rhetoric was the coin that paid for his keep,' permitting him leisure for serious literary projects."[40] Kirkham's presentation of Petrarch as a courtier *avant la lettre* is a most significant contribution to Petrarch studies because it recognizes how integral a public figure Petrarch had been for several of his patrons, despite his claims to the contrary. But she, too, falls into the trap of the poet's apparent "politics of the language" – that he uses Latin to engage in politics, and the vernacular to distance himself from it – by not connecting the implications of these speeches to his larger *ars poetica.* The appropriation of the Medusa myth in his poetry offers one angle by which this connection between Petrarch's poetry and politics can be viewed. He employs a strategy of poetic appropriation in his political rhetoric when addressing or discussing his relationship to the Colonna family and to King Robert of Naples, especially. This section examines how Petrarch undermines Colonna power by contaminating the figure of the patron with that of the beloved who lacks agency. As in the Medusa poems, the poet's intellectual masculinity confronts and overcomes political power, resulting in the feminization of the Colonna patrons.

Petrarch's relationship to the noble, Roman, Colonna family is well documented throughout his poetry, particularly through the figure of the column and puns on the Latin origins of the name, Columna.[41] Beyond the word play, Petrarch's figuration of the various male family members as columns evokes the family coat of arms, which prominently features a crowned column in the centre of the herald, and can be found on Colonna buildings throughout Rome.[42] In *RVF* 10, Petrarch opens the poem by using the figure of the column as a way of praising Giacomo Colonna, and his family in general:

> Gloriosa columna in cui s'appoggia
> nostra speranza e 'l gran nome latino,
> ch'ancor non torse del vero camino
> l'ira di Giove per ventosa pioggia, (1–4)

> Glorious Column on whom rests our hope and the great renown of Latium, whom even the ire of Jove in the windy rain has not yet turned aside from the true path.[43]

Petrarch mixes the sacred and the profane in his exaltation of the Colonna family. He initially pays homage to his patron's family by emphasizing the Roman roots of the blood line: he refers to the family by the Latinized form of their name – Columna – which he connects directly to Latium.[44] This appeal to their civic and familial pride is tempered by the allusion to Christ and the pillar of Pilate when Petrarch claims that "nostra speranza" (our hope) rests on the "gloriosa columna" (glorious column). "Columna" here evokes the scene of Christ's flagellation on the column before the crucifixion: the hope of mankind resides in the man tied to the column by the Roman guards. Thus, the Colonna are figured as the saviours of mankind, in whom the hope of humanity resides. This reading elevates the family to the status of moral exemplars, pillars of strength. The power of the Colonna seemingly derives from the etymology and connotations of their name, implicitly confirming, again, Dante's assertion in the *Vita nova* that "nomina sunt consequentia rerum" (names are the consequences of things) since not even Jove can make the Colonna stray from the "vero camino" (v. 4; true path).

The indestructible quality of the "columna" recalls an important property of the laurel tree, since that tree alone is impervious to even Jove's fury.[45] Thus, the Colonna are defined by a characteristic unique to the laurel, symbol of immortality and poetic inspiration. This figuration of the Colonna as a laurel-like column introduces the role of the poet in transforming ordinary objects into sources of poetic inspiration, a theme that he develops in the second quatrain where he transforms the urban domestic space of the Colonna family into a pastoral landscape:

qui non palazzi, non theatro o loggia,
ma 'n lor vece un abete, un faggio, un pino
tra l'erba verde e 'l bel monte vicino,
onde si scende poetando et poggia, (5–8)

here are no palaces, no theater or gallery, but in their stead a fir tree, a beech, a pine – amid the green grass and the nearby mountain where we climb and descend poetizing[46]

The civic space occupied by the Colonna is turned into a pastoral retreat that inspires poetry. The Colonna palaces, theatre, and loggia are transformed into the fir, beech, and pine trees situated near a mountain that Petrarch climbs and descends while writing poetry. The culmination of images presents the poet's ability to transform the symbols that represent the civic power of the Colonna – the column, now laurel-like, and their property – into the natural elements that inspire the poet. The transformations do not end there, however, since Petrarch also transforms himself into a nightingale who occupies the same space as his Colonna patrons:

levan di terra al ciel nostr'intellecto;
e 'l rosigniuol che dolcemente all'ombra
tutte le notti si lamenta et piagne,

d'amorosi penseri il cor ne 'ngombra:
ma tanto ben sol tronchi, et fai imperfecto,
tu che da noi, signor mio, ti scompagne. (9–14)

all these lift our intellects from earth to Heaven; and the nightingale that sweetly in the shadow every night laments and weeps // burdens our hearts with thoughts of love. But so much good you alone cut short and make imperfect, for you keep yourself, my Lord, far from us.

The Colonna family, initially described as a laurel-like column among pastoral surroundings, not only inspire the poet, raising his intellect to the heavens, but, most importantly, provide him (the "rosigniuol" of verse 10) with shade. This image of the poet resting beneath the shade of the laurel is a recurrent image in the *RVF* and is typically associated with Laura. In *RVF* 30, "Giovene donna sotto un verde lauro" ("A youthful lady under a green laurel"), the image of Laura beneath a green laurel in the incipit changes in the third stanza where Petrarch figures himself as an aging poet following "l'ombra di quel dolce lauro / per lo più ardente sole et per la neve / fin che l'ultimo dì chiuda quest'occhi" (vv 16–18; "the shadow of that sweet laurel in the most ardent sun or through the snow, until the last day closes these eyes").[47] The political implications of the column-as-laurel in *RVF* 10, while echoing the lyrical Laura, also recall Petrarch's description of the laurel tree in his coronation speech,[48] delivered from atop the Capitoline Hill, seat of Roman political (rather than poetic) power. In it, Petrarch discusses the significance of the laurel as crown to both Caesars and poets, in an attempt to delineate the role of the poet in the modern city. He claims that,

> Et preterea arbor hec umbrifera et quieti laborantium accommoda unde est illud [Horace] oratii XLIIII oda "Spissa ramis laurea fervidos / excludet ictus solis" et illud eiusdem oda XLVI "Longaque fessum militia latus / depone sub lauro mea," hoc secundum. Neque hec proprietas incongrue ad cesares refertur ac poetas ut illis post bellorum his pro laboribus studiorum requies promissa videatur.

> In the second place, the laurel tree is shady, and affords a resting place for those who labor. Whence come the lines of Horace in his 44th Ode: "Spissa ramis laurea fervidos/excludet ictus solis," and in his 46th "Longaque fessum militia latus / depone sub lauru mea." Not inappropriately is this property of the laurel associated with Caesars and with poets: for it may symbolize the rest that is in store for the former after their toils in warfare, and for the latter after their toils in study.[49]

In the coronation speech, the laurel tree is figured as providing shade for the political leader and poet, both of whom are rewarded with immortality for their respective labour. In *RVF* 10, however, the poet-nightingale is shaded by the "columna" and the various Colonna civic spaces that are figured as trees. Thus, the position of the patron in the analogy has changed in the poem: the "Colonna patron" is not figured as residing under the shadow of the laurel with the nightingale (Petrarch); rather he is the source of shade. The image of the patron shading the poet recalls Servius's commentary on Vergil's first eclogue, where he interpreted Tityrus as resting under the shade-protection of

Augustus. As Annabel Patterson has noted in her seminal work on the pastoral genre and ideology, this particular Servian allegory influenced later commentaries on Vergil's *Eclogues*, as well as readers like Petrarch.[50] Indeed, Petrarch's personal copy of the *Eclogues* includes Servius's commentary, and, as scholars have noted, Petrarch heavily annotated the first eclogue.[51] Thus, on the one hand, presenting the patron as a symbolic laurel tree figuratively acknowledges his role as Petrarch's *protettore* and implies a natural relationship between the poet-nightingale and his patron; on the other hand, the patron is denied the immortality associated with the political laurel crown through military triumphs, and is transformed into a source of inspiration that enables poetic production.

By attributing laurel-like attributes to the patron-as-column, the "Colonna patron" is aligned with the figure of Daphne, and by extension, Laura. The feminization of the patron leads to a loss of agency – the Colonna, like Laura, become a tool of poetic inspiration. Petrarch does not describe the accomplishments of the Colonna in his verses; rather, he describes what they have to offer him – the means and place to write his poetry and the raw materials for his subject. While the "Colonna patron" is denied a place under the laurel tree, and the immortality associated with the political laurel crown, in *RVF* 10 Petrarch figures himself as the nightingale with the power to bestow immortality upon the patron in his poetry. Hannah (Dolora) Wojciehowski has noted a similar strategy in the *Secretum*, where "Petrarchan pastoral can be said both to deny and to legitimate the humanist's relation to power, principally by obfuscating that relation."[52] Indeed, in the sonnet addressed to Giacomo Colonna, presenting the patron as the laurel-like column figuratively acknowledges his family's role as Petrarch's *protettore*, implying a natural relationship between songbird and tree in a tranquil environment that de-emphasizes any overt political benefits from such a union. It provides a masked justification for the poet's alliance with the Colonna. Furthermore, by associating Giacomo and the Colonna family with the symbols and rhetoric normally reserved for the beloved, Petrarch privileges the aesthetic over the political. This is most clear in the final tercet of the poem, where Petrarch laments the absence of the patron as though he were Laura. Yet, it is Petrarch's overt attempt at denying a political relationship with the "Colonna patron" by retreating into the allegorical mode of the pastoral that further emphasizes the political nature of the relationship, and, in turn, transforms his poetry into a political forum, as Annabel Patterson has read the pastoral genre, as noted above.

The association between the patron and the beloved through the properties of the laurel is such that the two figures seemingly become inseparable in later poems. In "Che debb'io far? che mi consigli, Amore?" (*RVF* 268; "What shall I do? What do you counsel me, Love?"), Petrarch seeks counsel from Amore in coping with the death of Laura: "invisibil sua forma è in paradiso, disciolta di quel velo / che qui fece ombra al fior degli anni suoi" (vv 37–9; "Her invisible form is in Paradise, set free from the veil that here shadowed the flower of her years").[53] The eschatological description of the beloved presents her as a holy figure, whose beauty on earth is surpassed only by her splendour in heaven. In the middle of the *planctus*, however, Petrarch confounds the figure of the beloved with that of the patron when she is figured as a *columna*:

> Più che mai bella et più leggiadra donna
> tornami inanzi, come
> là dove più gradir sua vista sente.
> *questa è del viver mio l'una colomna,*
> *l'altra è 'l suo chiaro nome,*
> *che sona nel mio cor sì dolcemente.*
> Ma tornandomi a mente
> che pur morta è la mia speranza, viva
> allor ch'ella fioriva,
> sa ben Amor qual io divento, et (spero)
> vedel colei ch'è or sì presso al vero. (45–55; emphasis mine)

> More beautiful than ever and more queenly she comes to my mind, as to a place where she shows the sight of her is most pleasing; *this is one column of my life; the other is her bright name, which sounds so sweetly in my heart.* But, remembering that my hope is dead, which was alive while she was in flower, Love knows what I become, and, I hope, she sees it who is now so close to the truth.[54]

Although the stanza is enclosed by descriptions of the poet's "donna," her identity is called into question when Petrarch claims that his livelihood is dependent upon two columns of support: that he will see her in death, and that her name resounds in his heart. Here, Petrarch plays on the figurative meaning of the *colomna* as a support ("sostegno"), yet the allusion recalls the previously discussed "gloriosa columna" of *RVF* 10. The intertextual allusion aligns the "Colonna patron" – "in cui s'appoggia nostra speranza e 'l gran nome latino" (*RVF* 10, 1–2; "on whom rests our hope and the great renown of Latium") – and the beloved as figures that sustain his life and give hope. "Columna," like the laurel tree, now evokes not only the patron, but also the beloved, intertwining the political and the apolitical.

The conflation of the identities of the "Colonna patron" and the beloved comes to full fruition in Petrarch's *tenzone* with Sennuccio del Bene where the patron is substituted into the poems as the *love object*. Petrarch's appropriation of the poetic practice that has come to characterize a significant amount of poetry in the Duecento simultaneously reinforces his place in the vernacular poetic tradition he praises in *RVF* 70 and 287 (the latter addressed to the same Sennuccio), while setting him apart from his predecessors. That is, with Petrarch's substitution of the patron for the beloved, not only is the Petrarchan lyric explicitly politicized, but implicitly the hierarchy between patron and poet is reversed as it is expressed through the symbolic relationship established between poet and his beloved that we have been exploring in this chapter. The *tenzone* begins with *RVF* 266, sent to Cardinal Giovanni Colonna:

> Signor mio caro, ogni pensier mi tira
> devoto a veder voi, cui sempre veggio:
> la mia fortuna (or che mi pò far peggio?)
> mi tene a freno, et mi travolve et gira.
>
> Poi quel dolce desio ch'Amor mi spira
> menami a morte, ch'i' non me n'aveggio;
> et mentre i miei duo lumi indarno cheggio,
> dovunque io son, dì et notte si sospira. (1–8)

My dear Lord, every thought draws me devotedly to see you whom I always see, but my fortune (what can it do to me that is worse?) keeps me reined in and wheels me and turns me about. // And then the sweet desire that Love inspires in me leads me to death so gradually that I am not aware of it, and while I call out in vain for my two lights, wherever I am there is sighing day and night.[55]

What is most striking about the quatrains is that the language is reminiscent of the way in which Petrarch laments the absence of the beloved: although Petrarch is far from the Cardinal, the patron is constantly in his mind, urging the poet to return to him. The connection between the patron and the beloved becomes more explicit in the second quatrain with the reference to "i miei duo lumi" (7; my two lights). Petrarch typically describes Laura's eyes as lights, as we find in *RVF* 189, "Passa la nave mia colma d'oblio" ("My ship laden with forgetfulness passes"), where her eyes function as the lights guiding him to the port: "i duo mei dolci usati segni" (12; "my two usual sweet stars"). Here, however, despite Giovanni's physical absence, Petrarch claims to see his eyes "dovunque io son, dí et notte si sospira" (14; "wherever I am there is sighing day and night"). This figures Giovanni as ever-present, and a source of light and inspiration. Like Laura, he is both everywhere and nowhere.

In the sestet Petrarch turns towards the political nature of the patron-poet relationship when he presents himself as chained to both patron and beloved by different degrees of "love":

Carità di signore, amor di donna
son le catene ove con molti affanni
legato son, perch'io stesso mi strinsi. (9–11)

Devotion to my lord, love of my lady are the chains where with much labor I am bound, and I myself took them on!

Augustinian *caritas* is distinguished from *amore* at the onset of the first tercet, yet both forms of love incarcerate the poet. In the case of Laura, the symbolic nature of the chains echoes *RVF* 76, "Amor con sue promise lusingando" ("Alluring me with his promises, Love") where Petrarch is ushered into a "prigione antica" (2; "former prison") by Amor who "die' le chiavi a quella mia nemica" (3; "gave the keys to that enemy of mine").[56] The analogy between Petrarch-as-prisoner and Laura-as-jailer does not hold up in this poem, however, since Petrarch claims that he chose to be imprisoned. Whereas throughout the poetic collection Petrarch regularly depicts himself as having been captured by Laura – assaulted by Love's arrows (*RVF* 2), netted by Laura's hair (*RVF* 59, 181) – here he is very explicit in expressing his freedom of choice and agency: "legato son, perch'io mi stesso mi strinsi" (11; "I am bound, and I myself took them on!").[57] Petrarch reminds Cardinal Colonna that the powerful patron did not hunt and capture him as prey, like the beloved; rather, Petrarch chose *him*, a patron who, unlike the beloved, does not possess the keys to Petrarch's prison. The symbolic significance of the keys, as seen in the sonnet addressed to his brother Gherardo at the beginning of this chapter, makes Petrarch's assertion all the more powerful.

The subtle reminder to Cardinal Colonna about the nature of their relationship strips the patron of the power normally associated with his station and calls into question the nature of the contract between the two. The implication of Petrarch's ability to *choose* his patron is that the decision to remain under the patronage of Cardinal Colonna is his, as well. This kind of power associated with Petrarch's will is reminiscent of one kind of "rhetoric of the will" that Wojciehowski has located in the poet's writings. In her reading of *Familiares* 7.7, the letter in which Petrarch tells Cola di Rienzo that he has changed his course and decided not to join him in Rome, she notes that,

> Petrarch vacillates between two positions on the will. The first is that men – and Cola in particular – are free to control their actions and their destinies; thus humans are accountable for their morality and their political choices. The second, in contrast, is that "eternal law" or "the stars" determine the course of human events, and that there is no point in raging or struggling against what cannot be changed … This final extant letter to Cola offers a clear example of how predestinarian arguments, far from precluding human action or power, can instead be construed as liberating (their utopian dimension), extending to the believer an alternative form of mastery.[58]

We see a similar vacillation in *RVF* 266. Petrarch recognizes the inevitable relationship between poet and patron, the necessary economy of exchange between the two. But he also acknowledges and reminds the patron that ultimately the decision to remain or leave rests with the poet. Thus, the chain that binds the poet to his patron would seem to be not binding at all – nor unique. The comparison of Petrarch's enchainment to both the patron and the beloved further weakens the tie to the patron in the final lines of the poem where, again, the Cardinal is presented in terms reminiscent of the beloved:

> Un lauro verde, una gentil colomna,
> quindeci l'una, et l'altro diciotto anni
> portato ò in seno, et già mai non mi scinsi. (12–14)

A green Laurel, a noble Column, the latter for fifteen, the former for eighteen years, I have carried in my breast and have never put from me.

What further complicates the double nature of this anniversary poem is the oscillation between the masculine and the feminine in verses 12 and 13. These verses form a gendered chiasmus that obscures the identities of Laura and Giovanni, and their respective anniversaries. At first glance, it is difficult to ascertain whether "l'una" refers to Laura or the "gentil colomna" (Giovanni). The same with "l'altro" – does it refer to the "lauro verde" (Laura) or the Cardinal? Since the *tenzone* with Sennuccio has been dated between 6 April and 23 June 1345, we know that the bond to Laura is eighteen years (since he fell in love with her in 1327), and to the Cardinal fifteen years (since he entered his service in 1330). Without this information, however, the final tercet is semiotically closed, open only to Petrarch, his patron, and, presumably, Laura. The contamination of their two identities is finalized in the last verse, where Petrarch claims that he holds both of their images in his heart ("portato ò in seno") – an iconic trope usually reserved for Laura, as we have seen in *RVF* 96, 5–7: "Ma 'l bel viso leggiadro che depinto / porto nel petto, et veggio ove ch'io miri,/ mi sforza" ("But that lovely smiling face, which I carry painted in my breast and see wherever I look, forces me").

It is striking that the final tercet presents the poem in a manner similar to what we find in Petrarch's fifteen *innamoramento* anniversary poems.[59] *RVF* 266 is unique in that it commemorates a double anniversary: Petrarch's first sight of Laura, and coming under the patronage of Giovanni Colonna. This is the only anniversary poem in which Laura is presented alongside a historical person other than Christ. This makes the patron part of the circular pattern that Gur Zak has identified in the *innamoramento* anniversary poems: "the poet fashions in the collection a type of personal ritual – circular and repetitive – that elevates the event beyond the ordinary passage of time and thus allows him to arrest the flux – to endow it with meaning – just as in the case of the commemoration of the crucifixion of Christ that supposedly took place on the same day he saw his lady [*RVF* 3]."[60] We have already seen how Petrarch associated the Colonna family with Christ in the poem sent to Giacomo Colonna (*RVF* 10). Here, the Christological reference is further strengthened when the patron is brought into the Laura-Christ analogy, and the occasion of Petrarch's entrance into the Cardinal's service is elevated to the same status as the *innamoramento* on Good Friday.

There is a more sinister side to this double-anniversary poem sent to Cardinal Giovanni Colonna. The intertwining of the political and the apolitical in this sonnet undermines Petrarch's political obligations to the Cardinal while seeming to elevate his obligation to the beloved. The inclusion of specific periods of time reveals Petrarch's obligation to his beloved as a more long-standing relationship than that with Giovanni. By lowering the status of the patron compared to that of a woman, and elevating the status of Laura above the patron, Petrarch essentially places them upon equal ground. The equality of their stature is recognized by Sennuccio del Bene in his response to *RVF* 266, which he wrote on behalf of the Cardinal. The sonnet, entitled "Responsio Sennuccio nostri" and copied into Vat.Lat. 3196, exploits the double referents of Petrarch's poem by urging the poet to return to Avignon to see both the beloved ("lauro verde") and the patron ("signor nostro"). The poem first opens with an exhortation to return to see Laura:

Oltra l'usato modo si rigira
lo verde lauro, ahi, qui dov'io or seggio
et più attenta, et com' più la [Laura] riveggio,
di qui in qui con gli occhi fiso mira.

Et parmi omai ch'un dolor misto d'ira
l'affligga tanto che tacer nol deggio;
onde dall'atto suo io vi richeggio,
ch'esso mi ditta che troppo martira. (1–8)

Beyond her usual wont, the green laurel turns toward the place where I now sit, and [is] more attentive; and the more I see her the more fixedly she looks in my direction, // and it seems to me now that a sorrow mixed with anger afflicts her so much that I must not be silent; therefore I call to you from her side, for she tells me that the suffering is too great.[61]

Although Sennuccio is writing on behalf of the Cardinal, he begins the response with a reference to the beloved: Petrarch's "lauro verde" awaits his return in Avignon. What is odd about the description is that Sennuccio claims to be able to see Petrarch's beloved ("*la* riveggio"), and she speaks to him ("mi ditta"). This is the only occasion in which one of Petrarch's contemporaries writes about Laura in a poem addressed to the poet himself.[62] Here, Laura enters into an economy of desire as a kind of currency exchanged between the two poets. She is no longer just the beloved of Petrarch but also of Sennuccio since he is able to discern her feelings from her outward appearance, and is able to put her into verse.

In the tercets Sennuccio implores Petrarch to return for the sake of Cardinal Colonna, who is presented as just as special as the beloved. Just as Laura has become the beloved of both poets, so too the patron is presented as belonging to both of them:

E 'l signor nostro in desire sempre abonna
di vedervi seder nelli suoi scanni,
e 'n atto et in parlar questo distinsi;

mei' fondata di lui trovar colonna
non potreste in cinqu'altri San Giovanni,
la cui vigilia a scriver mi sospinsi. (9–14)

And our lord still abounds in desire to see you sit at his table, and I have observed this in his words and in his manner; / / a Column better based than him you could never find in five feasts of Saint John, on the eve of which I undertook to write to you.

The Cardinal, just like Laura, desires to see Petrarch return to him. What is striking is the final description of the patron as *unique*: "mei' fondata di lui trovar colonna / non potreste in cinqu'altri San Giovanni" (vv 12–13). The depiction of the patron appropriates two important details that Petrarch often attributes to his beloved. First, the uniqueness of the patron recalls the notion, in *RVF* 159, that Nature created Laura from an Idea or ideal pattern: "In qual parte del ciel, in qual ydea / era l'exempio, onde Natura tolse / quel bel viso leggiadro, in ch'ella volse / mostrar qua giù quanto lassù potea?" (vv 1–4; "In what part of Heaven, in what Idea was the pattern from which Nature copied that lovely face, in which she has shown down here all that she is capable of doing up there?").[63] By recalling this poem and appropriating the uniqueness of the beloved for the figure of the patron, Sennuccio creates the analogy that just as Laura is Petrarch's soulmate (meaning there can be only one beloved), so too is the Cardinal Petrarch's only patron.

This analogy is reinforced by a second Petrarchan echo in the assertion that no other "colonna" can be found, not even in five other St Johns ("San Giovanni"). The comparison of the patron to a religious figure initially recalls the figure of Laura in *RVF* 16, "Movesi il vecchierel canuto et biancho" ("The little white-haired pale old man leaves"),

Et viene a Roma, seguendo 'l desio
per mirar la sembianza di Colui
ch'ancor lassù nel ciel vedere spera:

così, lasso, talor vo cerchand'io,
donna, quanto è possibile, in altrui
la disiata vostra forma vera. (9–14)

and he comes to Rome, following his desire, to gaze on the likeness of Him whom he hopes to see again up there in Heaven. // Thus, alas, at times I go searching in others, Lady, as much as is possible, for your longed-for true form.[64]

In the Petrarchan poem, the poet travels to Rome in order to see Veronica's veil – the true image of Christ – but instead finds himself searching for Laura's image in the visages of others. In the analogy, Petrarch presents Laura as a Christ-figure, further elevating her status and uniqueness, much as Dante did to Beatrice after her death, in the Veronica episode of *Vita nova* XL.[65] In Sennuccio's poem, then, the Cardinal is elevated to the status of a saint (San Giovanni). Yet the intertextuality does not end here, for in the presentation of Laura as Christ and Cardinal Colonna as John the Baptist, Sennuccio puts Petrarch in dialogue with another famous passage from Dante's *Vita nova.* In chapter XXIV of Dante's *libello,* Primavera (Giovanna) precedes the "true light" (Beatrice), granting Dante's beloved salvific powers.[66] By recalling Petrarch's pilgrimage sonnet, Sennuccio provides Petrarch with his own equivalent of the Dantean episode: Laura is his Christ-figure, the Cardinal his Giovanna/Primavera (female John the Baptist).

As a final example, we turn to *RVF 269,* "Rotta è l'alta colonna e 'l verde lauro," written in honour of Cardinal Giovanni Colonna at his death (3 July 1348). In this poem, Petrarch remembers not only the death of his patron but also that of his beloved:[67]

Rotta è l'alta colonna e 'l verde lauro
che facean ombra al mio stanco pensero;
perduto ò quel che ritrovar non spero
dal borrea a l'austro, o dal mar indo al mauro. (1–4)

Broken are the high Column and the green Laurel that gave shade to my weary cares; I have lost what I do not hope to find again, from Boreas to Auster or from the Indian to the Moorish Sea.[68]

The simultaneous remembrance of the deaths of the patron and the beloved is given a poetic dimension in the second verse, where Petrarch refers to the *service* they used to provide him: they both provided him with shade. Although this line can be read as "davano conforto," as suggested by Santagata,[69] the image clearly recalls the shadow's association with death in *RVF* 30, "Giovene donna sotto un verde lauro" ("A youthful lady under a green laurel"), and Petrarch's coronation speech and its metanarrative concerning the art of poetry. Thus, both the column and the laurel tree that once provided him with poetic inspiration are now dead. As a result, the uniqueness of the beloved is undermined by the notion that she was never the only one to provide the poet with shade (i.e., she was never *unique*). Giovanni, whose identity is now contaminated with that of the beloved, loses the symbolic power that once resided in the symbol of the column, his namesake. The figure of the patron has been feminized in his association with the beloved: not only is the "gloriosa columna" now "rotta" (broken, cut down in death), but his passing is memorialized alongside that of the female beloved. While the Cardinal is certainly elevated in his alignment with the beloved, the political significance of his life and his passing are de-emphasized in the double function of the lyrical planctus.

The feminization of the patron has potentially negative ramifications regarding political power, particularly in this case where the Colonna patron is a cardinal. This is most evident in the second quatrain, where the identities of the patron and the beloved are indistinguishable, and the nature of power is addressed:

Tolto m'ài, Morte, il mio doppio thesauro,
che mi fea viver lieto et gire altero,
et ristorar nol pò terra né impero,
né gemma orïental, né forza d'auro. (5–8)

You have taken from me, O Death, my double treasure that made me live glad and walk proudly; neither land nor empire can restore it, nor orient gem, nor the power of gold.

The use of "doppio thesauro" (5) conflates the two figures into one jewel with a double *signifié*. That Laura is referred to as a gem is not surprising, since Robert Durling has noted that throughout Petrarch's works, Laura is commonly associated with topazes and diamonds.[70] Furthermore, the representation of the beloved as a precious stone is a common trope of the medieval lyric tradition, yet it is an unconventional attribution for the patron.[71] Indeed, this double jewel has the same characteristics used to describe the effect of the beloved on the poet, as Petrarch claims here that it brought him not only happiness but also pride (Perarch walked proudly – "gire altero," [6]). Here, the patron is feminized and as a result is removed from active participation within the civic sphere, the forum reserved for men. The abrupt change in social hierarchy and its political ramifications are further supported by Petrarch's assertion that with the patron's death "et ristorar nol pò terra né impero" (7; "neither land nor empire can restore it"). The claim that, with the death of the patron and the beloved, his "double treasure" can never be restored, not through land or power or the physical possessions detailed in verse 8, goes to the heart of the problem addressed by Petrarch in his Latin works: that political power is transitory. Yet, what does the beloved have to do with land and political power?

The constant between the figures of the beloved and of the patron is their simultaneous subjugation under the discursive tyranny of the poet: the "column," which was once a pillar of strength, is now broken and feminized, and the beloved has lost all the attributes that once made her unique. In this light, the closing of the poem takes on a new meaning, one that points to Petrarch's understanding of patronage:

Ma se consentimento è di destino,
che posso io più, se no aver l'alma trista,
humidi gli occhi sempre, e 'l viso chino?

O nostra vita ch'è sì bella in vista,
com perde agevolmente in un matino
quel che 'n molti anni a gran pena s'acquista! (9–14)

But, since this is the intent of destiny, what can I do except have my soul sad, my eyes always wet, and my face bent down? // Oh our life that is so beautiful to see, how easily it loses in one morning what has been acquired with great difficulty over many years!

That the deaths of the beloved and the patron were destined is no novelty, nor is the image of the poet with downcast and moist eyes. The final tercet, however, exemplifies an underlying political theme that retrospectively politicizes the entire sonnet: death has stolen from him that which took him many years to procure. The general theme of unrequited love that marks the poetic collection excludes Laura as a possible acquisition, leaving only the patron, or rather, his favours, as the most logical possibility. Thus, just as death denies the patron his wealth, land, and power so too does his death rob the poet of his just deserts. This sheds light on Petrarch's movement within the patronage system and his oscillations between various patrons, since the patron is here represented as *useful* to the poet *only in life* – and thus dispensable.

In the poems dedicated to Petrarch's relationship to the Colonna family, the patron is treated like a beloved. He is both exalted and praised and simultaneously deprived of agency. When Petrarch repurposes the tropes and figurative language normally reserved for Laura to describe his patron, he recreates the power dynamic we find in the Medusa poems: though the beloved and patron might appear to wield power and influence over the poet, his intellect and art allow him to overcome them. As a result, we see the patron feminized not only in his poetic alignment with Laura but in the denial of agency that is associated with the feminine. As we saw in the *tenzone* with Sennuccio del Bene, Giovanni Colonna is figured as a currency exchanged between the poets, much as Laura is. While his death in 1348 is given even greater significance in its association with Laura's death – his lengthy friendship with Petrarch presented as just as important as the poet's love for Laura – Giovanni ultimately shares a eulogy with the woman whose presence already dominates Petrarch's poetry. These Colonna poems, then, come to signify something greater than personal or political friendships. In them we find subtle examinations of the nature of power, as well as moments where Petrarch not only investigates and negotiates his position in the ever-fraught politics of patronage but also expresses his vulnerability within that system. His rhetorical strategies in the poems examined above disguise an anxiety about his patrons that echoes *Familiares* 24.5, his letter to Seneca, written 1 August 1348 – only a few months after the deaths of Laura and the Cardinal. In this letter, Petrarch questions Seneca's choice to remain under the patronage of Nero, and criticizes his lack of prudence:

> Tu vero, venerande vir et morum, si Plutarcho credimus, incomparabilis preceptor, errorem vite tue, si non molestum est, mecum recognosce. In omnium seculorum crudelissimum principem incidisti et tranquillus nauta preciosis mercibus honustam navim ad infamem et procellosum scopulum appulisti. Cur autem illic hesisti, queso te? an ut in tempestate aspera magisterium aprobares? sed hoc nemo nisi amens eligit, neque enim ut fortis est perpeti, sic prudentis est optare periculum; (33–42)

> But you, O venerable sir, and if we believe Plutarch, incomparable teacher of morals, review with me, if you do not mind, the great error of your life. You happened to live under the cruelest ruler of all centuries, and like a peaceful sailor you guided your ship laden with precious cargo toward a dangerous and stormy reef. But I ask you, Why did you linger there? Perhaps to prove your skill in such a terrible storm? None but a madman would have chosen this course, for it is the role of a brave man to face danger, it is not the role of a prudent man to seek it.[72]

Petrarch's letter outlines the vulnerability of the intellectual whose livelihood depends on a patron and who does not exercise prudence. In the specific case of Seneca, the patron was a tyrant, and their relationship proved fatal to the philosopher. The life of Seneca serves as a reminder of the potential danger in patronage. Petrarch's poetic replaying of the confrontation between the poet's intellect and the (feminized) patron looks forward to the staging of invulnerability that Jane Tylus has located in late-Renaissance writers like Shakespeare, Benvenuto Cellini, Teresa of Avila, Torquato Tasso, Edmund Spenser, and Pierre Corneille, who "produced a complicated array of textual performances designed to protect themselves and their writing from the *vulnus* that late Renaissance authorities had the power to inflict."[73] In the next section, I examine how Petrarch's lyrical staging of the classical battle between sword and pen plays out in the Latin *Africa,* where the poet's alignment with the epic hero Scipio restages the battle between a masculine intellect, feminized patrons, and Medusan women.

Monstrous Women and Passive Rulers in Petrarch's *Africa*

Petrarch's *Africa,* the Latin epic poem centred on the exploits of Scipio Africanus in the Second Punic War, is arguably one of his most overtly political and self-promoting works.[74] Dedicated to King Robert d'Anjou of Naples, the nine books are as much about Petrarch's greatness as a poet as they are about the epic hero Scipio. Most importantly, as I examine in this section, the framing of the narrative pits the poet against the Anjou patron, with a love story serving as a model. In Book 5 of *Africa,* Petrarch restages the struggle of agency between the lyrical poet-lover's intellect and the beloved's petrifying gaze in the tragic love story between Massinissa and Sophonisba, and Scipio's intervention in their affair. Despite the more overtly political subject matter of the epic, allusions to the *RVF* characterize Massinissa, who struggles with his political allegiance to Scipio and his love for the conquered queen, Sophonisba, a Medusan female protagonist. As in the case of the Colonna patrons in the vernacular lyric collection, here Petrarch's paradigm of agency begins with the figures of two lovers that will become the model for his relationship to King Robert in the dedication of the book.

Sophonisba shares many traits with Vergil's tragic Dido. On the most basic level of narrative, both women function as obstacles to their lovers' political obligations. In the case of Aeneas, his sojourn with Dido delays his journey and destiny to found Rome. When Massinissa conquers Numidia and takes over as king, he ignores his alliance with Scipio by marrying the defeated queen, daughter of Rome's sworn enemy Hasdrubal. Ultimately, both Aeneas and Massinissa abandon their lovers to follow their political destinies, leading the women to suicide and the underworld. Despite these basic similarities, as Simone Marchesi has argued, Sophonisba evokes Dido primarily as a philological corrective to Vergil's historically inaccurate presentation of her in the *Aeneid*. Marchesi notes two important ways in which Petrarch corrects Vergil's Dido: (1) in *Africa* 3.424–7, the minstrel criticizes Vergil for having tarnished Dido's name and for having been overconfident in his art, and (2) in Book 5, Massinissa is overcome by love, but Sophonisba is not.[75] Indeed, if we look closely at the figure of Sophonisba in Book 5, Laura-as-Medusa is a closer archetype for her character than is Dido. From the moment that Massinissa enters into the capital city, Cirta, the presentation of the queen is couched in lyrical terms like those found throughout the *RVF*. In an extended *effictio* (vv 22–85), key elements of Sophonisba's beauty evoke Laura's image:

[...] Stabat candore nivali,
Frons alto miranda Iovi, multumque sorori
Zelotipe metuenda magis quam pellicis ulla
Forma viro dilecta vago. Fulgentior auro
Quolibet, et solis radiis factura pudorem,
Cesaries spargenda levi pendebat ab aura
Colla super, recto que sensim lactea tractu
Surgebant, humerosque agiles affusa tegebat (vv 22–9)

[...] And that brow,
as white as snow, might stir almighty Jove
to wonder and his jealous sister find it
more dangerous than any concubine

her errant spouse might cherish for her charm.
With brighter gleam than gold of any land,
putting the sun's own rays to shame, her locks
encircled by a fillet of light gold
and softly stirring in the gentle breeze,
formed first a frame for her slim, graceful neck –
a peerless, milk-white column, sweetly rising –
then spreading wide, in pleasing fashion twined,
encased her slender shoulders as they fell.[76]

Sophonisba's snowy-white forehead – "candor nivali/frons" – evokes Laura's "calda neve il volto" (*RVF* 157, 9), without the oxymoron so typical of Petrarch's vernacular lyrics. The emphasis on the whiteness of her skin is repeated in the description of her neck as a "colla ... lactea." The most striking similarity between the two female figures in this passage is the reference to the hair and its gesture towards the paronomastic play on Laura's name. The image of Sophonisba's long, flowing hair blowing in the gentle wind ("Cesaries spargenda levi pendebat ab aura") explicitly recalls the incipit of *RVF* 90, "Erano i capei d'oro a l'aura sparsi" ("Her golden hair was loosed to the breeze"). Petrarch here recreates the vernacular pun on "l'aura," as both wind and the beloved's name, in the Latin "ab aura," though it is admittedly more awkward in the Latin. Nevertheless, throughout the fifty-eight verses dedicated to describing Sophonisba's beauty, there is little deviation from the vernacular lyric tropes concerning Laura's beauty. By appropriating the tropes traditionally associated with Laura in his initial description of Sophonisba, Petrarch draws connections between the two female figures that will eventually move beyond the physical.

As we saw in the first section of this chapter, Petrarch's fixation on Laura's eyes is not limited to their beauty, particularly in the Medusa poems where the female gaze is the focus. In describing Sophonisba's eyes, Petrarch writes:

Lumina, quid referam preclare subdita fronti
Invidiam motura deis? divina quod illis
Vis inerat radiansque decor, qui pectora posset
Flectere quo vellet, mentesque auferre tuendo,
Inque Meduseum precordia vertere marmor,
Africa nec monstris caruisset terra secundis. (35–40)

How shall I tell you of her eyes? So clear
their radiance gleamed beneath her beauteous brows
that gods might covet them; her glance divine
cast all around her a compelling charm,
and where she wished to turn it she could rouse
desire or bend a will however firm
or to Medusan marble change the heart
of an admirer – nay, it is to wonder
that Africa has no second monstrous breed.[77]

Here we find two disparate descriptions of Sophonisba's eyes and their effects on others. They are described as divine ("lumina ... divina"), they irradiate charm ("radiansque decor"), and they bend the will of those around her ("mentesque auferre tuendo"). The shift from the luminous, visual quality of her eyes to the gaze (the verb, *tueor*) reintroduces the Medusan theme of the *RVF.* Not only is Sophonisba able to bend the most fervent wills of men, her gaze has the power to change men's hearts to Medusan marble – a reference to the monumentalizing power of Medusa's gaze as wielded by Perseus. Petrarch includes her in a "monstrous breed" of women who apparently possess the same powers as Sophonisba. Her inclusion in a lineage of gorgon-like women recalls Petrarch's insinuation in the *RVF* that all beloveds are Medusan. That is, his advice to Gianfigliazzi to look at his Medusan-beloved, rather than flee, makes Laura and Gianfigliazzi's beloved members of the same category of women.

The explicit use of "monstris" in the *Africa,* however, separates Sophonisba and her love story from the archetypical one created in the vernacular lyric collection. That is, whereas in the *RVF* the poet's ability to harness the monumentalizing gaze of the beloved empowers him, here the Medusan gaze is limited to the realm of love. That Sophonisba turns the hearts of men to marble, rather than the men themselves, symbolically privileges the love story over the lover himself. This differentiates her gaze from Laura's, particularly in the longer love narrative with Massinissa. The distinction is an important one when we consider the political position of Massinissa and how it differs from that of Petrarch as poet-lover. The love affair between the queen and Massinissa initially prevents him from fulfilling his political duties, much like that of Dido and Aeneas. The implication that his heart, rather than his entire being, is turned to Medusan marble foreshadows his eventual abandonment of Sophonisba at the end of Book 5. What will be immortalized in marble and in poetry is the love story, rather than Massinissa as a failed leader-turned-lover – a decidedly un-exemplary figure in an epic.

His abandonment of his political duties occurs instantly after Sophonisba delivers a heart-wrenching speech to her new captor.[78] When Sophonisba kneels before him to beg for mercy, she is able to "bend his will" and alter the course of events expected in such an encounter. She implores him to give her a worthy death rather than take her as a prisoner to be paraded before the Romans as the ultimate example of the spoils of war. Whereas Petrarch describes himself as able to gaze at Laura-Medusa and harness her power of monumentalization in his poetry, maintaining his position and identity as a poet, Massinissa is described as being overcome by Sophonisba's gaze, to the point of forgetting his martial duties:

> Immemor armorum iuvenis, cui Martius ardor
> Exciderat, gravidumque nove dulcedine forme
> Pectus, et insolitis ardebant viscera flammis, (107–9)
>
> Oblivious of arms, the youth, from whom
> all martial zeal had fled, with heart o'erwhelmed
> by new and unexpected images
> of sweetness, and within him all ablaze
> with flame unwonted […],[79]

"Martial zeal" confronts and loses to the "unwonted flame" of love that has now overcome Massinissa. The "new and unexpected images" coursing through his mind would seem to point to Sophonisba, but they also foreshadow the lyrical way in which the inner conflict between arms and love will play out. When, in a moment of solitude and introspection, Massinissa ponders his decision to marry Sophonisba and abandon his loyalty to Scipio, both beloved and patron are presented as competing Petrarchan love objects:

> […] gemitu sic longam concitus horam
> Exegit vario: nunc ora nitentia coram
> Cernere regine, nunc dulces fingere voces
> Ipse sibi, pedibus nunc oscula pressa manusque
> Leniter apprensas, lacrimosaque pectora flentis,
> Dulcibus undantesque oculos arsisse favillis.

At medias inter curas, ubi forte verendi
Frons aderat dilecta ducis, tanc improba tergum
Spes dabat, e domitis stabant precordia flammis. (183–91)

So for some time with lamentations long
and varied he continues; now he sees
before him the bright visage of the queen,
now he calls back her honeyed words,
feels once again her humble kisses pressed
upon his feet, the soft touch of her hand,
recalls the teardrops falling on her breast,
her dewy eyes yet glowing with sweet fire.
But when into such thoughts the Roman chief
with brow austere intrudes, then craven hope
takes flight and ardor in his heart is chilled.[80]

Massinissa has conflicting visions of Sophonisba and Scipio, whose images symbolize emotion and reason, respectively. The female beloved is characterized primarily through affect and her ability to bend his will. The image of her face is accompanied by memories of the persuasive, sweet ("dulces") words that convinced him to marry her, her kisses, soft touch, and tears. This emphasis on emotion is further symbolized as a burning in Massinissa's heart ("flammis"), which ardour is nearly extinguished by Scipio's image. The Roman leader represents reason, symbolized by his "brow austere" ("verendi ... frons"), which chills (tames) – but does not eliminate – Massinissa's desire for his beloved. In this sense, Sophonisba's presence seems to follow *RVF* 96 where the image of the beloved is ever present in the poet-lover's heart, and constantly inspires him. Here, however, the inspiration is misguided, and Scipio's brow and reason serve as a reminder of this mistake. Thus, the contrasting visions of Sophonisba and Scipio ultimately symbolize Massinissa's struggle between emotion (marrying the queen) and reason (returning to his political duties). There is a decidedly stoic undertone to this struggle, since ultimately a return to reason requires Massinissa to control his passions.

The potentially destructive nature of Sophonisba's all-encompassing love is later presented to Scipio and the readers explicitly through the example of her former husband, King Syphax. After having broken his political alliance with Scipio and the Roman cause against the Carthaginians, the defeated king is taken prisoner and transported to

Rome. There he explains his grave error to Scipio, laying blame on his queen, Sophonisba, and her control over him. The fallen king serves as an anti-exemplary figure about the dangers of allowing love to influence political decisions. The story also elucidates the political meaning of the "monstrous breed" of women to which Sophonisba belongs. As Syphax recounts,

Femina cum primum laribus fuit advena nostris,
Auspiciis invecta malis atque alite torva,
Tunc perii, periitque fides, et gloria nobis
Excidit ac sceptrum manibus diademaque fronti;
Prodita tunc tacitis arsit mea regia flammis.
Funereas tulit illa faces, potuitque dolosis
Flectere blanditiis animum, lacrimisque malignis
Hospitis illa sacri, fame, superumque deorum
Reddidit immemoremque mei. (348–56)

When in my house
an alien woman first set foot, she brought
omens of ill and augury of doom;
then did I perish and my majesty,
then from my hands the scepter fell and from
my brow the diadem. My palace in the grip
of a hidden flame already was afire.
She bore funeral torches. By her wiles
she bent my purpose; with her artful plaints
she made me heedless of my sacred friend [Scipio],
my name, myself, the great gods above.[81]

Syphax uses a series of contrasts in his description of Sophonisba's effect on him, thereby amplifying her control over him. The auguries and omens she brought to him are in opposition to Scipio's position as his "sacred friend" (hospitis ... sacri), pitting the queen against a political ally. The "hidden flame" (tacitis ... flammis) in his palace recalls Petrarch's description of his desire for Laura in *RVF* 207: "Chiusa fiamma è più ardente, et se pur cresce, / in alcun modo più non po celarsi" (vv 66–7; "A hidden flame is hottest, and if it grows it can no longer be hidden in any way),"[82] pointing to an all-consuming flame. In the vernacular poem, the hidden flames eventually escape through Petrarch's cries ("miei gridi," v. 74). In the case of King Syphax, the "hidden flames" are politicized, since his heart is represented by his palace, and the flames escape as "funeral torches" (funeraras ... faces) – a reference to the many deaths suffered by his troops and a foreshadowing of his death on foreign soil. In the end, Syphax's fate was sealed when he allowed the queen's "blanditiis" – her flattery and female "wiles" – to bend his will, a description explicitly linked to the earlier representation of Sophonisba-as-Medusa and the "monstrous breed" of women in Africa.

The king continues to lay blame on his queen, claiming she placed the helmet of war on his head and spear and shield in his hands: "Illa, / illa suis manibus misero tulit arma marito, / induit illa latus, capiti tum cassida caro, / Tum gladium dextre, clipeum dedit illa sinistre" (vv 356–9).[83] The control Sophonisba held over Syphax's will is symbolized by the repetition of "illa" (she) three times in the passage as an active subject, particularly in comparison to Syphax's use of the third person to speak about himself in this moment. *She* places the weapons "suis minibus misero ... marito" – into the hands of her wretched spouse. The King's auto-representation as an object of Sophonisba's will continues through this episode, as he describes to Scipio the first moments of battle in the third person, further emphasizing his lack of agency and reason, and then abruptly switches to first-person narrative in recognition of the errors he committed:

 Quando agmina campis
Contulimus stetimusque acie, fuit exitus ille
Erroris, michi crede, mei: placuisse prophanos
Amplexus fuerant huius primordia casus
Coniugioque hesisse fero. Proh! regia, vere
Regia et innumeris nuptura sine ordine coniunx
Regibus! (362–8)

 The trumpet called
and him, a-tremble, hating thoughts of war
she sent to dubious battle and compelled
him to attack you, though the gods denied
their favor. When the battle lines were formed,
then did my course of error reach its goal!
Such were the causes of my ruin: I joyed
Excessively in impious blandishments
And loved a savage wife. A queen indeed –

A queen disposed to wed a train of kings
Past counting, all in fickle faith espoused.[84]

The change in perspective further admonishes the queen while excusing Syphax of any culpability in attacking Scipio and his troops: she sent him into battle and forced him to attack his ally. Only when he describes his ruin does he return to first-person narrative, symbolizing his return to reason in the recognition of his grave error and inevitable fate. He closes by again placing blame on Sophonisba by presenting himself as merely one in a succession of kings to be felled by the love of Sophonisba. This final detail serves as a warning to Scipio about Massinissa's potential demise as Sophonisba's new husband, a warning upon which he acts when he sees Massinissa again.

When Massinissa returns to the Roman camp, after his marriage to Sophonisba and Scipio's talk with Syphax, Scipio explicitly reminds him of his political duty. He evokes Petrarch's "giovenil errore" of *RVF* 1 (v. 3; youthful error) when he admonishes Massinissa about the dangers of unbridled passion by telling him: "Precipue tamen hec nitide suspecta iuvente / Pestis, et etati pretendit retia nostre" (vv 403–4; "Youth in its early blossom / is subject to this evil, quick to spread / its nets to trap our unsuspecting years).[85] Scipio frames the struggle between emotion and reason with the issue of fame and immortality, telling Massinissa:

Gloria magna quidem magnum vicisse Siphacem;
Sed maior, michi crede, graves domuisse tumultus
Pectoris atque animo frenum posuisse frementi.
Preconem me virtutem memoremque tuarum
Semper habes; tua facta libens et dicta renarro. (418–22)

To vanquish Syphax is a glorious thing,
But doubt not it is greater to put down
Strong emotions raging in the heart
And hold tight the rein on the intemperate soul.
You'll have in me a herald of your virtues
And gladly I'll report your words and deeds.[86]

Scipio's message implies that Massinissa's past exploits – specifically, his conquest of Syphax – do not necessarily secure him positive fame if he cannot control his emotions. The Roman leader presents himself in a different political position than would be expected. He does not command Massinissa to action, as his leader, but rather places himself into the position of a "preconem" (praeconem; herald), responsible for disseminating official state proclamations. This places the burden of choice on Massinissa, who must decide whether to continue on his path towards memorialization as a lover, emasculated by the will of a woman, or as a political leader in charge of his destiny and reputation.

The emphasis on bridling passion carries into Scipio's more explicit advice, reminiscent of Petrarch's poem to his brother Gherardo on matters of love, examined earlier in this chapter. He commands Massinissa,

> Vince animum teque ipse doma, nec multa decora
> Commaculare velis unius crimine facti.
> Aspice quam fructus nichilo minor ira dolorque,
> Quantus ab obsceno tibi sit metuendus amore;
> Quid deceat regem, quam per se feda libido. (433–7)

> Now be master of your heart
> and of yourself; let not one lawless act
> besmirch your glory. Mark well how the fruit
> of waywardness, the wrath and woe it brings,
> should give you rightful cause to be afraid
> of an unwholesome love. Bethink you too
> of what becomes a king and bear in mind
> how vile a thing is passion itself.[87]

Massinissa's foray into love is presented as a loss of control and agency over his *animus* – the rational soul, which has been overcome by his *libido*. Love and passion are, thus, in direct confrontation with reason. By mastering his heart – controlling his passions – he will be able to get back on the right path to being a righteous king and ally to the Romans. The advice is similar to that given to Gherardo: take back control over your destiny from the beloved. Though Massinissa struggles with the decision, he ultimately does return to Scipio, and re-exerts his agency, bringing about the demise of his queen, whom he commands to kill herself so he may fulfil his political duties.

In this tragic love story, Scipio's intellect – his ability to look beyond Sophonisba's beauty and charm to recognize the inherent danger in her gaze – and his ability to control his own passions serve as a decidedly masculine (military) model for Massinissa. Aldo Bernardo has argued that Scipio represents human perfection for Petrarch, a "synthesis of all those values that were dear to him."[88] Indeed, Petrarch presents him throughout the epic as an idealized humanist model, particularly when compared to the lyrical Laura who, as Bernardo shows, represents human beauty and mankind's vulnerability to passion. The two figures would seem to exist as binary opposites, one representing ethics and reason, the other human passion and weakness. In this light, we can draw a parallel between the figure of Scipio and the authoritative Petrarchan voice of *RVF* 1, the one who writes from the place of wisdom, recognizes his "youthful error," and is (in part) a different man than he was before, as well as the one who advises both Gherardo and Gianfigliazzi on overcoming human passion with the intellect. Intellectual masculinity defines the epic hero of the *Africa* as much as it does the lyrical Petrarch-Perseus, and both are held up as exempla for readers.

The Massinissa-Sophonisba story is, thus, one of agency, of passive versus active rule. King Syphax is politically unseated by his inability to look at Sophonisba-Medusa and overcome her through reason. If not for Scipio, Massinissa would presumably have met the same fate. Scipio's intellect, his ability to learn from the mistakes of Syphax and teach Massinissa about the error of his ways, saved the young Numidian king. In the interlacing stories of these three male protagonists a pattern of gendered agency emerges: the love of Sophonisba politically emasculated Syphax and Massinissa, whereas Scipio's ability to look past her charm and recognize the danger of her ability to bend wills empowered him politically. His intellect is gendered masculine by the very nature of his political reasoning and prudence; by contrast, the Numidian kings are extensions of Sophonisba's desires. There is also a meta-poetic tenor to Scipio's role in the love story, since his identification as a potential "preconem" (herald) for Massinissa makes him a political parallel to the poet, further strengthening the Scipio-Petrarch parallel described above. In the dedication to King Robert of Naples in Book 1, Petrarch employs a similar strategy to Scipio's, pitting his active ability to memorialize Robert against the king's political accomplishments. At the beginning of Book 1, Petrarch addresses the monarch in a lengthy aside (of 72 verses) that praises the poet as much as it does the dedicatee. Most notably, he provides a series of reasons why he has not undertaken to write the epic about his patron:

> Ipse tuos actus meritis ad sidera tollam
> Laudibus, atque alio fortassis carmine quondam
> (Mors modo me paulum expectet! non longa petuntur)

Nomen et alta canam Siculi miracula regis,
Non audita procul, sed que modo vidimus omnes
Omnia. (40–5)

For with the praise that you have merited
I shall extol your exploits to the stars,
in a day to come perchance I may
sing of the King of Sicily, his fame
and his miraculous deeds, not yet well known
abroad but which we all have witnessed.[89]

Initially, it appears as though Petrarch is praising his patron: he has merited praise, he is famous, and his deeds are miraculous. So praiseworthy is King Robert that *someday* Petrarch will laud him in an epic ("carmine"; in a song). Yet, in praising Robert of Naples, Petrarch simultaneously undermines his accomplishments and, most importantly, renders him mortal. That is, the hyperbole used in characterizing his deeds as miraculous ("miracula") is undercut by Petrarch's claim that Robert's fame – a direct result of these miraculous deeds – is not known abroad. His fame is limited to his court; thus, although those around him might be able to attest to these deeds, he lacks an epic, and, by extension, immortality.

Petrarch goes on to explain that it is the practice of poets who undertake writing an epic to turn to ancient times for their subject matter. The excuse seems valid enough, were it not for the third reason given: that Petrarch's novice hand could not do justice to King Robert's greatness. The topos of humility employed here is a common rhetorical device, one that implies the poet's subservience to his patron, as well as a lack in poetic accomplishments compared to his political ones. However, when we examine Petrarch's reasoning more closely, we begin to ask whether it is King Robert who is lacking in the greatness required to become the subject of an epic, and especially, what role he plays in Petrarch's poetics, when the poet writes,

Nunc teneras *frondes humili* de stipite vulsi,
Scipiade egregio primos comitante paratus:
Tunc *validos* carpam *ramos*; tu nempe iuvabis
Materia, generose, tua, calamumque labantem
Firmabis, meritumque decus continget amanti
Altera temporibus pulcerrima *laurea* nostris. (65–70; emphasis mine)

> [...] For the nonce I pluck
> the *tenderest foliage* from a lowly bush
> and choose famed Scipio to share my course.
> One day I'll gather *sturdier boughs*, and you,
> most generous King, will help me with your deeds
> and lend more power to my faltering pen.
> *Another crown of laurel*, the most fair
> of all our times, will justly then reward
> with honor one who holds your person dear.[90]

Initially Petrarch seems to place Robert above him: he claims that his talents are not great enough to write an epic in honour of the king, so he has instead chosen Scipio from a "lowly bush" ("frondes humili"). The phrase "frondes humili" serves as the first of three *double entendres* linked to foliage in this passage that refer to both the military accomplishments of Scipio or Robert and Petrarch's poetic talents. In this first example, Petrarch claims that his poetic talents are too lowly to do justice to Robert; thus he has chosen a (seemingly) less accomplished epic hero, Scipio. As the passage continues, we find a second example when Petrarch imagines a day when he will possess "sturdier boughs" ("validos ... ramos"), and Robert's future deeds will become his subject matter. This is further supported by Petrarch's humble use of "calamum" – literally a small reed – to describe his pen. Although Petrarch seemingly undermines his poetic abilities while gesturing at Robert's potential greatness, the implication is that Robert has not yet reached these "sturdier boughs" where he would warrant an epic poem. Petrarch's allusion to his upcoming coronation, when an "altera ... laurea" will crown him, pits his poetic accomplishments against Robert's lack of the military laurel (i.e., lack of political accomplishments). It is not that Petrarch's "calamum" has yet to reach the apex of its abilities but rather that Robert has yet to accomplish the deeds worthy of a Petrarchan epic. Only his future deeds will enable Petrarch's supposedly "faltering pen" to rise to the occasion, implying that the king's future fame is contingent on Petrarch's future writings about him.

The dedication of the poem is meant to glorify King Robert, yet as we have seen, Petrarch praises him at the same time as he points out his shortcomings. The ambiguity in Petrarch's representation of Robert reflects the kind of ambiguity we found in his treatment of the Colonna in the *RVF*. Robert is an active ruler, whose fame and intellect are known throughout Italy, but he is also presented as a passive ruler dependent on Petrarch to immortalize him in writing. This is in contrast to Petrarch's active persona, most evident in comparing the dedication to the final book of the epic. After describing the victories of Scipio Africanus in the eight books that follow, Petrarch closes the epic by crowning himself (under the guise of the character "Franciscus"), and makes several moves that demonstrate the power of poetry over military or political power, and the way in which poetic agency is negotiated and appropriated. If in Book 1 he claims that the king is not ready to be immortalized in an epic, in Book 9 Petrarch shows that he has already reached the pinnacle of poetic accomplishment by inscribing himself into the epic. There we encounter Petrarch's epic hero, Scipio, and his biographer, Ennius,[91] on a boat leaving the African shores after his victories. Noting the poet's silence on the boat, Scipio implores Ennius to lift their weary hearts with sweet verse. Surprisingly, Scipio's biographer has no tale to tell, despite having, one may assume, witnessed the exploits documented in the previous books of the epic. Instead, Ennius describes his dream vision of Homer, who appeared to him while the outcome of the war was still in doubt to deliver two prophecies concerning the future of Latin arms and literature. First, Homer assures Ennius that Latium will ultimately succeed in the battle.[92] The second prophecy concerning letters is prompted when Ennius notices a young man in the distance who uncannily resembles Petrarch:

> Hic ego – nam longe clausa sub valle sedentem
> Aspexi iuvenem – "Dux o carissime, quisnam est,
> Quem video teneras inter consistere lauros
> Et viridante comas meditantem incingere ramo?
> Nescio quid, nisi fallor, enim sub pectore versat
> Egregiumque altumque nimis." (216–21)

> There in the distance I could see a youth
> seated within a valley closed by hills.
> I asked: "O cherished guide, disclose, I pray,
> who is it I behold taking his rest
> under the tender laurel? Lo, he seems
> about to bind his locks with those green fronds.
> I know not what he ponders in his heart,
> but surely it must be, unless I err,
> some high and noble purpose."[93]

Though the young man in the vision is not yet named, there are several clues that point to Petrarch: the youth is seated "within a valley closed by hills," an allusion to Vaucluse, Petrarch's preferred haunt, whose etymology means, precisely, a closed-off valley; he is preparing to crown himself with laurel fronds, a foreshadowing of Petrarch's own upcoming laurel coronation by King Robert. The reader's suspicion that the youth might indeed be Petrarch is soon confirmed by Homer's response:

Francisco cui nomen erit; qui grandia facta,
Vidisti que cunta oculis, ceu corpis in unum
Colliget: Hispanas acies Libieque labores
Scipiadamque tuum: titulusque poematis illi
AFRICA. (232–6)

He will be called Franciscus;
and all the glorious exploits you have seen
he will assemble in one volume –
all the deeds in Spain, the arduous Libyan trials;
and he will call his poem *Africa*.[94]

Homer is figured as an Adamic figure, whose power of language calls Petrarch into being. His prophecy inscribes Petrarch not only into the landscape of the epic poem but into Italian history, as the poet who returns the Latin muses from exile and who documents the life and travails of Scipio, the new Aeneas, in an epic poem that we, as readers, have nearly completed reading. By inscribing himself into his epic of origins, Petrarch constructs his own fame as the poet of a new republic and golden age; the age when the muses return to Italy. As Ronald L. Martinez has remarked in his reading of the final book of the *Africa*, "Victories require a contest, and it is the competition or *certamen* for the glory of poetic first place that chiefly guides Petrarch's autobiographical appropriation of epic."[95] The self-aggrandizement of such a metafictional move claims Petrarch for epochs that do not exist: both the past age of republican glory and an unknown future time of glory. That it will be a poet who ushers in this new age privileges the poetic over the military crown, thereby making King Robert reliant upon Petrarch for his fame, but figuring the poet as the agent behind his own immortality.

For writing the *Africa*, on 8 April 1341 Petrarch would receive his poetic laurels from King Robert, to whom he had dedicated his epic poem, in a public ceremony atop the Capitoline Hill, symbolic seat of Roman military power. A closer look at *Africa*, however, shows that Petrarch is playing a sort of Perseus, enlisting King Robert's power to help his own claim for renown while at the same time denying Robert self-agency. The self-coronation by Franciscus essentially refutes the symbolic necessity of the patron in the immortalization of the poet. By immortalizing himself, Petrarch emphasizes the notion that it is the poetic plume that bestows immortality upon the poet, not necessarily the patron. Hence, although the patron and the epic hero both require a poet for immortality, the poet does not require either the patron or the hero. From the classical *auctores* the poet receives eloquence, from patrons and heroes the subject matter. This discursive power play, so to speak, can be read as a critique of King Robert's own politics as practised in his Neapolitan court. Historians have long been fascinated with the prominence of patronage in King Robert's court, and, as Samantha Kelly has noted, "its function as an engine of royal propaganda."[96] Robert's rule, it should be remembered, happened only by default. The death of his brother, Charles Martel, heir apparent to the Angevin dynasty, put Robert in power and required, in a sense, legitimization. Kelly's scholarship elucidates a reign in which the patron-poet relationship became essential. Kelly catalogues the various ways in which Robert attempted to legitimize his rule: from the numerous sermons he wrote; to the attempt at having his deceased brother, Louis of Anjou, canonized; to filling his court with secular men of letters. As the historian notes, "As for the men who did attract royal patronage, their humanism turns out to consist largely of their friendship with Petrarch – a friendship which, in any case, started with Petrarch's visit and not in the 1320s."[97] Thus, Petrarch's treatment of Robert in the dedication of the *Africa* – as a passive ruler reliant on the poet – in comparison to his self-coronation as poet laureate at the end, seems to acknowledge Robert's attempt at legitimizing his political rule through artistic patronage, while simultaneously reminding him that it is the poet who crowns the king with immortality, revealing Petrarch's upcoming coronation by the king as purely ceremonial.

As has been explored in this chapter, the figure of Petrarch's Medusa is as multifaceted and as complex as that in Ovid's *Metamorphoses*. I have offered another reading of Petrarch's Medusa poems that recognizes Petrarch's alignment with Perseus after the slaying, when the disembodied head of Medusa becomes a poetic tool of self-aggrandizement. That Laura-Medusa has the ability to turn Petrarch into marble, rather than stone, points to the beloved's lack of agency, and that Petrarch can look at her repeatedly, and at will, nuances the paradigm of power between poet-lover and beloved that has generally characterized his lyric collection. There is no denying that the religious and eschatological implications of petrification that have been argued by several scholars elucidate an important aspect of Petrarch's writings about religion and his own battle with the double aspect of *gloria.* Indeed, it is an integral part of the myth the poet himself creates, not only within the lyric collection, but also in the *Secretum* and *Triumphi.* However, reading Petrarch's Medusa as solely an obstacle to *Paradiso* limits our understanding of the dimensional breadth of Petrarch's larger cultural project and œuvre. In particular, the traditional approach to Laura-Medusa has taken for granted both how closely Petrarch read his favoured classical authors – in this case, Ovid – and also the often intersecting trajectories of his vernacular and Latin cultural projects. By denying Laura-Medusa the power of agency in his vernacular poems, Petrarch is able figuratively to harness the power of immortalization, emphasizing the poetic process as a means towards this end – a preeminent topic in his Latin works. Petrarch's denial of Laura-Medusa's power over him mirrors the way in which he treats his patrons in examples presented from the *RVF* and the Latin *Africa*. Thus, the poet's encounters with Medusa and his recovery of the political use of Medusa in Ovid allow him to stage his relationship to his patrons and present patronage and love as similar systems of power ultimately controlled by the poet's ability to bestow or deny immortality upon others. The "monstrous breed" of women throughout Petrarch's writings provide the poet with the tools necessary to challenge his patrons. This new reading of Petrarch's Medusa supports the view of the elusiveness and mobility of Petrarch's poetry already discussed by scholars such as Marco Santagata and Enrico Fenzi.[98]

Albert Ascoli has noted a similar use of Medusa in Coluccio Salutati's appropriation (or rather, allegorization) of the myth in his *De laboribus Herculis,* noting that, "He [Salutati] allegorizes the shield [of Jove, upon which appears the head of Medusa] as well as Medusa herself, as poetic eloquence, the power of rhetoric to both illuminate and control."[99] The connection made between Medusa's head and the double nature of rhetoric – as a force that both illuminates (makes clear) and controls – is palpable in the figures of Petrarch's Laura-Medusa and Sophonisba. The poet's deliberate comparison between the art of poetry and the art of sculpting is more reminiscent of Petrarch's discussions of military power than of Neoplatonic love. Military heroes are immortalized in statues as visible examples of admirable behaviour, not beloveds. Yet, both are immortalized in poetry, something more durable than marble, since it is the poet's retelling of a hero's story that grants him fame and immortality; the image of the hero requires a narrative for exemplarity to take effect. The privileging of poetry and the poet's pen that begins in the Medusa poems of the *RVF*, and is restaged in the Sophonisba-Massinissa episodes of the *Africa*, thus emphasizes a theme that recurs throughout Petrarch's Latin works: that military power is transient, and the poet's pen immortal. A more comprehensive understanding of Petrarch's *ars poetica*, one that takes into account the intellectual intersections between his Latin and vernacular works, points to an emerging theory of the causality exerted by human art that informs his larger humanist project and that has consequences for later representations of gender, particularly in the writings of his humanist imitators. The issue at hand is one of agency and the way in which Petrarch turns inside out the relationship between those who have passive rule (Medusa, Sophonisba, the Colonna, King Robert) and turn men to stone and those who direct that passivity towards their own purposes (Perseus, Petrarch) and transform men into marble monuments. By aligning active rule with an intellectual masculinity – his own, that of other poets, and military leaders like Scipio and, eventually, Massinissa – and passive rule with the feminine, Petrarch inadvertently creates a gendered paradigm that will form the foundation of what I call humanist Petrarchism, to be examined in the following chapter.

2 In Laura's Shadow: Gendered Dialogues and Humanist Petrarchism in the Fifteenth Century[1]

Rara si vide a noi simil Phenicie
Qual rara e chi ben leggha et ben adopre
Non fenta Laura, o penta Beatricie.

Rarely has such a Phoenix been seen among us – / so rare is she who reads well and in her works truly / does not offend Laura or displease Beatrice.[2]

Giovanni Mario Filelfo, on the death of Isotta Nogarola[3]

In 1468, the Veronese Chiara Lanza Vegia asked Giovanni Mario Filelfo (1426–80) – son of famed humanist Francesco Filelfo and an accomplished humanist in his own right – to compose a book of poems in honour of the death of Verona's most revered female Latin humanist, Isotta Nogarola (1418–66). During her lifetime, Nogarola was held up as a paragon of both female erudition and chastity, a member of a small, elite group of female humanists to emerge in the Quattrocento as Italy's first generation of women writers. In addition to her lengthy Latin letter-book, composed of epistolary exchanges with prominent male humanists, she was the first woman to debate in public, on a topic normally reserved for theologians: the relative sin of Adam and Eve.[4] Filelfo's *Liber Isottaeus* praises the accomplished humanist in two distinct literary genres: a Latin biography, written in hexameters and dedicated to her brother Ludovico, and two vernacular *sonetti caudati*, an adaptation of the Petrarchan sonnet popular in the Quattrocento.[5] Filelfo's use of Latin for Nogarola's biography, in which both her chastity and her family are praised as much as – if not more than – her erudition, is in line with the linguistic cultural program favoured during the century.

The cultural shift to Latin imitation and composition among the literary elite granted Latin a gravitas and authority denied to the vernacular.[6] Furthermore, the Latin biography also contextualizes Filelfo's *Liber* within the tradition of Latin biographies of famous women, begun by Boccaccio in the Trecento and continued by Jacopo Filippo Foresti, who, incidentally, included Nogarola and her aunt, Angela, in his 1497 *De plurimis claris scelestisque mulieribus.*[7] The two vernacular *sonetti caudati* stand out not only because they are written in Italian, at a time dominated by Latin, but also because they align Nogarola with the two most famous figures of the Trecento lyrical beloved: Petrarch's Laura and Dante's Beatrice.

In the epigraph of this chapter – the first tercet of the poem "La pompa et l'oro, et questo viver frale" (Pomp and gold, and this frail existence) – Filelfo draws a parallel between Nogarola and Laura and Beatrice, emphasizing their connection as emblems of female chastity. By couching Nogarola's chastity in lyrical terms, Filelfo both defines her against her lyrical predecessors and also claims her for an earlier time, when women were the subject matter of art rather than producers of it. The opening reference to the phoenix (fenice), the mythological bird that cyclically regenerates from the ashes of its predecessor every 500 years, presents Nogarola as a woman (re)born from the ashes of Laura, in particular. While the phoenix often symbolizes the Christian afterlife – the resurrection of the soul in Paradise and, thus, an apt metaphor for Nogarola's death – it also holds a prominent place in Petrarch's *RVF* as a symbol for his beloved.[8] In *RVF* 321, for example, Petrarch asks, "E questo 'l nido in che la mia fenice / mise l'aurate et le purpuree penne" (1–2; "Is this the nest where my phoenix put on her gold and purple feathers" [500]). Laura's birthplace, Provence, is figured as her nest, the reference to gold and purple emphasizing her regal status. Furthermore, the phoenix's mythological association with the sun and Apollo highlights Laura's role as Petrarch's poetic muse.

Nogarola is an even rarer phoenix than Laura, however, given her ability to read and write – something not characteristic of the Trecento beloved but a feature of the new class of Quattrocento women humanists. Nogarola's identity as a female humanist is what makes her Filelfo's rare phoenix. She reads well ("ben leggha") and maintains her chastity in her writings, so much so that her intrusion into the traditionally male humanist sphere neither offends Laura nor displeases Beatrice ("Non fenta Laura, o penta Beatricie"). Filelfo's reassurance that the act of writing did not negatively impact Nogarola's chastity gestures, perhaps, at the controversy that had arisen during her lifetime: a 1439 anonymous invective against her that explicitly attacked her chastity through charges of adultery, promiscuity, and incest. The invective provoked a strong response from male humanists, who publicly defended Nogarola. As Anthony Grafton and Lisa Jardine have noted, "The charge that she is *unchaste* challenges the view that as a woman she can be a prominent humanist and remain a right living person ('the woman of fluent tongue is never chaste')."[9] Filelfo's poem participates, posthumously, in defending both her chastity and the field of humanism by negating the binary between writing and chastity.[10] In this regard, Filelfo presents Nogarola as both the reincarnation of a chaste Trecento beloved – Verona's very own Laura – and a Quattrocento female writer who symbolizes Italy's intellectual future.

The blurring of the line between an essentialist, fictional portrait of "woman" (Laura, Beatrice) and Nogarola as a speaking and writing subject points to the precise problem of representation theorized by Teresa de Lauretis: "The relation between women as historical subjects and the notion of woman as it is produced by hegemonic discourses is neither a direct relation of identity, a one-to-one correspondence, nor a relation of simple implication. Like all other relations expressed in language, it is an arbitrary and symbolic one, that is to say, culturally set-up."[11] Nogarola's accomplishments as a humanist, her voluminous literary output, and, indeed, her very subjectivity are at odds with the way in which she is represented in this poem as the (re)incarnation of the silent, chaste Trecento beloved. The notion of "woman," against which her historical portrait emerges, is produced by a decidedly Petrarchan amatory discourse. The tropes and topoi which made Petrarch's Laura a paragon of female beauty and chastity in his lyric collection could be easily appropriated by a male writer like Filelfo to describe real women, particularly in poetry. The fragmentary nature of the *RVF*, and especially of Laura's portrait therein, allowed Filelfo to recall her chastity without necessarily recalling her other defining features such as silence, haughtiness, her petrifying gaze, and so on.[12] Thus, both the form (*sonetto caudato*) and content (female chastity) of Filelfo's poem draw upon the authority of Petrarch to praise Nogarola, in terms easily recognized and understood by a contemporary reader.

Almost twenty years after Nogarola's death, another female humanist, Laura Cereta (1469–99), explicitly notes the effect that literary representations of Petrarch's Laura had on her own social reality as an intellectual. In a letter written to her uncle, Ludovico di Leno, on 16 July

1485, she provides a peculiar reason for having undertaken humanistic studies. She writes: "Ego potius omnen hanc insumpsi operam mihi, ut Laurae nomen, miro Petrarcae preconio cantatum, novior altera in me custodiat aeternitas" ("I took on all this work myself so that the name of Laura, so wondrously celebrated by Petrarch, might be preserved in a second and quite new immortality – in me").[13] Here, the reasoning behind Cereta's intellectual drive is reminiscent of the "rare phoenix" of Filelfo's poem. She recognizes that the name Laura has come to symbolize a fictional portrait of woman that does not reflect her own reality. Through her humanist writing she imagines herself rising from the ashes of Petrarch's Laura to read and write well, thereby reinscribing the name "Laura." Cereta's attempt to recuperate the name that had come to symbolize, on the one hand, unrequited love, and on the other, feminine virtue highlights the difficult, transitional moment in Italian history when the first generations of women writers had to compete with centuries of essentializing representations of woman.[14] Her attempt to break from the portrait she had inherited and instead make the name "Laura" symbolize female erudition, points to the precise problem between representation and self-representation that founds De Lauretis's work, mentioned above.

Although Cereta does not state explicitly the reasons behind her aversion to being identified with Petrarch's beloved, they are not difficult to surmise. In *RVF* 366, Petrarch closes the lyric collection by referring once again to Laura-Medusa, but this time presenting her as an obstacle to his salvation. His final turn towards the Virgin Mary is a symbolic rejection of Laura, something he was famously unable to accomplish in the *Secretum.* Laura rarely speaks in Petrarch's writings; her general silence is a testament to her chastity and reminder of the unrequited love that defines her relationship to the poet. When she speaks, she often relays a religious message to the poet-lover, as in *RVF* 359 when she consoles Petrarch after her death, asking him, "Sì forte ti dispiace / che di questa miseria sia partita / et giunta a miglior vita?" (vv 18–20; "Does it displease you so much that I have left this misery and have come to a better life?" [556]). In another example, *RVF* 190, she communicates with Petrarch through a sign placed upon her sleeping body: "Nessun mi tocchi" ("Let no one touch me"), a warning that recalls Christ's words to Mary Magdalene, "Noli me tangere" ("Do not touch me"), at the Resurrection. Here, however, Laura is silent, the sign serving as a mediating function, a mouthpiece for a higher message.[15] The Laura that emerges from the *RVF,* in particular, but also from the

Triumphi and *Bucolicum carmen*, is a static figure, much like the "agnoli dipinti" (painted angels) in Filippo Balducci's cave described in Boccaccio's *mezza-novella* of *Decameron* 4.1: a representation of a woman that is completely divorced from the historical reality of women.

If we compare the reference to Laura in Filelfo's poem to that of Cereta, we see how the power of the name resides in what it evokes: female chastity rather than erudition. Cereta's distancing from her lyrical predecessor is not simply an abstract or imagined association, however. Her epistolary exchange with male humanists uncovers a pattern of discursive parallels drawn between Cereta and the figure of Petrarch's Laura. Throughout Cereta's letterbook, we find Petrarchan tropes translated into Latin and used to praise the female intellect, engage in intellectual conversation, and profess love to a woman, often sight unseen. Petrarchan amatory rhetoric and paradigms of desire embedded in the *RVF* become the vehicle for intellectual exchange between men and Laura Cereta, but this circumstance is not limited to her case alone. Indeed, we see the same discursive pattern in the letterbooks of Isotta Nogarola and Cassandra Fedele (1465–1558), and in poems and letters written to and about Alessandra Scala (1475–1506). In the so-called "Secolo senza poesia," Petrarchan poetry, it would seem, functioned as a social discourse between male and female humanists, a culturally hegemonic system of signs that, less than a century after Petrarch's death, elevated his poetry to the status of a classic.

This chapter identifies and explores what I call "humanist Petrarchism": a social discourse founded on the translation and adaptation of Petrarch's amatory tropes into humanist Latin. When used in correspondence with women, these adapted translations release the latent political issues of agency and power embedded in Petrarch's vernacular poetry and tied into gendered identities. Although female humanists were revered and brought into the otherwise restrictive and elite world of humanism, the male humanists' appropriation of Petrarchan amatory rhetoric points to an anxiety surrounding the public arrival of educated women as both interlocutors and intellectual equals. By recalling Petrarchan amatory tropes in their letters, male humanists echo the paradigm established in chapter 1 whereby the "masculine intellect" aligns learned men with power while disempowering a feminine intellectuality. Though Ciceronian imitation reigned in the age of humanism, Cicero's letters to various friends provided a model for male *amicitia* and epistolary exchange, not for male-female intellectual exchange or friendship. Indeed, the fact that there was no classical model to follow opened up a space for linguistic experimentation when writing to educated women.[16] During this same century, humanists were theorizing and debating the merits of Ciceronian versus eclectic imitation in the so-called Ciceronian Quarrel – a debate that would continue well into the sixteenth century.[17] What we see in these female letterbooks is that humanist Petrarchism filled a practical need for male humanists when Ciceronian Latin failed to provide a paradigm of male-female *amicitia*, making otherwise neo-Ciceronian letters necessarily eclectic. But, just as women were excluded from Cicero's political writings, so too did they risk being excluded from the dominant discourse of his neo-Latin humanist imitators when the language used to address and describe them was grounded in Petrarchan amatory rhetoric.[18]

Born under the shadow of Petrarch's Laura, the female humanist may have gained a voice through her writing, but she found herself objectified by her male interlocutors much as the silent, chaste beloved of the Petrarchan lyric had been. When Lauro Quirini (1420–75) wrote "amor enim relationem avet" ("love, indeed, longs for a beloved") to Nogarola, he was honouring her erudition in a Latin encomium, but he couched his praise in terms that Petrarch used to address his fictional beloved.[19] Indeed, this language is intensely reminiscent of the language used by Angelo Poliziano (1454–94) in the Greek epigram to Alessandra Scala: "I have found, I have found what I wanted, what I have always been seeking, what I was asking for from Eros, what I was even dreaming of ..."[20] Poliziano believes he has found his beloved in the female humanist, yet his portrayal of her is at odds with the praise he bestows upon her for her mastery of Greek. Margaret King has long argued that educated women during the Renaissance were viewed as members of a "third sex" – neither male nor female but "other." In her discussion of Cassandra Fedele, she remarks that, "she, too, had overcome her sex, had created a man within her womanliness and had become a creature of ambiguous identity, belonging to a third and unknown sex beyond the order of nature. The learned women of the Renaissance, in the eyes of their male contemporaries and friends, ceased, in becoming learned, to be women."[21] Contrary to King's assessment, I would argue that it is precisely because they became learned, and thus more "masculine," that male humanists treated them discursively as more "feminine." Petrarch's *RVF* provided a cornucopia of tropes ready for imitation and steeped in essentialist representations of male and female identities. Thus, humanist Petrarchism resignified the female humanist as "woman," and consequently reified her traditional place in the social and "natural" hierarchy.[22] In the letters from her male humanist colleagues, the learned woman of the Quattrocento thus becomes the embodiment of Laura.

Scholarship has long recognized the use of commonplaces in Renaissance texts written *about* women, but has not generally done so in texts written *to* them.[23] Humanist Petrarchism reveals a tense moment in the intellectual history of women. At the same time that these learned women were praised widely for their humanistic accomplishments, they were discursively treated as silent, chaste Petrarchan beloveds. They were both members of an elite humanist culture and outsiders at the same time, as Virginia Cox has noted:

> Whatever her initial novelty and threat value, by the late-fifteenth century, the "learned lady" was a familiar and sanctioned enough figure to have been co-opted as a kind of "national treasure," routinely boasted of by compatriots as an honor to her city and her kin. True, these women were adopted more in the role of mascots than fully integrated members of the professional humanistic community; women's existential "otherness" in the period was such that things could have hardly been any other way. Allowing for this, however, the writing woman did have a place by 1500 in Italian literary culture, even if that place was more of the nature of a pedestal or niche than a genuine "seat at the table."[24]

I agree with Cox about the pedestal-dwelling function of women's writing; however, I seek to discern male writing's use of the lyrical paradigms of power to generate the "existential 'otherness'" responsible for the marginalization-by-reification that Cox and I both identify. In this sense, one is reminded of a question De Lauretis has posed in a rather different context that nonetheless resembles our own: "How did Medusa feel seeing herself in Perseus' mirror just before being slain?"[25] This chapter explores the humanist text as if it were Minerva's shield, a symbol of prudence and wisdom, and poses the same question about the fifteenth-century female humanists: how did they respond when looking at their reflection in the Latin humanist text?

Isotta Nogarola: Ciceronian *Amicitia* and Petrarchan Love

Isotta Nogarola's humanist letterbook is the most voluminous example of female erudition to emerge from the Quattrocento. She was born into a wealthy family that fostered and promoted female education. Sarah

G. Ross has used the Nogarola family as an example of what she calls the "intellectual family"during the early modern period. She explains that, "Sponsored and often educated by their learned fathers, women authors of the fifteenth and sixteenth centuries enjoyed and capitalized upon the cultural legitimacy and patriarchal sanction – or representation – afforded."[26] Indeed, several generations of women writers stem from the Nogarola blood line.[27] Isotta Nogarola's aunt, Angela Nogarola (ca 1400), was a Latin poet whose poetry is extant, though unfortunately not much biographical information about her has survived.[28] At the insistence of their mother, Bianca, both Isotta and her sister, Ginevra (1417–64), received a humanist education from their private tutor, Martino Rizzoni, student of famed humanist Guarino da Verona.[29] Bianca was often praised for emphasizing her daughters' education, as we see in a letter written by Giorgio Bevilacqua to the Nogarola sisters on 3 April 1436. After calling the sisters the reincarnation of the Muses and the most educated (classical) women,[30] Bevilacqua attributes their accomplishments to their mother, calling her a "mulier generosissima" (most generous woman) and the "effigiam Corneliae" (effigy of Cornelia).[31] While the young Nogarola sisters enjoyed a considerable amount of fame for their intellect and Latin composition, their lives took different paths after Ginevra married in 1438 and abandoned her humanist career. Isotta Nogarola never married, nor did she enter a convent; instead, thanks to the financial support of her family, she devoted herself entirely to humanistic studies, becoming the most prolific female writer of the century. As a result of her unimpeded, lifelong commitment to her studies, her letterbook documents her intellectual maturation from the beginning of her studies to the end of her life, providing us with a sustained portrait of her career as a humanist.[32]

Nogarola's Latin letters are carefully crafted examples of classical erudition, in both letter and spirit. Particularly in her earliest letters, her imitation of Cicero is elegant and commendable in her attempt to forge literary friendships with men. As with Cicero's *De amicitia* and three volumes of *Epistolae ad familiares*, her letters employ a classical rhetoric of affection and friendship, tempered by modesty, revealing her well-founded understanding of the humanist epistolary genre from the earliest years of her career. This is exemplified in a series of letters from 1436 or 1437 that she exchanged with another of Guarino's students, the Venetian nobleman Giorgio Bevilacqua.[33] After having received his gift, a book on the death of St Jerome,[34] she sends him a letter expressing appreciation and a mutual, Ciceronian affection for him. She opens the letter by expressing relief that Bevilacqua's previous silence was due to his dedication to his studies, rather than, as she had feared, his lack of regard for her. She then writes:

> Quo cum ita sit, nos maximis molestiis et doloribus liberasti, cum in epistola tua nullam apud me, *quantum me amares*, dubitationem reliquisti. Nam profecto eas laudes, quas de nobis scriptura prosecutus es, sine *amore* haud vere scribere non potuisse. Etsi tibi verbis non potero, amore certe tacito respondebo; etenim tua ad nos ingens in dies fama me tanto *tui desiderio* afficit, quod unam solam inter dolorem hunc consolationem assequor, ut *nostrum utriusque desiderium* crebris et longis epistolis leniatur. (emphasis mine)

> And so, you have freed us from great sorrow and anxiety, since your letter has left me no doubt of *how much you love me*. Really, you could not possibly have written the praises you lavished on my writing without *love*. And though I shall not be able to respond to you in words, I shall respond unfailingly with *a wordless love*; for your excellence, which appears greater to us each day, affects me daily with such a *great desire for you* that I seek only one consolation for the longing – that *our desire for each other* may be assuaged by long and frequent letters. (translation amended)[35]

At first glance, the repetition of "love" and "desire" – as both nouns (*amor, desiderium*) and verbs (*amo*) – might seem immodest in a letter written by an unmarried woman to a man outside her family. But the Ciceronian intertext of the passage reveals the affectionate language as synonymous with a mutual esteem between the two humanists, rather than the kind of explicitly erotic love associated with, for example, the letters of Abelard and Héloise. Indeed, the similarities between Nogarola's letter and Cicero's letter to Trebonius in December 46 point to Nogarola's attempt at mediating her voice and desire for literary kinship through Cicero's model of male *amicitia*.[36] There are three clear examples to note. The first line of the citation above echoes Cicero's "nullam enim apud me reliquisti dubitationem quantum me amares" (par. 1; "for you have left me in no doubt how much you love me"). Then, her subtle evocation of the topos of ineffability – that she will not be able to respond in words – alludes to Cicero's declaration that he will repay Trebonius's affection by returning it: "cui quidem ego amori utinam ceteris rebus possem, amore certe respondebo" (par. 3; "I wish I could repay your affection in all other ways, but at least I shall repay it with my own"). The last example is the role of letter writing in consoling the two during one another's absence. As Cicero writes, "meque tanto desiderio adficis ut unam mihi consolationem relinquas, fore ut utriusque nostrum absentis desiderium crebris et longis epistulis leniantur" (par. 1; "Missing you as sorely as I do, you leave me only one consolation – that long, frequent letters will mitigate the sense of loss we both feel in each other's absence"). Nogarola's almost verbatim imitation of these Ciceronian declarations of affection and friendship for Trebonius grounds her letter in Ciceronian *amicitia* and makes humanistic intellectual conversation the cornerstone of her relationship to Bevilacqua.

When imitated by a woman, the subtle homoerotic undertones of Ciceronian *amicitia* – much discussed by scholars – produce a similar sexual tension in male-female epistolary exchanges.[37] However, the erotic undertone is diminished in Nogarola's letter when she goes on to describe Bevilacqua's gift – a piece of devotional literature – as a "declarationem amoris" (lines 15–16; declaration of your love). Given the very religious nature of the book, *amor* takes on a meaning of *caritas,* since the gift is meant to ameliorate the soul. Again, Nogarola's choice of phrasing is taken directly from Cicero when he thanks Trebonius for the gift of a book of Ciceronian witticisms. In his letter, Cicero writes, "liber iste quem mihi misisti quantam habet declarationem amoris tui!" (par. 2; "this book you have sent me, what a declaration of your affection!"). Both the gift Cicero received and the one received by Nogarola are meant to flatter the recipient, though Trebonius's gift appeals to Cicero's ego and Bevilacqua's to Nogarola's religious devotion. As Margaret King has explained, Nogarola often received gifts of a religious nature, and many of her contemporaries viewed her as a holy woman.[38]

The closing of the letter repeats the Ciceronian nature of their friendship, this time explicitly attributing her words to him. She writes,

> Quamobrem tuam verbis Ciceronis profectionem amore prosequar, reditum saepe exspectem, absentem memoria colam, omne desiderium litteris mittendis accipiendis leniam.
>
> And so, I shall lovingly adorn this parting from you with Cicero's words: I shall impatiently await your return, remember you while you are gone, and by sending letters, I shall allay my desire to receive them.[39]

She mimics the tone of Cicero's letters to his many friends, where male friendship is founded on a distinct form of love – *amicitia*

– requited only through epistolary exchange. Thus, the Ciceronian undertones, while admittedly still erotic, privilege a sense of deep kinship and admiration over that of erotic feelings.

While one of Cicero's concerns in *De amicitia* is delineating the boundaries of affection between (male) friends, the notion of a spiritual kinship, which founds Cicero's theory of *amicitia*, does not seem to translate linearly into male-female friendship. The framework within which women writers like Nogarola worked to establish literary friendships with men was a model that excluded women, since Ciceronian *amicitia* was a political relationship. As Grafton and Jardine have noted, a humanist education for women was an end in itself rather than a means to a political career, as was the case for young male aristocrats.[40] The same rhetorical question they pose – "education for what?" – can be transposed to the act of women's imitating the Ciceronian model. That is, what could be gained from Ciceronian imitation if political *amicitia* was out of the reach of the female humanist? Thus, Cicero's theorizing over the limits of affection between male friends takes on a new meaning in Quattrocento epistolary exchanges between men and women. The issues of morality and female chastity were ever present. Indeed, while Nogarola maintained a Ciceronian frame in her letters to her male peers, they did not always respond in like manner. In certain cases, we see a distinctly Petrarchan rhetoric employed in letters addressed to Nogarola, where Ciceronian affection is replaced by Petrarchan professions of love. The *RVF* supplied numerous examples of a male intellectual addressing a woman using terms of endearment and spiritual kinship and expressions of longing similar to what we find in Cicero. But the codified nature of the *RVF*, the silence of Laura, and her domination by the poet-lover make its imitation in humanist letters push the boundaries of the limits of affection between "friends." Gender complicates and problematizes the practice because, as we shall see, humanist Petrarchism does not create a level playing field between the male and female humanist. The paradigms of power between poet-lover and beloved/feminized patrons examined in chapter 1 are rooted in the amatory language of the *RVF*, and within a humanist letter they risk silencing the female voice and re-objectifying her as an object of desire.

An early example of humanist Petrarchism can be found in renowned humanist Lauro Quirini's (1420–75?) earliest letter to Nogarola.[41] Quirini, a student and classmate of Leonardo Nogarola at the University of Padova, sent her a letter sometime between 1448 and 1452 praising her accomplishments and advising her on philosophical studies. Although he had never met the young female scholar and knew her only by reputation, Quirini opens the letter in an affectionate Ciceronian fashion claiming, "Pudor nescio quis paene subrusticus Isota insignis feminarum nostri temporis maxima gloria ad hanc usque diem me tenuit, ne tibi antea scriberem, quam tacito quidem, sed certe plurimo amore colebam" ("Some sort of almost boorish shyness, remarkable Isotta, greatest glory of women of our age, has restrained me to this day from writing to you, whom, although silently, I have certainly cherished most affectionately").[42] The initial topos of modesty is frequently employed by male and female humanists alike: his bashfulness ("pudor") prevented him from reaching out to her, even though he has silently and affectionately cherished ("colebam") her. He elevates her status by calling her the "greatest glory of women of our age" while lowering himself when he describes his modesty ("pudor") as "subrusticus" – clownish, boorish, awkward. The specific phrasing Quirini uses – "Pudor nescio quis paene subrusticus" – is taken from the incipit of Cicero's letter to Lucius Lucceius, circa 12 April 55: "Coram me tecum eadem haec agere saepe conantem deterruit pudor quidam paene subrusticus quae nunc expromam absens audacius" ("Although I have more than once attempted to take up my present topic with you face to face, a sort of shyness, almost awkwardness, has held me back").[43] While Quirini's opening phrase is conventional, by adding the detail about Nogarola's fame he ultimately blames his "pudor ... subrusticus" on a sense of intimidation. This is an important deviation from the Ciceronian letter, which centres on Lucceius's role in increasing Cicero's fame. In his letter, Cicero urges Lucceius to complete the history of Cicero's consulship, as promised, expressing his impatience to finally see himself praised by the famed historian.[44] Cicero is hardly intimidated by his friend; rather, his bashfulness is in how to remind his friend of an unfulfilled promise. By citing Cicero's incipit, Quirini recalls a letter between two intellectuals who both have something to gain from their friendship.

The theme of literary friendship subtly threads through the letter, particularly when Quirini praises Nogarola's intellect. He congratulates her on being admitted to the group of famous learned women of antiquity, whom he briefly lists: the Sibyls, Aspasia, Sappho, Proba, Amesia, Hortensia, and Cornelia. Rather than discuss them all at length, he instead focuses on another learned woman, the philosopher Hypatia (ca 375–415):

> Sinesius ergo eximius philosophus Hepatram philosophia praeceptricem habuit, quam tanta laude tantisque praeconiis effert, ut conctos illius temporis philosophos excoluisse magnopere affirmet. Iuer igitur es tu quoque, Isota praeclara, summis laudibus prosequenda, quippe naturam, ut sic dixerim, tuam superasti.
>
> Synesius, a distinguished philosopher, had as his teacher Hypatia, whom he exalted with such praise and such declarations as to demonstrate that all the philosophers of that time enthusiastically admired her. Rightly, therefore, you should also, famous Isotta, receive the highest praises, since you have indeed, if I may so speak, overcome your own nature.[45]

Hypatia was the head of the Neoplatonic school of Alexandria, where she taught philosophy and astronomy.[46] In this respect, she is an apt exemplar for Nogarola, who is embarking on a new course of study in philosophy. In addition, as Virginia Cox has noted, the general practice of comparing Quattrocento female humanists to learned women of antiquity legitimized the emergence of women writers in this century. She has argued that Quirini's use of Hypatia – a philosophical example – distinguishes his Venetian humanism from that of the Florentine Leonardo Bruni, who tended towards rhetorical-poetic-theological exampla.[47] I would also add that the comparison between Nogarola and Hypatia further legitimizes Quirini's attempt at forging a literary friendship with Nogarola, since Hypatia was known to have corresponded at length with her student Synesius. Thus we see in Quirini's example above a model of male-female intellectual friendship grounded in philosophy and expressed in letters. Their relationship is made platonic when he claims that Nogarola has surpassed her sex ("naturam ... tuam superasti"), making the issue of their respective sexes a moot point. From this example, it would seem that Ciceronian *amicitia* was possible between the two because Nogarola was no longer a woman.

After this initial establishment of friendship between them, Quirini spends the bulk of the letter detailing which philosophers Nogarola should read, and what she has to gain from these studies. He closes the letter with a series of statements that move away from Ciceronian *amicitia* and educational advice towards a Petrarchan paradigm of desire. He begins by stating, "Itaque tibi spondeo fide Athica, quod si iniurato non credis, per ventum et humum tibi iuro me tuam dulcem memoriam inter arcana pectoris servare" ("I promise you, therefore, with Attic faith

– in the event you would not believe me without this vow – by wind and earth I swear to you that I preserve your sweet memory within the secret places of my heart").[48] The pledge to preserve her memory ("memoriam") recalls Petrarch's *RVF 96*:

> Io son de l'aspectar omai sì vinto,
> e de la lunga guerra de' sospiri,
> ch'i' aggio in odio la speme e i desiri,
> et ogni laccio ond'è 'l mio cor è avinto.
>
> Ma 'l bel viso leggiadro che depinto
> porto nel petto, e veggio ove ch'io miri,
> mi sforza; onde ne' primi empii martiri
> pur son contra mia voglia risospinto. (1–8)

> I am so vanquished by waiting and by the long war of my sighs, that I hate what I hoped for and my desires and every noose with which my heart is bound. // But that lovely smiling face, which I carry painted in my breast and see wherever I look, forces me, and I am driven back just the same into the first cruel tortures.[49]

In a manner characteristic of Petrarch, the poet-lover here portrays himself as battle torn and without hope. Although he has been conquered in the "war of ... sighs" ("guerra de' sospiri") of the first quatrain, and despite his disdain for the hope and desire he feels, there is a driving force described in the second quatrain that throws him back into torment, albeit against his will: the "lovely smiling face" ("bel viso leggiadro") that he carries in his heart. Within Petrarchan poetics, this face – the face of Laura – not only keeps him in the battle of love, but, most importantly, it is the image that inspires and drives the poetic process. Thanks to the portrait, the absent beloved is eternal in his heart and, by extension, eternal in the landscape not only through the paronomastic play on *laura-lauro* (Laura-laurel tree/crown) that is prevalent throughout the collection but also through the poet-lover's projection of the portrait, as he states, "everywhere I look" ("ove ch'io miri"). This image establishes the symbolic and metaphysical relationship between Petrarch and his beloved Laura by making her ever present, as image and as inspiration, yet completely unattainable.[50]

Although reminiscent of Petrarchan poetics, Quirini's use of "memoriam" is unusual. First, there is no indication that he had ever *seen*

Nogarola. The faculty of sight was generally considered a necessary precursor to the *innamoramento,* as first theorized by Giacomo da Lentini: "Amor è un[o] desio che ven da core / per abondanza di gran piacimento; / e li occhi in prima genera[n] l'amore / e lo core li dà nutricamento" (Love is a desire that comes from the heart / through an abundance of great pleasure; / the eyes first generate love / and the heart gives it [love] nourishment).[51] In addition, and more importantly, the evocation of this lyric commonplace undermines the stated purpose of the letter, which is to praise Nogarola's intellect and encourage her to further study. This Petrarchan conceit begins a series of encapsulating evocations that transform Nogarola into a beloved-like figure of the Petrarchan lyric. Quirini goes on to say that, despite the delay in his writing to her – as he has already explained at the beginning of the letter – he has been moved to write by his conscience and his affection for her, claiming that he will maintain his affection for her as long as she wishes. He justifies this devotion through a kind of dictum of love: "Amor enim relationem avet" ("Love, indeed, longs for a beloved").[52] The use of the verb *aveo* depicts not so much the act of seeking as the act of longing and desiring. The use of "relationem," from "relatio" – literally a carrying back or bringing back – used in philosophical and grammatical discourse, could be translated literally as "relation." Although an abstraction, the desire of love to find a relation(ship) necessitates an object that, in the context of the letter, is Nogarola. When this notion of a relationship is coupled with the use of a strong affective verb like *aveo,* we are left with a statement reminiscent of a poet-lover's claim: Love desires a beloved.

The move from an encomium to suggestions of future studies in philosophy to proclamations of love is surprising, yet it echoes a specific tension found in Petrarch's appropriation of the Apollo-Daphne myth in his lyrics. That is, in the Petrarchan pursuit of the beloved Laura, the laurel tree (lauro) and the laurel crown (alloro) are intrinsically joined through paronomasia. Quirini employs the same rhetorical word play with his first name, Lauro, recalling the Petrarchan pursuit of letters and beloved. He implores Nogarola, "Laurum ergo tum plurimis aliis causis amare debes, tum vel praecipue quod simper virescit, ob id enim Apolloni tuo deo sapientiae consecrabat gentilitas" ("Therefore, you should love *Lauro* [the laurel tree], among many other reasons, particularly for this, that it is always green, for which reason the pagans consecrated it to Apollo, your god of wisdom").[53] Among the many (unspoken) reasons for which Nogarola should love *Laurum,* Quirini emphasizes the fact that it (the laurel tree) is evergreen ("simper virescit"), for which reason it was consecrated to Apollo, god of wisdom, as he states, but also god of poetry. The possessive qualifier "*tuo* deo sapientiae" (*your* god of wisdom) implies that Nogarola's appreciation of Apollo might be different from that of others, like Quirini. His assertion that she should love *Laurum* therefore serves a double purpose: he praises and encourages her by telling her to love the laurel tree, consecrated tree of her god Apollo and symbol of study and fame, while simultaneously telling her to love him, Lauro. The use of the double entendre echoes the Petrarchan paronomastic play on Laura's name that enables the poet to love both fame and the beloved simultaneously within his poetics.

At first glance, the analogy seems to grant Nogarola the power of subjectivity: if Lauro is Laura, then Nogarola is Petrarch, the pursuer of the beloved and of fame. However, Quirini continues to speak from the position of privilege. That is, only he is able to switch between subjectivity and objectivity. By grounding the language in a narrative of desire, Quirini inscribes himself as the beloved who explicitly encourages his pursuer. In other words, he embodies the male poetic fantasy of the beloved reciprocating love and desire. This reinforces the metaphysical relationship between Quirini and Nogarola already described in the beginning of the letter when he confessed to carrying her "memoriam" in his heart. Her role as a figure of the beloved is made definitive in the closing of the letter when he writes, "Vale et me, ut cupio, ama" ("Farewell, and I entreat you, love me").[54] The pursuit – the chase – is in the letter, and the original intent of encouraging her towards philosophical studies is overshadowed. Quirini grounds his praise in a Petrarchan language of desire, thereby undermining his purported praise of Nogarola's intellectual accomplishments. His praise arises ultimately from the female humanist's ability to *inspire love* in Quirini, as did the lyrical beloveds before her. She is treated not as an intellectual equal – a Ciceronian *amica*, or a modern Hypatia – but rather as an object of affection.

Literary allusions and Petrarchan topoi abound in letters sent to other female humanists in praise of their intellect, several of which will be examined in the remaining sections of this chapter. In each case, the female humanist's intellectual accomplishments are met with reductive praise grounded in Petrarchan desire. As a result, the learned woman is figured as somewhere in between her historical reality and a literary ideal about woman. The Latin humanist epistle reflects the highest level of learning, the medium through which the humanist displays his/her mastery of the classics and Latin composition. Yet, what is reflected to the female humanist is not what is expected: not the image of an educated woman equal to her male humanist colleague but rather an object of desire without a voice – a poetic beloved. The next sections examine more explicit examples of this metamorphosis of the female humanist into a literary beloved, in the case studies of Cassandra Fedele and the young female humanist Alessandra Scala.

The Spectacle of Woman: Cassandra Fedele's Oration for Bertuccio Lamberti

Cassandra Fedele was born in Venice in 1465 and at a very young age was renowned for her mastery of Latin and Greek under the tutelage of the Servite monk Gasparino Borro.[55] As in the case of Isotta Nogarola, Ciceronian *amicitia* is a defining feature of Fedele's letters, though she seems to prefer *De amicitia* over Cicero's letters to friends. References to the friendship of Laelius and Scipio are thus sprinkled throughout her letters addressed to prominent members of her extended family and notable humanists like Angelo Poliziano and Bartolomeo Scala of the Medici circle in Florence, as well as the Paduan academics and poets Giovanni Aurelio Augurello and Paolo Ramusio. What is most remarkable about Fedele's letterbook is the lengthy correspondence she had with male and female patrons, from Queen Isabella and King Ferdinand of Spain to Duke Lodovico Maria Sforza, King Louis XII of France, and Beatrice d'Este, to name a few. In this respect, her network extended beyond the confines of humanist circles, and so we see in her letterbook the figure of both a female humanist writer and a would-be courtier.[56] This, in addition to the numerous public lectures she delivered, presents us with a learned woman who, by the end of the Quattrocento, had a formidable public presence and reputation. Although she lived well into the sixteenth century, after marrying the physician Gian Maria Mappelli in 1498/9, her humanistic output virtually came to an end until she was widowed in 1520. In 1556, at the age of ninety-one, Fedele delivered her final public oration in Venice to celebrate the visit of Queen Bona Sforza of Poland. She died two years later, and was given a state funeral in Venice – a public testament to her illustrious humanist career and the prominent place she held in the city's culture.

A defining moment in Fedele's early career was her 1487 public oration at the University of Padua, in honour of her cousin Bertuccio Lamberti's graduation in philosophy.[57] Before a distinguished group of liberal arts faculty, students, and members of the graduating class, the twenty-two-year-old Fedele embarked on a philosophical discourse about the transitory nature of worldly goods and the ennobling effects of philosophy on the mind and soul, as exemplified by her cousin. Seemingly aware of the novelty of the spectacle of a young woman expounding on this topic to a distinguished and educated audience of men, Fedele modestly opens her oration by praising the men and their status, before declaring her worthiness to be there:

> Forti animo incipienti timere decorum esset, amplissimi patres, academiae moderatores, vosq; [vosque] viri ornatissimi, cum ego sim coram tanto virorum confessu, titubare ac minus minusq; [minusque] mihi constare deberem. Sed hoc minime fortissimum decere cognovi. Timiditas itaq; [itaque] finem accipiat. (193)

> Gracious fathers, officers of the academy, and gentleman worthy of the highest honor, if it were fitting for me to be afraid, now that I have bravely plunged in and stand here in your presence in this great assembly, I would stutter and stammer, and I would gradually lose my composure. But I know that my coming here is fitting, though it is by no means very brave. So let the fear end here. (155)

Her opening address is formulaic with its use of the superlative to elevate the status of the audience: "ampl*issimi* patres" and "viri ornat*issimi*." She hints that one might be fearful in front of such an esteemed crowd of men, but she herself is not. She will not stutter or stammer ("titubare") in fear before them, because she knows her presence is warranted on this occasion. Indeed, the repetition of "timere" from the opening line in the final, hortatory subjunctive, "timiditas itaque finem accipiat" ("so let the fear end here"), downplays the uniqueness of her public oration by placing her on the same level as the men in the audience. As Diana Robin has noted, in her letters Fedele often uses the diminutive to lower her station, referring to her letters as "literulae," her mind as "ingeniolum," her voice as "vocula."[58] In this oration, however, we find no traces of these topoi of modesty that would otherwise characterize her authorial voice.

She continues to justify her presence there as an intellectual equal by calling attention to her sex and what has been denied to her because of it:

> etsi non dubitem plerisq; [plerisque] vestrum facinus audax videri posse, quod ego et virgo et cui per aetatem altior nulla eruditio contingere potuit, neq; [neque] ingenij memor, in tantam eruditorum hominum lucem, et praefertim in ea urbe, in qua his temporibus (ut olim Athenis) liberalium, atrium studia florent oratura processerim. (193)

> I am well aware than many of you may think it outrageous that I, a young girl to whom higher learning is denied, would come before an assembly of men so learned and so luminous and not worry about my sex or talent in speaking, especially in this city where the liberal arts are flourishing now as they once did in Athens. (155)

When she refers to herself as "virgo" she highlights both her sex and (young) age. On the one hand, this further praises the audience of, especially, the "amplissimi *patres*" by playing into the familial trope: she is a young virgin before esteemed father figures. Yet the repetition of "eruditio" in this passage subtly critiques the academic system that would deny women entry but invite them to speak publicly at such an important and symbolic event. That is, she qualifies "virgo" with the statement that she has been denied a university education ("cui per aetatem altior nulla eruditio contingere potuit"). "Eruditio" is taken as a formal, university education in this context, rather than the more general sense of learning or erudition. She refers to the second connotation, however, when she again addresses the audience as "in tantam eruditorum hominum lucem" – the men are "learned" and "luminous." Her use of the more general term "homo" (mankind, people), instead of the earlier exclusively male terms "pater" (father) and "vir" (man), levels the intellectual playing field. "Homo" is all-inclusive and does not limit erudition to only the men in the crowd whom she is addressing. While she might have been denied a formal university education, she is erudite, like all those men who are present at the graduation ceremony.

Throughout the oration, Fedele emphasizes the intellect as the one true virtue, leaving the question of age and gender (sex) aside. While she praises her cousin's academic achievements, she does so in such a way that the two of them are presented as comparable. Through a string of rhetorical questions, she remarks that intellectual virtue is a tangible thing;

> Sed quid attinet magis in coniuncto meo genus laudare, quam mores? Quam studia optima? Quam ingenium docile varium, promptum, capax? Memoriā [memoriam] tenacissimam? Bonarū [bonarum] artium

praecipuum amorem? ... quam immaturo aevo cernitis, tam maturum virtute cognoscetis: quae nisi omnibus aperta fuissent minime in tanto caetu proferre auderem. (195–6)

But what quality or characteristic is it more important to praise in my kinsman than his character? How shall I praise his excellent studies? How do I speak of his mind, which is capacious, alert, flexible, and open to learning? His tenacious memory? His special love of the liberal arts? ... you see here a man who is as mature in virtue as he is young in years. And had this virtue of his not been apparent to all, I would never have dared to extol it in so great an assembly. (156)

Fedele deploys the topos of ineffability in praising her cousin, passing over in silence any evidence she might give to prove his accomplishments and dedication to humanist study. Instead, the proof of Bertuccio's virtue resides in his intelligence, which is being honoured with a degree in philosophy. When she claims that he is "as mature in virtue as he is young in years," she echoes her self-presentation as a "virgo" at the beginning of the oration, providing another example of erudition that is not limited to the "amplissimi patres." She will go on to philosophize about the transitory nature of worldly things, including beauty, claiming that the achievements of the mind and soul are eternal and should thus be praised, as she has undertaken to do. Eloquence, specifically, is the marker of a great mind when she claims that "orationem enim bestijs homines praestant" ("it is speech that makes men superior to all animals" [197]). As earlier, here Fedele chooses the more general and inclusive term "homo" in her distinction, not relegating eloquence and rhetoric exclusively to the realm of men.

The closing of the oration is her most explicit move towards including herself among the distinguished, learned male scholars in the audience. In an aside to herself, the century, and the city of Padua, she draws attention both to the accomplishments of Paduan humanists and to her own:

O te igitur felicem Cassandram, cui hisce temporibus nasci contigit. O beatam aetatem nostram, O urbem praeclarā [praeclaram] Patavij, quae doctissimorum virorum copia exuberas. Definant iam omnes, definant inquam vetera mirari. Deus Optimus Maximusque hoc in loco omnium studia gentium florere voluit, ac aeternitati cōmendata [commendata], consecrataque esse. (200)

And so in conclusion, happy are you, Cassandra, since you were fortunate enough to be born in these times, and you, blessed era of mine, and you,

> famous city of Padua, graced in your bounty of learned men. May everyone now cease – yes, I say cease – to marvel at antiquities. God almighty has granted that the studies of all nations should flourish in this one place and be commended and consecrated for all eternity. (158–9)

Fedele first congratulates herself for being born in an age that saw the rebirth of classical letters and humanistic accomplishments. By invoking her name – Cassandra – she draws attention to her sex much as she did in the beginning of the oration when she referred to herself as "virgo." But here, it is not as a young girl standing before older men but rather as a humanist in her own right who has just delivered a philosophical oration at an all-male institution. She distinguishes herself from the "doctissimorum virorum copia" (bounty of learned men) in Padua, congratulating the century and city for both its educated men (*viri*) and women (Cassandra). Thus, when she commands all to cease marvelling at antiquity, we can read it both as praise for the accomplishments of the men in the audience, who have surpassed the ancients, and as a strategy for setting herself apart from the static women of the "famous women" tradition widely popularized by Boccaccio.[59] The performative effect of her speech is that no longer must humanists only read about educated women and orators, for now they can see and hear them, as the men of the audience have just done.

One defining feature of Fedele's oration is thus the sense of erudite community she presents, and her inclusion in it. Epistolary reactions to her oration pick up on this thread, but treat the subject matter in a much different manner. Angelo Tancredi's 1488 letter following her oration, for example, depicts his personal response to her oration as a communal and shared experience among all the men in the audience. In praising her intellect, Tancredi re-identifies her as woman by reverting to the language and paradigms of Petrarch's *RVF*. He tells her that before writing to her, he visited the renowned humanist Francesco Negri to discuss Fedele's oration and get his opinion on her eloquence. He then relates that,

> Illum tamen cantantem pro immortalibus tuis laudibus carmina qualiacumque forent, et suspirantem atque dolentem video, pudetque etiam temporum, et miseriarum nostrarum clamantem, quod neque ocij, neque quietis … (150)

> When I see him he is still singing poems to your immortal praises. He sighs, grieves, and is ashamed of our times and our wretchedness, and shouts that he has had no peace or serenity … (translation amended)[60]

Negri's praise of Fedele comes in the form of sung poems ("carmina"), accentuated by his sighs ("suspirantem"), grief ("dolentem"), and the shame he feels ("pudet") for their wretched times ("miserarium nostrarum"). This combination of emotions in a poetry of sighs recalls Petrarch's *RVF,* and especially his iconic opening sonnet:

> Voi ch'ascoltate in rime sparse il suono
> di quei sospiri ond'io nudriva 'l core
> in sul mio primo giovenile errore,
> quand'era in parte altr'uom da quel ch'i' sono (1–4)

> You who hear in scattered rhymes the sound of those sighs with which I nourished my heart during my first youthful error, when I was in part another man from what I am now.[61]

Petrarch's sense of interiority in this poem places the notions of shame, grief, and regret squarely upon his own shoulders – that is, it was his "youthful error" (including his love for Laura and his desire for fame) that led to his wretched state, for which he is chastised by St Augustine in the *Secretum.* Negri however projects an outward disappointment in the wretchedness of contemporary life; his shame is directed at the times and not at himself or his own errors. In Petrarch, Laura is the source of his existential crisis, and the closing of the first poem includes a small beacon of hope when he writes of "'l conoscer chiaramente / che quanto piacer al mondo è breve sogno" (13–14; "the clear knowledge that whatever pleases in the world is a brief dream"). Human wretchedness, for Petrarch, ends with death. For Negri, however, Fedele represents the only positive thing in their age.

Tancredi seconds Negri's praise of Fedele, marking her as a turning point in humanism, and representative of great things to come. He continues, remarking that,

> Cassandra, tu illa es, cui facile cedant Romani scriptores, cedāt [cedant] Graij: *Nescio quid maius in toto nascatur orbe.* (150)

> Cassandra, you are the one before whom the Roman writers and the Greeks would gladly bow. "I don't know whether anyone greater has been born in the whole world." (68)

That Fedele represents a change in humanism is signalled by the unattributed citation, which I believe comes from Propertius. While not verbatim, the citation in Tancredi's letter – "Nescio quid maius in toto nascatur orbe" – bears a striking resemblance to Propertius's famous line "Nescio quid maius nascitur Iliade" (2.34.66; I don't know if something greater than the Iliad is coming into being [my translation]). Propertius here expresses optimism about the composition of a post-Homeric epic – the *Aeneid* by his close friend Vergil – and the start of a new Roman epic tradition. The elegiac citation became commonplace, as several scholars have noted that the imitation of this Propertian verse functioned as a kind of prophetic or "prequel" reference to forthcoming works and major changes in Western literary traditions.[62] The seamless transition from recounting Negri's response to Tancredi's support and amplification of his praise presents a communal response to the oration. By juxtaposing Negri's channelling of Petrarch's pessimism and grief, told through a poetry of sighs, and Tancredi's Propertian hope, both men signal a shifting of the tides: Fedele, as a learned woman, represents a new chapter in Quattrocento humanism, though as we shall see, not without consequence.

Immediately following the Propertian citation, Tancredi characterizes Fedele as something divine and nymphlike, thereby claiming the female humanist for a different reality – that of "woman." He co-mingles a Vergilian allusion and a Petrarchan codification of said allusion when he writes,

> Aut diva es certe Virgo, quando minime vox hominem sonat, aut Nympharum sanguinis una … Te verò gloriosissime orantem disputantemque in hac Antenorea Artium liberalium Palaestra philosophantes cum summa attentione, ut ad miraculum usque procederet, intuemur, & os, vultum, virginea totius corporis lineamenta, & facta non humana cernimus, sed divina. (150)[63]

> Surely you are divine, maiden, since your voice hardly sounds human, or you are related to the nymphs by blood … Indeed, we all gazed with rapt attention, as in the presence of a wonder, as you spoke and debated with the philosophers at this Antenorean podium for the liberal arts. And we observed a face, expression, and the maidenly lines of your entire figure that were not human but divine. (68)

Tancredi's description emphasizes the spectacle of Fedele's oration, something that she herself had downplayed in her lecture, as was examined above. His initial reaction is parallel to that of Aeneas when, about halfway through book I of the *Aeneid,* he encounters his mother, Venus – disguised as a huntress – in a forest. When Venus asks Aeneas if he has seen her sister huntress, Aeneas, taken in by her beauty, replies: "o – quam te memorem, virgo? Namque haud tibi vultus / mortalis, nec vox hominem sonat; o dea certe! / An Phoebi soror? An Nympharum sanguinis una?" (1.327–9; "but by what name should I call you, maiden? for your face is not mortal nor has your voice a human ring; O goddess surely! Sister of Phoebus, or one of the race of Nymphs?").[64] Aeneas does not recognize his mother, but does glean from her beauty and voice that she is not human. He questions whether she might be Diana, the chaste huntress and sister to Apollo. Tancredi's appropriation of this scene presents Fedele's oration as an apparition, and as something divinely inspired. While he elevates her status to that of something more than human, the effect is that her humanistic accomplishments and eloquence are undermined as having been divinely inspired.

This Vergilian episode was codified by Petrarch in his descriptions of Laura, who was inherently associated with Daphne (a naiad) as well as Diana (chaste goddess of the hunt whose entourage was made of nymphs), and less frequently Venus. In *RVF* 90, Petrarch draws directly from the Aeneas episode, not only in the description of Laura's golden hair blowing in the wind but also in the description of her gait and voice: "Non era l'andar suo cosa mortal / ma d'angelica forma, et le parole / sonavan altro che pur voce humana" (vv 9–11; "Her walk was not that of a mortal thing but of some angelic form, and her words sounded different from a merely human voice" [194]).[65] In the *Aeneid,* Venus's appearance to Aeneas serves to remind him of his true path: she tells him Dido's story, convincing him to leave the Carthaginian queen in order to fulfil his duty. Thus, in Vergil the encounter between Venus and her son is prophetic, while in Petrarch's version the parallel between Laura and Venus contributes to her uniqueness. Petrarch's influence on Tancredi's description of Fedele is most noted in his use of the poetic device *effictio* to describe her beauty. Tancredi introduces the more detailed description of her beauty by claiming to recount a collective response. He shifts to the first person plural – "intuemur" (we gazed) and "cernimus" (we discerned) – midway through his praise of her. He says that all the men in the audience were enraptured by Fedele, gazing at her as though in the presence of a wonder or miracle ("ad miraculum"). The content of her oration is passed over completely in favour of the collective response to her beauty. Not only was her voice "divine" but also, as he claims, her "face, expression, and the maidenly lines of your entire figure … were not human but divine." By the end of the letter, what we see is praise for her mythical beauty and voice, without any reference to the content of her speech.

The final compliment paid to Fedele is one concerning poetry, and her fitness to become a source of poetic inspiration: "at si infantissimus ego homunculus onus tuarum laudum aggredi velim, quod tantopere praestantissimi nostrae tempestatis Vates, non secùs ac Aethnae onus subire recusant" (151; "But if I, a tongue-tied little man, wish to take up the burden of praising you, how can the most distinguished bards of our time refuse to assume this burden as well, be it as heavy as Mt. Aetna?" [68]). Tancredi invokes the topos of ineffability in a manner characteristic of Fedele's own letters: he is merely a "homunculus" who cannot do her justice. Thus, he places the burden on the "vates" (poets) to sing her praises. The letter closes with the request that she accept the gift of a poem sent by Negri, whom he refers to as "Favorinus." Retrospectively, then, the Petrarchan lyrical evocations throughout the letter take on a more significant meaning. The collective male response to Fedele's oration, her characterization as a divine, nymphlike creature whose beauty strikes men with awe and leaves them tongue-tied, relegates Fedele to a lyric environment that excludes her from meaningful humanist discourse. That only a poet could properly praise her reclaims Fedele as an object of art rather than a producer of it. The significance of her oration, her attempt to include herself in the larger humanist sphere, merely contributed to the spectacle of the public, learned woman, rather than destabilizing it.

This characterization of Fedele as a Petrarchan beloved is not limited to Tancredi's and Negri's assessment of her eloquence. In an undated letter by Girolamo Broianico da Verona, we find a similar shift from praising her intellect through classical allusions to complimenting her beauty through Petrarchan tropes. He writes,

> Te ergo unam ex Cornelijs Procijsque nobilibus Romanis mulieribus sanctissimis, unamque è Pisistrati filiabus moribus sanctis ornatis esse conspiciebam. Cassandra apellaris nomine, proprie & vere inquam Cassandra es forma, atque pulchritudine. Lucretiae enim mulieri pudicissime non cedis, Helenae forma tibi est pulchrae, quam … oculis inspicere nolebant, ne in eius concupiscentiam inciderent … indicat, glauci oculi instar divinarum lampadam fulgentes. Cor … tuum … & … incessus tuus, qui tanto cum decoro a te fieri solet, ut Dea potius, quam Virgo praediceris.

> I have seen that you alone have been graced with the venerable character of the noble Roman women of the Cornelii and Porcii and the daughters of Pisistratus. Your name is Cassandra, but I say, truly you are Cassandra in your demeanor and beauty. For you are second neither to Lucretia, nor to Helen, whose beauty you possess, and whom no one wished to gaze upon lest they should fall madly in love with her. Your shining blue eyes are like divine stars ... your heart ... the way you walk, which ... is so graceful that you are declared not to be a mere girl but a goddess.[66]

As is common with letters written to female humanists of this century, and as I have previously examined in the case of Isotta Nogarola, Broianico compares Fedele to the illustrious women of antiquity. In the style of the *De mulieribus claris* tradition, he compares various aspects of Fedele to famous, classical women. She has the character – read, intellect – of the Cornelian and Porcian women, whose clans included Cornelia Scipionis Africana (who educated her sons, the Gracchi) and the female Stoic Porcia Catonis (daughter of Cato of Utica, second wife to Caesar's assassin Brutus).[67] Her beauty, and by extension her chastity, is compared to that of Lucretia and Helen, with the reminder that there was no defence against their beauty. Broianico then turns to the Petrarchan convention of *effictio,* using a series of Petrarchan conceits to describe her beauty. The comparison between her eyes and stars is a typical Petrarchan conceit, as we see in numerous poems: *RVF* 189, "Passa la mia nave colma d'oblio" ("My ship laden with forgetfulness passes"), the nautical poem where her eyes function as guiding stars ("Celansi i duo mei dolci usati segni" [v. 12]; "My two usual sweet stars are hidden" [334]); *RVF* 157, the epitome of *effictio* where he describes her face, noting "hebeno i cigli, et gli occhi eran due stelle" (v. 9; "ebony her eyebrows, and her eyes two stars" [302]); and *RVF* 200 where we read about Laura's starry brow ("li occhi sereni et le stellanti ciglia" [v. 9]; "her clear eyes and starry brows" [346]). The reference to the divine way in which she walks repeats the earlier Vergilian-inspired convention previously discussed in *RVF* 90,"Non era l'andar suo cosa mortal / ma d'angelica forma ..." (vv 9–10; "Her walk was not that of a mortal thing but of some angelic form ..." [346]). The objectification of Fedele's beauty, through poetic tropes codified by Petrarch in the previous century, comes at the expense of her intellect. She is simultaneously the figure of classical women of antiquity, renowned for their intellect and/or modesty, and the new Laura, famed for her beauty and chastity.

In this letter whose original intent was to praise Fedele's intellect, we see Broianico's discourse turn from Latin humanist conventions to vernacular Petrarchan ones. As with Tancredi's response to Fedele's oration, the female humanist's beauty and her potential to inspire love in men are privileged over her intellectual accomplishments. While including her in a genealogy of illustrious women of the past (including Petrarch's Laura) elevates her status, it also runs the risk of memorializing her as a spectacle of woman rather than a humanist equal to her male peers. In the letters examined above, there is no intellectual engagement with the ideas expounded in Fedele's oration or other works, no challenge or affirmation of her ideas. Rather, the emphasis is on the emotional reaction she elicits from her male peers. Where there is no precedent for male-female correspondence, Petrarchan conceits and tropes fill a need for finding a linguistic model that adequately expresses a sense of awe and wonder when confronting a learned woman. Fedele, like other learned women in the century, performs a role that is founded in fictional representations of woman. These representations – especially when entrusted to a male correspondent – ultimately relegate the female humanist and her innovative role to the restrictive category of "woman." This performance of gender is most explicit in the Greek poems exchanged between Angelo Poliziano and Alessandra Scala – Fedele's stand-in – discussed in the next section.

Performing Woman: The Greek Epigrams of Alessandra Scala and Angelo Poliziano

One of Cassandra Fedele's great admirers was the renowned poet and humanist Angelo Poliziano of Lorenzo de' Medici's Florentine circle. In 1491 Poliziano and Giovanni Pico della Mirandola visited Fedele in her home in Venice, and were astonished by her learning. Poliziano was so impressed by her that he subsequently wrote to Lorenzo de' Medici and, with Pico, campaigned to have her accepted into their Florentine Academy and Court.[68] After their initial meeting, Fedele sent Poliziano several letters, to which she never received a reply. Finally, in 1493 Poliziano responded, excusing his delay and silence by evoking the *Aeneid* episode previously examined: when they met he was dumbstruck, like Aeneas when he saw his mother, Venus, emerge from the woods dressed as a mortal woman.[69] He was so dazed that apparently he could not even read Fedele's letters. So instead he took them to Alessandra Scala and asked her to read them aloud to him, and to an audience of his humanist peers:

her father, Bartolomeo Scala (1430–97), Marsilio Ficino (1433–99), and Giovanni Pico della Mirandola (1463–94). By having Scala, herself a young humanist, perform the letters, as if she were reciting a part in a play, Poliziano claims he was able to recreate Fedele's combination of learning and beauty:

> Alexandram Scalam domi conveni, coramque ipsius parente legendas ei tuas litteras dedi; quas illa ita distincte, scienter, modulate, suaviter pronuntiavit, ut ipsam te tua verba recitantem, liniamentis (quod dicitur) omnibus expresserit. Pellectis rogavit agerem gratias, debere tibi plurimum professa, quae tanti se faceres. Pater ipse stilum non mediocriter laudavit; idem Marsilius fecit, idem Picus …

> I came to Alessandra Scala's home, and personally gave her and her father your letters to be read; which [letters] she recited distinctly, skilfully, rhythmically, sweetly, with the result that, reciting your words, she represented you with all her features, as they say. With the letters having been read through, she asked me to thank you, having professed that she owed much to you, for showing your esteem for her. Her own father praised her style in no uncertain terms; Marsilio [Ficino] did the same, as did Pico [della Mirandola] …[70]

Poliziano emphasizes the spectacle of the event and gives no indication as to the content of the letters Fedele sent to him. Rather than engage her in a meaningful dialogue, he instead describes Scala's recitation and pronunciation with a string of adverbs praising her acting ability – distinctly (with precision), skilfully, rhythmically, sweetly. Scala's performance was so well executed that Poliziano claims she was able to impersonate Fedele in all her features ("liniamentis … omnibus"). In her reading of this passage, Lisa Jardine has noted that, "This effects the metamorphosis of the individual talented woman into a *genus* of representatives of female worth."[71] Indeed, Scala's acting out of Fedele's letters implies a universal connection between all educated women that would allow one to be easily substituted for another. That Fedele's words are embodied by another woman also asserts a necessary relation between women and the body, which distracts and detracts from the intellect. As we observed earlier in Tancredi's reaction to Fedele's oration, here Poliziano's response to and assessment of Scala's performance is presented as a communal judgment. Furthermore, by sending a description of the spectacle to Fedele, Poliziano attempts to include her as a spectator alongside Pico, Ficino, and the others.

The gendered connotations of the split position in which Poliziano is placing Fedele, as both the viewer and the object of her own spectacle, can be productively understood in the same terms in which female cinema spectatorship is read by De Lauretis: "How can the female spectator be entertained as subject of the very moment that places her as its object, that makes her the figure of its own closure?"[72] Was the purpose of Poliziano's response to entertain Fedele, or was it to show her that her worth lay in the spectacle of her learning, rather than her actual intellect? The emphasis on the actress Scala's physical features and the performativity of pronunciation in Poliziano's description points to the audience as being awestruck and impressed by her beauty and her voice rather than by the content of what she was reciting. That is, Fedele's voice was silenced by Scala's performance, the content of her letters overshadowed by the spectacle of the learned woman reciting a script written by her female peer. While it is true that, in the end, the women's identities were conflated into one, as an archetype of the *genus* identified by Jardine, Poliziano's intervention does more than simply conflate the female voices. His letter acts as a screen that, instead of recognizing and re-proposing Fedele's performative subjectivity as he had received it from her letter, splits it into two distinct object positions: her agency is all but lost, and she becomes the spectator and object of her own spectacle.

The balance of Poliziano's letter to Fedele focuses on the past and present accomplishments of her stand-in, the young Florentine Alessandra Scala. I hesitate to say accomplishments because, as is typical of the letters Poliziano sent to Fedele, the emphasis is placed on the effect Scala's accomplishments had on Poliziano. He devotes only one phrase to praising Scala's erudition: "Dies ea noctesque in studiis utriusque linguae versetur" (She is immersed day and night in studies of both languages).[73] This is a distinguished form of praise, since Scala, like Fedele, was one of very few women learned in Greek at the time. This compliment, however, is undermined by the remainder of the letter, which discusses yet another spectacle: her performance as Electra in the Sophoclean play of the same name. Poliziano recounts that,

> ipsa Electrae virginis virgo suscepit, in qua tantum vel ingenii vel artis vel gratiae adhibuit, ut omnium in se oculos atque animas una converteret. Erat in verbis lepos ille atticus prorsum genuinus et nativus, gestus ubique ita promptus et efficax ita argumento serviens, ita per affectus varios decurrens, ut multa inde veritas et fides fictae diu fabulae accederet.

> This virgin herself took on [the role of] Electra the virgin, in which she applied so much of [her] temperament or rather art or even love, so that she turned the eyes and souls of all on her alone. There was an Attic grace in her words, genuine and inborn, her posture open and efficacious everywhere, serving her proof, running through various emotions, so that much of the truth and faith of long standing fables came to be in it.[74]

Poliziano's initial description of being dumbstruck when he met Fedele recurs here in the description of the audience's response to Scala's interpretation of Electra – a detail that could not have escaped Fedele's attention. All eyes and souls were turned to her whose posture ("gestus") was so convincing that it made the fiction of the play believable. In this moment the figure of Electra contaminates the figure of Scala, for, Poliziano claims, "Nec tamen Electrae sic meminit ut Alexandrae sit oblita" (Electra is not remembered so that Alessandra be obscured).[75] The parallel structure of the two theatrical episodes – Scala first acting as Fedele and then as Electra – strips the female humanists of their identity through *contaminatio.* In other words, Scala can just as easily imitate Fedele as she can Electra. Both Fedele and Electra are figured as parts in a play, and Scala's accomplishments in Greek are reduced to her ability to recite and "play the part."

Scala, indeed, plays many roles for Poliziano, including a poetic beloved, as we see in a series of Greek epigrams he exchanged with her. Poliziano's *Epigrammatum Graecorum* 28 describes Scala's performance as Electra, repeating several details from the letter he sent to Fedele, but presenting her in a new, lyrical light:

> Ἠλέκτρην ὑπέκριν᾽ ὁπότ᾽ ἄζυξ ἄζυγα κούρην
> κούρη Ἀλεξάνδρη τήν γε Σοφοκλεΐην,
> θαμβέομεν πάντες πῶς εὐμαρὲς Ἀτθίδα γλῶτταν
> ἤπυεν ἀπταίστως, Αὐσονὶς οὖσα γένος,
> πῶς δέ γε μιμηλὴν προΐει καὶ ἐτήτυμον αὐδήν,
> τἀκριβὲς ἐντέχνου τήρεε πῶς θυμέλης,
> πῶς ἦθος δ᾽ ἐφύλαττεν ἀκήρατον· ὄμματα γαίῃ
> πήξασ᾽ οὐδ᾽ ὁρμῆς ἤμβροτεν, οὐ βάσεως·
> οὐδ᾽ ἀσχημόνεεν φωνὴν βαρύδακρυν ἱεῖσα,
> βλέμματι μυδαλέῳ σὺν δ᾽ ἔχεεν θεατάς.
> πάντες ἄρ᾽ ἐξεπλάγημεν· ἐμὲ ζῆλος δ᾽ ὑπένυξεν
> ὡς τὸν ὅμαιμον ἑῇς εἶδον ἐν ἀγκαλίσιν.

> When Alexandra played the part of Sophocles' Electra – one virgin playing the part of another – we were all astonished at how easily she spoke the Attic tongue without stumbling, though being Ausonian by birth, and at how she projected a convincing and authentic voice, and at how carefully she observed the customs of the artful stage, and at how she kept the character [of Electra] pure. Fixing her eyes upon the ground, she missed the mark neither in effort nor in her steps; nor did she disgrace herself by projecting a voice heavy with tears, but with wet eyes she stirred up the audience. We were all struck dumb: and jealousy stung me when I saw the brother in her arms.[76]

The spirit of the epigram is true to the description above of Scala's performance as both Fedele and Electra. Her ability to imitate the essence of her character so naturally impressed the audience as much as her skills in Greek recitation. Scala is presented as a kind of paradox: Ausonian (Italian) by birth, but seemingly (ancient) Greek; her voice is "convincing" yet "authentic"; she was both Alessandra Scala and Electra. The final verses of the epigram describe something not present in the letter, however: the metamorphosis of the learned woman into Poliziano's beloved. While the entire audience of men was dumbstruck by her performance, Poliziano was overcome by jealousy "when I saw the brother in her arms." Poliziano's purported jealousy over Scala's embracing the male actor on stage is unexpected, to say the least. For one thing, in the final scene of Sophocles' *Electra*, the tragic female heroine embraces her brother after they have committed matricide. They are united by filial revenge, and not sexual desire.[77] Yet Poliziano's reading of the visual scene denotes the same kind of poetic fantasy present in Petrarch's *RVF* 78, where the poet expresses jealousy of Pygmalion and his female statue:

> Quando giunse a Simon l'alto concetto
> ch'a mio nome gli pose in man lo stile,
> s'avesse dato a l'opera gentile
> colla figura voce ed intellecto,
>
> di sospir' molti mi sgombrava il petto,
> che ciò ch'altri à più caro, a me fan vile:
> però che 'n vista ella si mostra humile
> promettendomi pace ne l'aspetto.

> Ma poi ch'i' vengo a ragionar co·llei,
> benignamente assai par che m'ascolte,
> se risponder savesse a' detti miei.
>
> Pigmalïon, quanto lodar ti dêi
> de l'imagine tua, se mille volte
> n'avesti quel ch'i' sol una vorrei

> When Simon received the high idea which, for my sake, put his hand to his stylus, if he had given to his noble work voice and intellect along with form // he would have lightened my breast of many sighs that make what others prize most vile to me. For in appearance she seems humble, and her expression promises peace; // then, when I come to speak to her, she seems to listen most kindly: if she could only reply to my words! // Pygmalion, how glad you should be of your statue, since you received a thousand times what I yearn to have just once![78]

RVF 77 and 78 concern a (now lost) portrait of Laura painted by Simone Martini (1284–1344) that was so lifelike that Petrarch attempted to speak to it. Petrarch's jealousy of Pygmalion concerns the ability to embrace the female statue – a creation of art, much like Simone Martini's painting – not converse with it.[79] In Poliziano's case, it is jealousy over the apparent reciprocation of desire that brings about jealousy: he sees another man in Scala's arms. As was the case with Lauro Quirini's pun on his name – *Laurum* – in his letter to Isotta Nogarola, Poliziano projects himself into the scene as the object of Scala's affection, revealing his privileged status through the oscillation between subjectivity and objectivity. Scala-as-Electra is displayed as an object of Poliziano's desire, a beloved who fulfils the fantasy of reciprocation by embracing another man. Such a lyrical evocation de-emphasizes her performance by turning the reader's attention to Poliziano's feelings of desire and jealousy. At this textual moment Scala becomes his silent, chaste, and desired beloved, just like Petrarch's portrait of Laura and Pygmalion's statue.[80]

Poliziano sent a total of six Greek epigrams to Scala, all depicting unrequited love and desire.[81] They display a conflicting portrait of the female humanist as both the incarnation of a beloved and an accomplished female intellectual and colleague (she is, after all, able to read the Greek poetry, and reply in like manner). Upon close examination of their poetic exchange, we see Poliziano evoke Petrarchan imagery and topoi that essentially metamorphose her into his beloved, while she explicitly denies such a characterization. This conflict of unrequited love emerges from the poetic *tenzone* between the two, beginning with Poliziano's *Epigrammatum Graecorum* 30. The epigram is enclosed in lyrical evocations of unrequited love, and although Poliziano makes reference to Scala's erudition, as we shall see, her status as a learned woman is undermined by her inscription as a beloved:

Εὕρηχ᾽ εὕρηχ᾽ ἣν θέλον, ἣν ἐζήτεον αἰεί,
  ἣν ᾔτουν τὸν Ἔρωθ᾽, ἣν καὶ ὀνειροπόλουν·
παρθενικὴν ἧς κάλλος ἀκήρατον, ἧς ὅ γε κόσμος
  οὐκ εἴη τέχνης, ἀλλ᾽ ἀφελοῦς φύσεως·
παρθενικὴν γλώττῃσιν ἐπ᾽ ἀμφοτέρῃσι κομῶσαν,
  ἔξοχον ἔν τε χοροῖς, ἔξοχον ἔν τε λύρῃ·
ἧς πέρι Σωφροσύνῃ τ᾽ εἴη Χαρίτεσσί θ᾽ ἅμιλλα,
  τῇ καὶ τῇ ταύτην ἀντιμεθελκομέναις.
εὕρηκ᾽, οὐδ᾽ ὄφελος· καὶ γὰρ μόλις εἰς ἐνιαυτὸν
  οἰστροῦντι φλογερῶς ἔστιν ἅπαξ ἰδέειν.

I have found, I have found what I wanted, what I was always seeking, what I was asking for from Eros, what I was even dreaming of: a maiden whose beauty is pure, and whose form is not derived from artifice, but from a simple nature; a maiden pluming herself upon both tongues, excellent in dances, excellent on the lyre; concerning whom there might be a contest between Prudence and the Graces, dragging her in different directions, this way and that. I have found her, but this is not helpful: for only with difficulty is it possible for one in a blazing frenzy to see her once in a year.[82]

Poliziano's message cannot be overstated: he has found, in Scala, the maiden he has always wanted, for whom he has searched, from whom he has requested love, and about whom he has always dreamed; in other words, he has found his soulmate. The profession echoes Petrarch's *RVF* 15, "Io mi rivolgo in dietro a ciascun passo" ("I turn back at each step") where the poet asks rhetorically, "Talor m'assale in mezzo a' tristi pianti / un dubbio: come posson queste membra / da lo spirito lor viver lontane?" ("At times in the midst of my sad laments a doubt assails me: How can these members live far from their spirit? But Love replies to me: Do you not remember that this is a privilege of lovers, released from all human qualities?").[83] The Neoplatonic notion of two souls belonging to one body makes the relationship between poet and beloved undeniable. Poliziano's depiction of Scala's beauty, as created by nature rather than art, also recalls the Petrarchan lyric, particularly *RVF* 248, where the poet urges others to come and admire Laura's beauty and virtue before her death, and claims her unique beauty to be an invention of nature: "Chi vuol veder quantunque pò Natura / e 'l Ciel tra noi, venga a mirar costei" ("Whoever wishes to see all that Nature and Heaven can do among us, let him come gaze on her").[84] Because the beauty of the beloved is unique, it could only have been created by nature, not by artifice. Poliziano reinforces the notion that he has always been searching for Scala by including this minor, yet telling, detail concerning her beauty.

What distinguishes her from the figure of Petrarch's Laura, however, is the detail that establishes her specifically as a female humanist: she is "a maiden pluming herself upon both tongues" (παρθενικὴν γλώττησιν ἐπ' ἀμφοτέρησι κομῶσαν). She commands both languages, Latin and ancient Greek – a compliment we have encountered before. But Poliziano's praise of her impressive erudition is undermined by the end of the epigram where Poliziano describes their relationship as one of unrequited love: "I have found her, but this is not helpful: for only with difficulty is it possible for one in a blazing fury to see her once in a year" ("εὕρηκ', οὐδ' ὄφελος· καὶ γὰρ μόλις εἰς ἐνιαυτὸν / οἰστροῦντι φλογερῶς ἔστιν ἅπαξ ἰδέειν"). In one sweeping move, Poliziano explicitly defines Scala as his beloved. By enclosing the epigram in Petrarchan evocations, Poliziano detracts from the praise he bestows upon her command of Latin and Greek. This is further compounded by his consistent references to her as *maiden* (παρθενικὴν) throughout his epigrams, emphasizing her youth and virginity despite the praise he bestows upon her humanist accomplishments. Poliziano's use of the term "maiden" not only denies Alessandra the dignity of womanhood but gestures at her sexuality (chastity).

Scala's reply to Poliziano challenges his understanding of love and of soul mates:

Οὐδὲν ἆρ' ἦν αἴνοιο παρ' ἔμφρονος ἀνδρὸς ἄμεινον,
  κὰκ σέθεν αἶνος ἔμοιγ' οἷον ἄειρε κλέος.
πολλοὶ θριοβόλοι, παῦροι δέ τε μάντιές εἰσιν.
  εὗρες ἄρ'; οὐχ εὗρες γ', οὐδ' ὄναρ ἠντίασας.
φῆ γὰρ ὁ θεῖος ἀοιδός "ἄγει θεὸς ὡς τὸν ὁμοῖον"·
  οὐδὲν Ἀλεξάνδρῃ σοῦ δ' ἀνομοιότερον.

ὡς σύ γ' ὁποῖα Δανούβιος ἐκ ζόφου ἐς μέσον ἦμαρ
καὖθις ἐπ' ἀντολίην αἰπὰ ῥέεθρα χέεις.
φωναῖς δ' ἐν πλείσταις σόν τοι κλέος ἠέρ' ἐλαστρεῖ,
Ἑλλάδι, Ῥωμαικῇ, Ἑβραικῇ, ἰδίῃ.
ἄστρα, φύσις, ἀριθμοί, ποιήματα κύβρις, ἰατροὶ
Ἡρακλῆν καλέουσ' ἀντιμεθελκόμενα.
τἀμὰ δὲ παρθενικῆς σπουδάσματα παίγνιά τ' αἰνῶς,
Βόκχορις εἰ κρίναις, ἄνθεα καὶ δρόσος ὥς.
τοιγὰρ μήτ' ἐλέφαντος ἐναντία βόμβον ἀείρω
αἴλουρον Παλλὰς καὶ σύ γ' ὑπερφρονέεις.

Nothing was better than praise from a wise man, and the praise from you – what glory it brought me! Many are the soothsayers, but few are the prophets. Did you find [something]? You did not find [anything], nor did you have a dream. For the divine bard said, "God leads [one] to the similar"; but nothing is less similar to Alexandra than you. Since you, at least, like the Danube, from the West to the South, and again to the East, pour out sheer streams. And in the greatest number of tongues your glory plies the air: in Greek, in Latin, in Hebrew and in your own tongue. The stars, nature, numbers, poems, law tablets and doctors call you Heracles, dragging you in different directions. But my pursuits are those of a maiden, very much games, just like flowers and dew, if you should judge them as Bokchoris [would]. Therefore, let me not hum before an elephant: you, like Pallas, look down upon a cat.[85]

Scala challenges Poliziano's application of Neoplatonism and Petrarchan desire to their relationship when she asks, "Many are the soothsayers, but few are the prophets. Did you find [something]? You did not find [anything], nor did you have a dream. For the divine poet said, 'God leads [one] to the similar'; but nothing is less similar to Alexandra than you." Her message is clear: she is not his soulmate because their souls are dissimilar. In addition, she exposes his use of Neoplatonic rhetoric as empty and malleable by invoking her name, which Poliziano never does in his epigram to her. She reclaims her identity through this rhetorical move: she is neither Cassandra Fedele, nor Electra, nor Poliziano's παρθενικήν (maiden; virgin), and intimates that the epigram he wrote could have been sent to anyone. Furthermore, in the process of undoing Poliziano's characterization of her as his beloved, Scala redefines herself as a learned woman by calling on the authority of the "divine bard" (θεῖος ἀοιδός). Although the "divine bard" usually refers to Homer in the Hellenist tradition, Scala echoes Plato's theory of soulmates in the *Symposium,* upon which Poliziano relied in his declaration that he had found "her," the one whom he had always desired. In the space of a single epigram, Scala breaks from the mould and refuses to become Poliziano's beloved. Although Poliziano continued to compose and send her more Greek epigrams, there is no indication that she ever responded to him, as implied in *Epigrammatum Graecorum* 48, where he writes, "Ἂν μηδ᾽ εἰσαθρεῖν, ἂν μηδ᾽ ἔξεστιν ἀκούειν,/ ἆρ᾽ οὐδὲ γραπτῆς τεύξομ᾽ ἀποκρίσεως" (If I am permitted neither to look at you, nor to hear you, will I not receive a written reply?).[86] One could perhaps say that Poliziano did indeed get what he had hoped for, but not in the way he would have liked. In the end, ironically, Scala did appropriate one essential characteristic of her Petrarchan female predecessors: silence.

The Essence of Woman: Humanist Petrarchism and Female Intellectuality

The advent of publicly recognized and active learned women in this century, and the extensive intellectual networks of which they were a part, signals an important moment in both the history of Italian letters and the larger intellectual history of women. For the first time we see women debating and orating in public, often at institutions of higher learning, exchanging letters and poems with the most prominent men of the century, and making their voices heard on important theological, social, and political issues. In this respect, the transition from the Trecento to the Quattrocento might appear abrupt. In the span of less than a century, Italy progresses from an illustrious literary program headed by the Florentine *Tre Corone,* and particularly Dante and Petrarch's idealized representations of silent women and feminine virtue, to a humanist Latin tradition characterized as much by its women writers as by their male peers. While women like Isotta Nogarola, Cassandra Fedele, Laura Cereta, and Alessandra Scala were highly esteemed and regarded as jewels of their respective cities – and the Italian peninsula – their entrance into the humanist and public spheres was not without friction or uncertainty. While the anonymous invective against Isotta Nogarola, discussed at the beginning of this chapter, is an extreme example, what I have tried to show in my analysis is a more subtle manifestation of the anxiety surrounding the public emergence of the learned woman. In the absence of a classical model to follow, we see male humanists adapting Petrarchan tropes and conceits to their new social reality, which included women interlocutors, alongside more conventional comparisons to the illustrious women of antiquity. While on the one hand comparing female humanists to Petrarch's Laura elevates their status and praises their chastity and beauty, it also runs the risk of devaluing the female intellect. By translating Petrarchan topoi into Latin, male humanists – however unwittingly – released the underlying political issues of agency and power embedded in Petrarch's vernacular poetry examined in chapter 1. Humanist Petrarchism, thus, reinforces the dominance of the male intellect and disempowers a feminine intellectuality. As a social discourse, it has embedded within it a power struggle reminiscent of Petrarch's treatment of his feminized male patrons. Petrarch's masculine intellect is thus appropriated by these early male imitators, in a medium and language not traditionally associated with Petrarchism, and a full century earlier than its accepted periodization.

Humanist Petrarchism, as it permeates the Latin humanist epistle, enacts a fictionalized power dynamic as a way of subverting the female presence in active – or, rather, visible – civic roles. We must analyse the contamination of these letters to the female humanists by Petrarchan courtly love rhetoric in a manner similar to that suggested by Robin Lakoff through her "hierarchies of grammaticality" wherein "the acceptability of a sentence is determined through the combination of many factors: not only the phonology, the syntax, and the semantics, but also the social context in which the utterance is expressed, and the assumptions about the world made by all the participants in the discourse."[87] By employing Petrarchan rhetoric in his correspondence with a female humanist, the male humanist recalled clearly established paradigms of desire that deny a woman a voice and active participation in the civic sphere.[88] In the Latin humanist epistle she is put back in her place, so to speak, after having transgressed the societal boundaries set for women through her studies and participation in the humanist world. This place, woman's place, is the place of literature where she was always already an object.

What is striking is the lack of Petrarchan rhetoric in female humanist responses to men professing their poetically inspired love, desire, and admiration for them. Consistently, Petrarch-inspired letters are met with Ciceronian responses, or, as in the case of Scala, poems explicitly denying the paradigm of desire that would have her play the part of the lyric beloved.

The circumscription of female intellectuals as beloveds in humanist correspondence suggests that the female intellectuals examined here were not held to the same standards as their male colleagues. Joan Kelly claimed that "The Florentine humanists in particular appropriated only the classical side of their predecessors' thought, the side that served public concerns. They rejected the dominance of love in human life, along with the inwardness and seclusion of the religious, the scholar, the lovesick poet."[89] This chapter calls this long-held assertion into question by highlighting instances of cross-contamination between the Petrarchan lyric and neo-Latin humanism, and by exposing the role of humanist Petrarchism in the political history of women.[90] It suggests that we need to re-evaluate the way in which scholars have envisaged and defined Petrarch's influence on fifteenth-century humanism and ethics up until now, and the way in which we have historically understood the trajectory of neo-Latin humanism as separate from the development of the vernacular poetic movement that pervaded the sixteenth century: the genre and language changed; the issues did not.

In the context of this chapter, Kelly's question, "Did women have a Renaissance?" is more relevant than ever: how did the male humanists' discursive attempt to contain their female counterparts within the role of the Petrarchan beloved affect the female intellectual's arrival in the humanist sphere of letters? Laura Cereta both answers and further complicates this line of inquiry in a letter to Bibolo Semproni dated 13 January 1488, where she both attacks the male assumption of female inferiority and places equal blame for women's lack of schooling on women themselves.[91] To a long list of learned women of antiquity she adds her fellow Quattrocento female humanists, gesturing at a shared fate of silence in what she calls a "muliebris respublica" (republic of women): "cu[m] quibus Nicolosa Bononiensis, Isotaque Veronea & Cassandra Veneta sub silentii corusca luce transibunt" ("and accompanying them [the learned women of the past] Nicolosa of Bologna, Isotta of Verona, and Cassandra of Venice will pass away under a shimmering light of silence").[92] The oxymoron "shimmering light of silence" highlights the tension surrounding the figure of the Quattrocento female intellectual: she gains a voice through her writing yet is symbolically silenced by discursive containment as a Petrarchan beloved. While these women did not respond to their male peers using Petrarchan rhetoric, the next chapter examines how they engaged in humanist Petrarchism but to a very different end: to express marital love and female friendship.

3 Laura Speaks: Sisterhood, *Amicitia*, and Marital Love in the Female Latin Petrarchist Writings of the Fifteenth Century

Sollicitata precibus tuis, non potui non obtemperare tibi, Germana, cujus ad amatum vultu[m], atque ordinatos mores ante animu[m] semper fero.

While I have worried about your request, I could not refuse to oblige you, sister, whose dear face and orderly ways I always carry with me in my heart.

Laura Cereta to Nazaria Olympica, 1486[1]

In the opening of the last chapter, we saw how Laura Cereta claimed to have undertaken humanist studies in order to give the name "Laura" a new immortality. In her letter to the nun Nazaria Olympica – her friend and intellectual mentor – her attempt to distance herself from the figure of Petrarch's Laura inherently challenged both the symbolic nature of the beloved and the Petrarchan poetic tradition that had created it. Emerging from the shadow of a Trecento lyric tradition wherein Dante's dictum "nomina sunt consequentia rerum" (names are the consequences of things) seemingly ruled the day, Cereta does not deny a theoretical relationship between a name and the concept it signifies. Rather, she accepts and then repurposes it to her needs: through her accomplishments, "Laura" will now signify erudition. If we think of it in terms of the phoenix in Filelfo's poem to Isotta Nogarola, this new incarnation of Laura might have been born from the ashes of her predecessor, but she is not one and the same.

The letter to Nazaria Olympica is an important one for Cereta's letterbook. Diana Robin has already discussed the importance of its autobiographical nature and how it sets the tone for the entire collection. She reads this letter as a conversion narrative, one that details Cereta's birth, symbolic death, and spiritual rebirth.[2] I would add that within the larger narrative of conversion we find a smaller but not less significant story of death and rebirth within the episode of Cereta's birth – specifically, the symbolic death of Petrarch's Laura and her regeneration as a new figure of the educated woman. As we see below, the laurel tree figures prominently in her mythology of origins, but it is a tree divorced from its association with Petrarch's beloved:

> Natam igitur me quarto mense, ante quam curreret millesimi quadringentesimi Saluatoris annus septuagesimus, fatis ex domesticis annalibus compertum habeo. Aruerat jandudu antea ex niuali saeuientis hyemis gelu nostra laurus, quae politarus horti frondentis procacibus ramis umbrabat. Hujus inditum nomen ipsa retinui, quare dulci hac appellatione: dehinc semper ex frequēti [frequenti] ore omnium domus una resonuit, adeo pientissimis parentibus carior, alternis omnium ulnis ridibunda gestabat: Usu namque euenit, ut preciatissimu[m] habeat, quem quisque primum genuit filium. (146-7)

> It is well established from our family records that I was born in the fourth month before the coming of the seventieth year in the century one thousand four-hundred of our Savior. Our laurel tree, which shaded with bold branches a polished and burgeoning garden, had grown shriveled and dry in the wake of the icy frost that followed a brutal storm. I myself kept the name with which this tree was endowed. And thus, the whole house rang constantly with this sweet appellation, and I, who was carried around alternately in their arms, became for my adoring parents their most precious source of delight, for parents usually favor their firstborn child. (24)

The symbolism surrounding Cereta's birth is hard to ignore. The laurel tree in her family's garden was destroyed by a hard frost. She describes it as "shriveled" and "dry" – a stark contrast to the myth that it is evergreen and indestructible, save for Zeus's thunderbolts. Its death ushered in her birth, finding a new immortality in her since she was named after it and would, as we know, go on to thrive as an intellectual. In this manner, Cereta founds her biography by going back to the origins of Petrarch's myth – the laurel tree itself, symbol of poetic immortality and erudition – passing over in silence its incarnations as Daphne and Petrarch's Laura, symbols of chastity and unrequited love. Indeed, she further distances herself from that model in the detail concerning her parents' affection towards her: the familial home echoes with her name, and her relationship with her family is characterized by physical affection. What we see in both examples from this letter is Cereta's rewriting of Petrarchan conceits concerning the laurel-Laura paradigm. She does not outright deny the connection, but instead privileges the intellectual properties of the laurel, rather than those associated with Petrarch's beloved, when she reinscribes her name.

The same pattern of imitating Petrarchan conceits while denying the constraints they impose on the figure of woman (silence, chastity, etc.) is present in the incipit of the letter, cited in the epigraph. Olympica had asked Cereta to write a letter about her life. When Cereta finally completes the request, she imitates Petrarch's *RVF* 96 when she says to Olympica, "Sollicitata precibus tuis, non potui non obtemperare tibi, Germana, cujus ad amatum vultu[m], atque ordinatos mores ante animu[m] semper fero" ("While I have worried about your request, I could not refuse to oblige you, sister, whose dear face and orderly ways I always carry with me in my heart"). Though Cereta had difficulties in writing her autobiography, the image of her "sister" (germana) propelled her forward, in the spirit of Petrarch's claim in *RVF* 96 that, "Ma il bel viso leggiadro che depinto / porto bel petto, et veggio ove ch'io miri, / mi sforza" (vv 5–7; "But that lovely smiling face, which I carry painted in my breast and see wherever I look, forces me").[3] Cereta's imitation of this Petrarchan trope is vastly different from that in Lauro Quirini's letter to Isotta Nogarola, examined in the previous chapter. In Quirini's letter, Nogarola's image inspired love in him, much like the original Petrarchan citation. Here, however, Cereta adds a detail to the original Petrarchan verses that connotes work: Olympica's "orderly ways" (ordinatos mores). The image of Olympica recalls a work ethic that serves as an inspiring example to Cereta. The emphasis on work is significant in two distinct ways. First, as a nun, Olympica's "orderly ways" are directly connected to her regimented life in the convent. As mentioned in the previous chapter, Cereta was first educated in a convent; thus her work ethic in her studies would bear a resemblance to Olympica's. Second, throughout Cereta's letterbook she compares her writing to weaving a tapestry, a laborious, detail-oriented act that is traditionally seen as women's work.[4] Contrary to traditional depictions of weaving as a way of keeping women's hands from being idle, for Cereta it is intellectual work and an art that requires practice. Thus, the female humanist's imitation of *RVF* 96 foregrounds inspiration in the intellect, rather than in desire or a supernatural inspiration, as we find in Petrarch. The image of Olympica establishes and nourishes an intellectual relationship between the two women.

Though the female humanists examined in the previous chapter did not reply to their male peers using Petrarchan tropes or conceits, several of them did engage in a version of humanist Petrarchism when writing to other women and their spouses. This chapter thus provides a counterpoint to the conclusions of the second chapter by highlighting the ways in which female humanists adapted Petrarchan tropes to different ends than their male colleagues: to establish a model of female sociality, political *amicitia*, and marital love. While the previous chapter showed how male humanists deployed Petrarchan rhetoric to both praise and limit the political power of women's writing, this chapter turns to a kind of female Petrarchan response by Costanza Varano (1426–47), Cassandra Fedele, and Laura Cereta. These women adopt Petrarchan rhetoric to mount a complicated defence, accepting the praise but not the limitations, as in the Cereta example above. In the first two sections I examine two kinds of female friendship expressed through humanist Petrarchism: first, Costanza Varano's letter and poem to Isotta Nogarola, where Petrarchan tropes express female friendship through a notion of sisterhood, and second, Cassandra Fedele's letters to Queen Isabella of Spain, where we find the self-portrait of a female Petrarchan courtier who recalls Petrarch's political poetry in order to form a female version of Ciceronian *amicitia*. In this manner, Fedele channels the political Petrarch of chapter 1 and anticipates the figure of the female courtier in Castiglione's *Il Cortegiano* (1528). In the final section, I analyse Laura Cereta's Petrarch-inspired love letters to her husband, Pietro Serina, to show how she adapted Petrarchan rhetoric to express a form of requited marital love devoid of the Petrarchan religious tension that presents the woman as an obstacle to the man's Christian salvation. In the end we see how these early female Latin Petrarchists were able to extract the political undertones of Petrarch's poetry to carve out a space for women and women's issues in the male-dominated world of humanism. They challenged social, moral, and religious expectations by overturning prescriptive ideals about women. And they did so by adapting the otherwise restrictive language of Petrarch to express social realities beyond the codified space of the lyric and of other literature depicting the idealized essence of woman.

In Friendship's Footsteps: Female Petrarchan Friendship and Intellectual Sisterhood in the Letters and Poems of Costanza Varano

Costanza Varano (1426–47) was the daughter of Pier Gentile da Varano, lord of Camerino, and Elisabetta Malatesta. Like Isotta Nogarola, she had a strong female presence in her life that nurtured her studies: that of her maternal grandmother, Battista da Montefeltro

Malatesta (1384–1448), the dedicatee of Leonardo Bruni's treatise on female education *De studiis et litteris* (published between 1405 and 1429).[5] Varano received a broad humanist education, producing letters and poems which she exchanged with prominent male and female humanists alike, and delivering several public orations – like her grandmother before her – the first at the young age of sixteen.[6] What most distinguishes her writing from that of her female contemporaries and predecessors is what Holt Parker has called "Latin as an instrument of the state": she used her skills and accomplishments as a humanist to publicly defend her family's interests and safeguard their patrimony.[7] Her letters and poems are thus more overtly political than those of many of the female humanists in this century, her imitation of Cicero a testament to both her style and a political agenda.

Among the many letters to kings, popes, and lords we find a 1442 letter and poem to her contemporary, Isotta Nogarola.[8] The letter is written in the style of *De mulieribus claris,* and the poem amplifies the praise begun in prose. In her encomium, we see an eclectic mix of classical citations alongside (unattributed) Petrarchan conceits to praise Nogarola's erudition and establish a friendship between the two women. At the beginning of the letter, Varano tells Nogarola that she read her letters over and over again and began to feel a strong affection for her. She expresses her affection for Nogarola in terms of a Ciceronian model that links love to the act of letter writing. She writes, "stilo orationis commota sum quanto tui amore afficiar significare litteris meis, quamquam et id parum concinne tum, pro ingenii tenuitate, tum quia in eloquentia parum admodum versata sum" ("I was moved by the style of your speech to express how much I am affected by love for you in a letter, although without style, both because of the meagerness of my talent and because I am little experienced in eloquence"). Here, as we saw previously in Nogarola's letters, Varano's love for Nogarola stems from esteem for her eloquence and accomplishments. In praising Nogarola she employs the topos of modesty, contrasting Nogarola's command of eloquence and diction to her own meagre talent and lack of eloquence.

The conventional aspect of her letter continues as she cites lessons from classical authors that she claims Nogarola has internalized: following Lactantius, she does not neglect "bona animi" (the goods of the soul), and like Cicero, she is propelled by a desire for thought and knowledge, which Quintilian also espoused in his *Fundamentals of Oratory.*[9] Recalling these three authors both praises the life of the mind that Nogarola leads and also displays Varano's own erudition. She then loosely adapts

Petrarch's *RVF* 96 to describe how steadfast Nogarola is in abiding by these classical lessons, writing "has omnes sententias in pectore collatas diligenter semper ipsa servasti" ("Having diligently collected all these ideas in your heart, you keep them always"). The idea that Nogarola keeps these lessons "in pectore," which in turn serves as a constant source of inspiration in her life, recalls the image of Laura in Petrarch's heart, and serves as another example of how this particular Petrarchan trope was easily adapted by humanists of both genders. Varano repeats this Petrarchan conceit in the opening verses of the accompanying poem: "Est, Isota, meo tua dulcis epistola fixa / pectore nec poterit quam longa abolere vetustas" (vv 1–2; "Your sweet letter, Isotta, has been fixed / in my breast and no age, however long, will be able to destroy it"). In both instances, symbols of the intellect are fixed in the respective female humanist's heart. The Petrarchan trope enables Varano to create a lineage of erudition and inspiration, starting with the writings of Lactantius, Cicero, and Quintilian fixed in Nogarola's breast, and ending with Nogarola's letters memorialized in Varano's breast. Nogarola's letters are equated with the lessons of the classical authors Varano cites, something emphasized later in the poem when she writes, "luminis est etiam prisci tibi flamma reposta / mentis in arcano" (vv 11–12; "The flame of the ancient light has been placed safe / in the hidden recesses of your mind").

The idea of a lineage that begins in antiquity and passes through Nogarola to Varano is a strong theme that characterizes the letter and poem. In the letter, Varano compares Nogarola to the learned women of the past, stating that, "unde fit ut non impar iudicanda sis superioribus illis dominabus doctissimis, quarum illa aetate non parva fuerat multitudo: quales fuere Aspasia, Cornelia Scipionis, Elphe, et aliae quas non est hic narrandi locus" ("So it comes about that you are to be judged not inferior to the most learned ladies of old, of whom there was no small multitude in the former age: such as Aspasia, Cornelia daughter of Scipio, Elphe,[10] and others whom this is not the place to mention"). Varano singles out women famous for their learnedness and, most importantly, women who transmitted their knowledge to others. According to Plutarch, Aspasia – the companion of Pericles – hosted a salon in Athens that included such notable philosophers as Socrates.[11] Cornelia educated her Gracchi sons and, as mentioned in the previous chapter, Nogarola's mother, Bianca, was often compared to her. Nogarola is included in this lineage as an example of their age, since her letters have inspired and instructed Varano. Thus, we see that Varano is careful and deliberate in her choice of famous women who have something in common beyond erudition. They, like Nogarola, imparted their knowledge to others who learned from them. While in the letter Varano claims that Nogarola is equal to these women, in the poem she further praises Nogarola by claiming that, "hac aetate viros superas celeberrima doctos" (v. 7; "In this age you are the most famous for surpassing learned men"). Here, Varano compares Nogarola's intelligence to that of men famed for their learning – a gesture at another popular genre of encomia in praise of men, the *De viris illustribus* (famous men) tradition initiated by Petrarch (and continued by Boccaccio) in the previous century.[12] Nogarola's learning, thus, surpasses that of exemplary men and women of both antiquity and the Quattrocento.

The closing of the poem reinforces the lineage of famous women who pass down their knowledge when Varano looks into the future and imagines a "soror" (sister) who will someday continue the tradition of female erudition begun by Nogarola. She writes,

et si quam omnipotens concessit forte sororem,
o faustam, poterit tua post vestigia recto
sumere calle viam facilique venire volatu
Parnassi ad sacros lattices et docta sororis
munere blandiquo componet carmina plectro.
egregiam scribet prosam plaudentibus astris. (15–20)

And if the Omnipotent allowed by chance any sister,
O lucky girl! She will be able later on in your footsteps
to take the way with the right path and come with easy flight
to the sacred waters of Parnassus, and taught by her sister's
gift she will compose poems with a sweet-speaking plectrum,
she will write exceptional prose as the stars applaud.

There are two things of note in these verses that are quite remarkable. First, the repetition of "soror" creates a kinship between women that is based not on bloodlines but on a shared engagement with the intellectual life.[13] The future educated woman imagined by Varano is a sister to Nogarola and to herself. In this imagined community erudition is passed down as though it were a genetic trait, but here it is not restricted to blood relations. Instead, Nogarola, who is also referred to as a "soror," leaves a gift (*munus*, v. 19) for her intellectual descendant that will show her the way to Parnassus. What is striking is the way in which Varano humanizes Nogarola and educated women as a *genus*. Nogarola is not presented as a muse or Corycian nymph venturing back home to Parnassus; rather, she is a woman who through her studies reached the peaks of the mountain and then left her "vestigia" (footsteps) for her intellectual descendants to follow.

The image of Nogarola's "vestigia" brings us to the second remarkable facet of these verses: Varano's rewriting of Petrarch's *RVF* 35, "Solo e pensoso i più deserti campi" ("Alone and filled with care"), a poem that clearly lays out the poet's approach to imitation. In Petrarch's poem, he figures himself as a solitary poet avoiding the footprints of the ancients:

Solo et pensoso i più deserti campi
vo mesurando a passi tardi et lenti,
et gli occhi porto per fuggire intenti
ove vestigio humana la rena stampi. (1–4)

Alone and filled with care, I go measuring the most deserted fields with steps delaying and slow, and I keep my eyes alert so as to flee from where any human footprint marks the sand.[14]

In this poem we see Petrarch's complicated relationship with his predecessors. On the one hand, he recognizes that his poetic path is a recreation of those that came before him, but in imitating them he claims to try to avoid their precise footsteps.[15] This is typical of Petrarch, who simultaneously presents himself as part of a longer poetic lineage while setting himself apart.[16] Varano negates such a solitary process when she describes the future sister's relationship to Nogarola: "poterit tua post vestigia recto / sumere calle viam facilique venire volatu / Parnassi ad sacros latices …" (vv 16–18; "She will be able later on in your footsteps / To take the way with the right path and come with easy flight / To the sacred waters of Parnassus …"). The future sister does not avoid Nogarola's "vestigia," as Petrarch did – instead, she will be able to follow them. The juxtaposition of "callis" (footpath) and "via" (the way) reinforces the female lineage and each member's responsibility to pass on her knowledge to future sisters. Petrarch's avoidance of his predecessors' footsteps leaves him alone in his own thoughts, with Amor as his only companion (vv 12–14: "Ma pur sì aspre vie né sì selvagge / cercar non so, ch'Amor non venga sempre / ragionando con meco, et io co·llui"; "but still I cannot seek paths so harsh or savage that Love does not always come along discoursing with me and

I with him"). In Varano's poem, we find a virtual community of women that embraces, rather than denies, the accomplishments of its female predecessors, and recognizes those accomplishments as integral to the success of past, present, and future learned women.[17]

In the Latin letter and accompanying poem to Isotta Nogarola, we see Petrarchan tropes repurposed and recontextualized in order to build the foundation for female intellectual friendship. Petrarch's poems about poetic inspiration – the image of Laura in his heart (*RVF* 96), his avoidance of any "vestigio" (*RVF* 35) – are also poems of isolation. The latter poem needs no further explanation in this respect, since it explicitly presents the poet as (purposefully) isolated. *RVF* 96 sets the stage for a different kind of isolation, since Petrarch is able to project the image in his heart outward into the world, for only his eyes to see: "et veggio [il bel viso] ove ch'io miri" (v. 6 "[I] see [her beautiful face] wherever I look"). Thus even in company, he self-isolates in his thoughts about the beloved, as we see most clearly in the pilgrimage poem *RVF* 16, "Movesi il vecchierel canuto et bianco" ("The little white-haired pale old man leaves"), when he seeks out Laura's face in the crowd of women.[18] Varano's imitation of these poems reinscribes them as integral parts of a community that does not begin and end with one woman. The image in Nogarola's and Varano's hearts is of letters, a symbol of erudition and model of imitation. The footsteps of predecessors do not evoke anxiety in the modern writer; they inspire imitation and a sense of intellectual continuity.[19] Nogarola, Varano, and future learned women are bonded through an intellectual sisterhood, wherein each sister is responsible not only for maintaining current ties but especially for laying the groundwork of future relationships, real and virtual.

Female *Amicitia*: Cassandra Fedele and the Language of Female Patronage

One remarkable and unique aspect of Cassandra Fedele's letterbook is her continued correspondence with powerful female patrons within and beyond Italy's borders. These letters offer us a rare glimpse into the world of female patronage and female courtiers in its earliest stages, before writers like Castiglione theorized on the place of women in Italian courts. Indeed, it may seem strange and mildly anachronistic to talk about female courtiers in the Quattrocento, but this is the portrait of Fedele that emerges from instances of correspondence with powerful women like Beatrice d'Este (1475–97), wife of Milanese ruler Ludovico

Sforza "il Moro"; the two daughters of Ferdinand I of Naples, Beatrice of Aragon, Queen of Hungary (1457–1508), and Eleonora of Aragon, Duchess of Ferrara (1450–93); and, especially, Isabella I of Castile, queen of Spain (1451–1504). Fedele's epistolary relationship with the Spanish queen, for example, spans a decade – by far the lengthiest correspondence between a female humanist and female head of state during this century. While their exchanges are full of mutual admiration and praise for their respective accomplishments, they are primarily characterized by Queen Isabella I and King Ferdinand II of Aragon's desire and request for Fedele to join their court, and Fedele's hope of becoming a female courtier *avant la lettre*. Unfortunately, both an unnamed illness and, eventually, politics seem to have got in the way of Fedele's hoped-for move to the Spanish royal court. In several letters, Fedele describes an illness that has delayed her move to Spain. Diana Robin has noted that the French invasion of Italy in 1494 and the ensuing war between France and Spain for control of the Italian peninsula may have ultimately dashed any hope that Fedele could join Queen Isabella's court.[20] After 1495, we have no extant letters between Fedele and Isabella I, leaving the issue an open mystery.

Although Fedele never did join the Spanish queen's court, nevertheless her letters to Isabella I are a rich example of the kind of linguistic experimentation required of a humanist embarking on uncharted territory. In Fedele's letters we see something akin to a model of female *amicitia* that had no precedent or classical source from which Fedele could draw. While she could, and did, include many humanist topoi of modesty in addressing the queen, the hierarchical and political differences between the two women required Fedele to develop a new rhetoric of patronage. Her letters to Isabella I are characterized by the repetition of bird and shadow imagery, which recalls Petrarch's own use of the images in his poems to the Colonna, and his Coronation Speech, examined in chapter 1. Yet, as we shall see in this section, Fedele repurposes these images to equalize her relationship with queen, rather than surpass her. Thus, female *amicitia* – while founded on politics and mutual benefit, with the queen claiming Fedele for her court, and Fedele holding a position as female courtier – is not antagonistic or competitive, as we find in Petrarch's poetry, as well as his Latin works. Instead, it creates a female intellectual kinship based on mutual respect and female erudition.

In the early letters to Isabella I, Fedele is careful not to appear too audacious in writing to the queen. In her letter of October 1487, she heads off any criticism of her correspondence with the queen by presenting Isabella I as a source of inspiration for both men and women writers.[21] In the opening lines, Fedele praises the queen for her virtues and her deeds, in terms reminiscent of both Cicero's letters and Petrarch's *RVF*. She writes,

> Si quis forte Regina Invictissima me ad te scriber miratur, & audaculam me nuncupet, eius quidem sententiam reprehendi (ni fallor) posse existimo, cum tuae divinae potius quam humanae virtutes egregiaque facinora ad ea discribenda non modo literatos, verumetiam me literarum studijs incensã [incensam] invitent, pelliciant, necnon incendant, me praefertim, cum tuas continué audiam celebrari virtutes.

> If anyone should perchance be surprised that I write to you, invincible queen, and if he should call me a bold little woman, then he can – unless I err – be criticized for his opinion since your divine rather than human virtues and your extraordinary deeds would invite, entice, and seduce not just literary men into describing them but even me who am fired up by the study of literature.

Fedele pays homage to Isabella I's station by addressing her as a "Regina Invictissima" (Invincible Queen), while deprecating herself as an "audaculam" (a bold little woman). The use of the diminutive as a topos of modesty further elevates Isabella I while also minimizing the (hypothetical) accusation of audacity by an unknown man. Indeed, Fedele presents the possible accusation as unfounded by claiming that Isabella I's virtues and actions warrant such attention. Here, her phrasing recalls Petrarch's codification of the mingling of the human and divine (based on Aeneas's encounter with his mother), and the affectionate and erotic tone of Cicero's letters, both examined at length in the preceding chapter. When Fedele describes the queen's virtues as "divinae potius quam humanae" ("divine rather than human"), she changes the emphasis of Petrarch's *RVF* 90 – "Non era l'andar suo cosa mortal / ma d'angelica forma, et le parole / sonavan altro che pur voce humana" (vv 9-11; "Her walk was not that of a mortal thing but of some angelic form, and her words sounded different from a merely human voice)"[22] – from the female gait and voice to female virtues. While the characterization of her virtues as "divine" gestures towards the *De mulieribus claris* tradition, risking making the queen a figure of an otherworldly woman, Fedele humanizes her by referring to her "egregia facinora" – extraordinary deeds – which, throughout the letter, she ties to military campaigns and the defence of the Christian faith.[23] Thus while her virtues may be divine, her actions are not miraculous but commendable. Fedele still plays with the Petrarchan co-mingling of the human and divine, but here she privileges the human accomplishments of the queen on behalf of her kingdom and faith.

This distinction between Isabella's divinely inspired virtues and worldly accomplishments for the Christian faith is important because it alters her figure as a source of inspiration for writers. Fedele claims that her virtues and deeds "would invite, entice [pelliciant], and seduce [incendant] not just literary men into describing them but even me who am fired up [incensam] by the study of literature." The homoerotic tone of Ciceronian *amicitia* is here mimicked in Fedele's use of "pellicio" (to entice, coax), coupled with the repetition of the verb "incendo" (to inflame, arouse, seduce). She first claims that Isabella's virtues and deeds "seduce" men into celebrating her in letters, and then that she herself is "incensam," playing on the literal and figurative meaning as inflamed and seduced. Though she states she is "fired up" by literary studies, the parallel structure of *incendant-incensam* in the sentence implies that she, like other male writers, has also been seduced by the queen's virtues and deeds. Having laid the foundation for something akin to what we might call female *amicitia,* Fedele closes the letter by offering her services to the queen: "Sciasque velim pro mea in te observantia pro tuarum rerum claritudine me in praeconijs magnitudineque tuarum rerum nunquam defuturam" ("I would like you to know that in serving you and the fame of your reign I shall never be wanting in acclaiming the greatness of your deeds").[24]

As Fedele's relationship to Isabella I develops, her rhetoric of patronage changes, moving away from a more classical Ciceronian model to become more experimental and judicious in its imitation of Petrarchan tropes. A recurrent trope is the use of bird and shadow imagery to represent the relationship between the female humanist and her female patron. Like Petrarch in his poem to the Colonna (*RVF* 10), and in his Coronation Speech, Fedele presents herself as a bird under the shadow of the queen. Unlike Petrarch, however, she is not uniquely the bird in the analogy: both she and the queen are birds, sharing a familial kinship. This bird-shadow imagery characterizes the letters written after Isabella I's invitation for Fedele to join her court in 1488.[25] In an undated letter, for example, Fedele presents the queen as a bird, whose wings will harbour and protect the female humanist.[26] She writes,

> Relinquam ergo propinquos, affines, ac dulcissimam Patriam: haec omnia praetermittam, ut felicitate iam diu exoptata sub umbra alarum tuarum perfrui valeam. Duo quippe in hac vita mea immortalem ac beatam recidere posse arbitror. Alterum literarum suave ac liberale ocium, cui a tenella aetate perpetuo me dedicaram; alterum autem animum mentemque meam totam me denique tibi unice tradidisse, ut coram fortitudinem tuam coeterasque immensas virtutes contempler ac admirer.

> Therefore I shall abandon my kin, friends, and my native city. All these I shall relinquish so that I may enjoy the happiness I have long desired, under the shade of your wings. I believe I can render myself immortal and happy in this life in two ways: one, through the dedication of my life to literature, a goal to which I have devoted myself from a tender age on; the other, through my complete commitment to you, mind and soul, to the end that I may admire and contemplate your fortitude and the rest of your magnificent virtues and in your presence.

Fedele figures the queen as a bird when she imagines finding happiness "sub umbra alarum [tuarum]" (under the shade of [your] wings). The analogy is familial, religious, and political. First, Fedele introduces the imagery with a statement about her personal sacrifices in joining the queen's court: she will have to abandon her family, friends, and native city of Venice. Her familial network, however, would be replaced by the queen and her court, making the shadow of the queen's wings a form of protection, and the court a new nest-home for the female humanist. In this light, the image of Isabella I as a bird is maternal, a replacement figure for Fedele's loss of family and all things familiar. Furthermore, the expression "sub umbra alarum" is liturgical, a direct citation of the opening of an entreaty for the Lord's protection in Psalms 17: 8–10: "Sub umbra alarum tuarum protege nos" (Protect us under the shadow of your wings [my translation]). Isabella I is thus figured as the protector not only of Fedele and the members of the royal court but, most importantly, of the Catholic world.

The combination of bird imagery and the explicit citation of Psalms 17: 8–10 in Fedele's letter pays homage to the royal coat of arms for the Crown of Castile: an eagle perched atop a scroll inscribed with the words "sub umbra alarum tuarum," which Isabella I maintained throughout her life, with some variation. As Elizabeth Lehfeldt has shown, Isabella I's association with the eagle was fundamental in the construction of her political legitimacy, particularly after the death of her brother, Henry IV (1425–74), king of the Crown of Castile, nicknamed "the Impotent."[27] Isabella I's religious adviser and confessor, Hernando de Talavera (1428–1507) – who would become archbishop of Granada in 1493 – figured the eagle prominently in a sermon he sent to her. As Lehfeldt discusses in her article, the original sermon that Talavera delivered to the monastery Santa María del Prado in Valladolid contained no references to the eagle. When Isabella I requested a copy of it, however, he added political advice to the young queen, using the eagle as a legitimizing symbol of her power. The eagle was sacred to both her patron saint, John the Evangelist, and her father, King John II of Castile (1405–54), whose powerful reign was an example to her. Rafael Domínguez Casas has noted that the biblical inscription was also placed underneath the eagle shortly after the death of Isabella I's brother in 1474, and, most importantly, was minted onto gold *excelentes* after she and King Ferdinand had signed the Concordia de Segovia on 15 January 1475.[28]

Thus, Fedele's portrayal of Isabella I as a bird coincides with, and adds to, the dynastic mythology surrounding and legitimizing the queen at this time. Her presentation of Isabella I as a literal bird recalls Petrarch's *RVF* 10, where he depicts the Colonna family as a literal column under the shadow of which he resides. In both cases, the writer draws from the patron's respective coat of arms and places him/herself under his/her patronage through shadow imagery. In addition, in both Petrarch's *RVF* 10 and his Coronation Speech (where the laurel tree shades the poet), as well as in Fedele's letter, artistic immortality is associated with the patron's shadow. Fedele makes explicit reference to this when she claims that she will gain immortality in two ways: by continuing her studies, and by serving Isabella I. Fedele's appropriation of the Petrarchan tropes distances her from Petrarch's model of power, however. Whereas Petrarch figures himself as a peripatetic "rosigniuol" under the Colonna-column's shadow, here Fedele portrays Isabella I's court as a new nest to replace the one she will leave behind. As we see in the subsequent examples, however, Fedele – like Petrarch – also figures herself as a bird preparing for flight.

In a letter written in July 1492, Fedele discusses the plan to have her move to the queen's court.[29] She mentions how honoured she is by the invitation, and by the queen's audience. Upon hearing news of the invitation from the queen's orator, Girolamo Leone, Fedele claims she asked her uncle Niccolò Franco, the archbishop of Treviso, to carry a letter to the queen. Realizing that the letter had never arrived, Fedele decides to write again, and figures herself as a bird, waiting for Isabella I's command to fly to her. She writes,

> Ex his igitur intelliges, me litterarum studijs deditam tuae Maiestati unice inservire cupere. hoc mihi quidem plurimum exoptabile est, tametsi mihi grave esse fatear affines, propinquos, ac dulcem Patriam relinquere. malo tamen tibi Regina omnium Virtutum decus, fidei Christianae auctrix, ac totius terrarum orbis tutela, me subiectum esse. Tuum igitur est imperitare: meum vero mandata exequi. quibus acceptis ad te advolabo, nedum veniam interea me ut servulam commissam habeas.

> Therefore I decided to write again, and from this letter you will learn that I, who am devoted to the study of literature, wish only to serve Your Majesty. This is very much my hope, even if I should admit that it is hard for me to leave my family, those near to me, and my sweet native city, still I would prefer to be your subject, O Queen, who are the emblem of all the virtues, the guarantor of the Christian faith, and the protectress of the entire earth. Therefore it is yours to command, mine to follow your commands, and when I have received your order, still I will not come to you – I will fly. In the meantime, know that I am your servant.

The passage opens with Fedele's reminder that she is dedicated to both her literary studies and serving Isabella I, which she had previously used in reference to her own immortality. As in the last letter, too, she refers to her sacrifice of her family ("affinos"), neighbours ("propinquos"), and her "dulcem Patriam" (Venice, but also Italy). She further emphasizes her devotion to the queen by this time admitting how difficult it will be for her to leave Venice. Fedele also repeats the idea of Isabella I as a nurturing, protective figure when she calls her the "tutela" (protectress) of the world. While the major themes of the last letter are present here, one major change is the bird imagery, which Fedele uses to describe herself when she writes "ad te advolabo" (I will fly to you). The verb "volo" (here, "advolo") recalls the wing imagery of the last letter, creating a kinship between Fedele and Isabella I, who are both figured as birds. While Fedele does not specify the species of bird, her emphasis on her immortality as a writer in these letters recalls the figure of Petrarch's "rosigniuol," and the classical associations between the nightingale, poets, and poetic immortality. If Isabella I is the bird (eagle) whose wings shade and protect the female humanist, Christendom, and the whole world, then Fedele is the nightingale awaiting her call. The repetition of "ad" in "*ad* te *ad*volabo" connotes a sense of haste and urgency on Fedele's part to join the queen's court.

This same image of avian flight recurs in a 1495 letter, where Fedele excuses her delay in joining the queen because of an (unnamed) illness.[30] Again, she uses the verb "advolo" when she writes,

> Intellecta ab Reverendo Fratre Augustino tibi deditissimo tua de me opinione, ut me scilicet ad tuam conferrem Amplitudinem, advolassem quidem ni gravi valetudine oppressa essem, qua nec sum adhuc penitus levata.

> Now that I know, through the agency of your very devoted servant the reverend brother Agostino, that I should come to Your Highness, I would indeed have flown to you, were I not to have been impeded by serious illness from which I have not yet completely recovered.

This letter is significantly shorter than the previous ones, as well as less detailed. Fedele does not repeat the detail concerning her emotional difficulty in leaving Venice but instead focuses on an illness that has prevented her from making the journey. Had she not been ill, she would have flown to the queen ("advolassem"). While this illness impeded her journey, political turmoil seems also to have played a part in the delay. Fedele goes on to say that the "turbulentissimis temporibus" (turbulent times) and Italy's preparations for war have made her trip inadvisable, stating that, "non enim hisce turbulentissimis temporibus, & praesertim Italia bellis flagrante mihi virgunculae spatiari licet, nec tu quidem sapientissima persuaderes" ("for in these most turbulent times and particularly with Italy preparing to go to war it is not advisable for me, a young maiden, to take so much as a stroll, nor could even you, most prudent one, persuade me to do so"; translation amended). The political reality of the Italian peninsula – as mentioned above, the French invasion of 1494, and subsequent war between France and Spain for control of Italy – grounds Fedele, as we see the contrast between her desire to fly to the queen and the danger in her even walking ("nec … spatiari licet") in Venice. From the description in this letter, it would appear that by 1495 Fedele's hopes of joining Isabella I's court, as her resident humanist, had come to an end.[31] Over the course of Fedele's ten-year correspondence with Queen Isabella I of Castile, her rhetoric of female patronage developed into an original language of female *amicitia*. In her earliest correspondence we see her imitating the erotic undertones of Ciceronian *amicitia* alongside Petrarchan allusions, in an attempt to find her authorial voice in an unprecedented socio-political arena for woman writers and would-be courtiers. Petrarch's writing about patronage offers her a model that is easily adaptable to the contemporary mythography legitimizing the queen's reign. The shadow and bird imagery allows her both to maintain a political relationship between female patron and humanist and also to create a close kinship between the two women. In the case of Fedele, humanist Petrarchism re-enacts his more political poems, while avoiding the combative elements examined in chapter 1. What is seen in Fedele's Petrarchan imitation is an attempt at establishing a political relationship with the queen rather than a more theoretical examination of the hierarchy between patron and humanist, or the nature of political versus artistic power. Female kinship, it appears, is the foundation of female patronage in Fedele's letters and the relationship established through humanist Petrarchism. As the final section of this chapter shows, humanist Petrarchism will become a vehicle for describing another kind of kinship – marital love – in Laura Cereta's letters to her husband.

Petrarchan Love: Laura Cereta's Letters to Her Husband

Laura Cereta's marriage to Pietro Serina was brief – eighteen months – but it had a marked impact on her humanistic writings. Although we do not know much about Serina's biography, what we do know comes directly from Cereta's letters. From a letter dated 13 August 1485 we know that he was a merchant with a shop in Venice, and that the shop burned down.[32] Though the physical distance between their home in Brescia and his shop in Venice was not great, nevertheless she often describes her frustration with his frequent absences from her. His death was marked by her many letters of mourning in which we see the figure of a woman devastated by loss but unwilling to play the role of the classical self-sacrificing, grieving widow described in Ovid's *Heroides* and Boccaccio's *De mulieribus claris*. Just as her autobiographical letter to Nazaria Olympica provided us a glimpse into Cereta's personal life, so do her letters to and about her husband give us a rare look into their marriage. The tone of her letters ranges from playful and erotic to frustrated and, after his death, devastated and sad. What is remarkable is Cereta's imitation of Petrarch's poetry to express this full range of emotions in an intimate and highly personal manner. The Petrarchan topoi and conceits are masterfully and subtly threaded throughout the tapestry of her letters. They seamlessly work together with her more personal and original professions of her feelings, without standing out as lyrical topoi. In her letters to her husband before his untimely death, she repurposes them to describe something inconceivable in Petrarch's paradigm of desire and power: requited love marked by brief periods of absence and longing. In this group of letters, we find unrequited love as a temporary state of being, and the Petrarchan topoi as expressions of hope for her absent beloved's return to her.

On 14 July 1485, Cereta sends her husband a playful letter in response to an earlier one he wrote accusing her of neglect.[33] Diana Robin has noted the flirtatious tone of the letter thanks to the use of judiciary rhetoric and the depiction of husband and wife as lawyers in a court arguing their respective cases.[34] What is also worth noting in this letter is the way in which Cereta reassures her husband that her humanist friendships are not more important than her marriage, primarily by playing the part of the Petrarchan beloved, Laura. In order to defend herself from his accusation that she neglects him while devoting attention to her humanist correspondents, she raises him onto a pedestal while distancing herself from other humanists. She writes,

> Agis me socordiae, & ream aggrederis longi silentii, velutque ad extraneos scribens, Te praeterierim solum, tanquam oblita: quum potius prae caeteris doctis honoratum tibi gradū [gradum] ascribam,

> You charge me with laziness and attack me for my long silence as though I were a defendant in court. You act as if I were the sort of person who would write to strangers and only neglect you, as though I were forgetful of you when in fact I accord you a place of honor above that of other learned men.

Here, Cereta attempts to bridge the gap between her humanist writings and those of a more personal nature addressed to her husband.[35] She frames the second line with a reference to male humanists, first presenting them as "strangers" ("extraneos") – emphasizing a lack of kinship or intimacy with them – and then as "other learned men" ("caeteris doctis") who are ranked lower in her life than Serina. She in fact equalizes them, claiming to give her husband a place of honour above these learned men. The qualifier "other" ("caeteris") places Serina on the same intellectual level as her male humanist correspondents. He is above them, however, due to the love he shares with Cereta.

In order to further emphasize that her first loyalty is to him, and not other humanists, Cereta presents herself as the Petrarchan beloved whose nets are a powerful tool for catching a lover:

> a quo quamquam pro honore tuo quidquid habeo doctrinae suscepisse me glorior, ad haec tamen pro aliqua excusatione Epistolaria blandimenta non dederim, ne forte impunitatis spes ulla possit esse peccanti. Semper enim blandimentorum auceps fallendae amicitiae retia distendie.

> And although I might boast that I have received whatever learning I have from you for the sake of your honor, still I won't offer further epistolary flattery in place of an excuse in any hope that there could be impunity for one who has committed an offense: for the hunter of false friendships uses flattery to set up her nets.

Again, Cereta places her husband on the same intellectual level as humanists by claiming to have learned everything from him. The tone abruptly shifts when she refuses to continue flattering him. The hunting metaphor she uses to end the game of flattery plays on the Petrarchan conceit of the female beloved laying traps to catch a lover. When she writes, "Semper enim blandimentorum auceps fallendae amicitiae retia distendie" ("for the hunter of false friendships uses flattery to set up her nets") she evokes an iconic image of Laura from *RVF* 59, "Perché quel che mi trasse ad amar prima" (Although that which first drew me to love [my translation]). In this poem, Petrarch claims to have been ensnared in Laura's hair: "Tra le chiome de l'òr nascose il laccio, / al qual mi strinse, Amore" (vv 4–5; "Amid the locks of gold Love hid the net with which he bound me" [translation amended]).[36] The similarities between Cereta's hunting metaphor and Petrarch's poem place the female humanist in the position of the lyrical beloved attempting to snare a lover. In Cereta's letter, however, her metaphor serves as an anti-example of sorts. That is, since she had already caught him in her net of love, she claims she will not re-use her nets for false purposes by continuing to flatter him, for flattery only leads to "false friendship" ("fallendae amicitiae"). Cereta's reference to the friendship between husband and wife again reinforces her attempt to place Serina in the same category as her male humanist correspondents, while elevating their marital relationship. Amyrose Gill has worked extensively on marriage and friendship in the Quattrocento, and has noted the self-consciousness of Cereta in negotiating her position as humanist and spouse.[37] In

Cereta's letterbook, Gill focuses on the interplay between the languages of friendship and marriage, arguing that Cereta focuses her readers' attention on "the reciprocal relations – mutual love, communication, and duty – that govern both spousal and friendship bonds" (1099). Indeed, as examined above, Cereta's reassurances to her spouse that she does not value other educated men over him privileges their relationship over her humanist network, making husband and wife emotional equals. While references to reciprocity and friendship can be found throughout her letters to Serina, as noted by Gill, Cereta's expressions of mutual love are grounded in Petrarchan amatory rhetoric. She shifts blame onto her husband by portraying him as the absent Petrarchan beloved when she writes,

> Innocentiae vero incentiuum est Iudex neque enim deceo absque Iudice ab absente deferri, quum videatur contra eum, qui absit, insimulatio suspecta; aliter enim possent incusari vel Dei.

> But really, the motive separates innocent from the guilty. And I should not be summoned to a court without a judge by a plaintiff who is absent, since the alleged offense seems to have been committed against him who is absent. Otherwise you might as well blame the gods.

Cereta twice accuses her husband of being an absent beloved, as we note in the repetition of "absente" (absent) and "absit" (he who is absent). The use of the third-person singular in this passage further distances Serina from Cereta. It is an abrupt shift from earlier parts of the letter where she addresses him directly in the second person, to reassure him that she is not neglecting him. In this manner, Serina becomes the absent (male) beloved of Cereta's letter, his purported neglect of his own making.

Despite Cereta's insistence in her letter to Nazaria Olympica that she is not Petrarch's Laura, in her letters to Serina she often takes on the lyric persona, as we saw above in her repurposing of Petrarch's female nets imagery. In her 22 July 1485 letter to Serina, she expresses a profound frustration with their marriage, placing herself in the role of the silent, Petrarchan beloved at odds with her humanist identity.[38] She writes,

> Ut sive *sileam*, sive scribam mox probro mihi & reticentiae dentur, & litterae. Ego quo scopulo *iste ventus* erumpat parum assequor. Atsi tamen judice te,

> *silentium* est sermone rusticius, hoc mihi medium superest, ut de hinc, vix allevatis labiis *insusurrem*. Nam, quando fari redarguebat me *pudor ille virgineus*, iubebas, horrabaris ipse me saepe trepidulam, velem tandem a perfusa formidine pectus eximere: nunc autem vel secura sermonis a culpa non absum, velut argumento cavilleris, quod vel *taceam* irata, vel loquar impulse, quum neutrum veritatis facies admittat. (emphasis mine)
>
> May I be endowed with both eloquence and reticence, so that I can either be *silent* or respond promptly to your reproach. I too seldom reach the heights where *that wind of yours* gusts forth. But still, if my silence is more boorish than my conversation in your judgment, I have a compromise: and that is *to whisper* and to allow these lips to speak freely. For when you ordered me to speak, that *virginal shame* of mine caused me to refuse. You yourself urged me, though I was often trembling, to desire to free myself from the fear in which it was drowning. Now, however, though uninhibited by my speech, I am not free from blame either. It is as though you pick arguments with me because either *I'm silent* when I'm angry or speak when I feel impelled to, though apparently neither option is permitted.

In this passage we see Cereta's frustration about balancing silence with speech in responding to Serina. Her frustration stems from her husband's commands that she speak, when she finds herself slipping into the role of a silent, submissive beloved. Several keywords stand out that hark back to the figure of the lyrical beloved. The accumulation of words pertaining to silence – "sileam," "silentium," "taceam" – is juxtaposed with a reference to her "pudor … virgineus" (virginal shame), which prohibited her from speaking on Serina's command. She presents herself as having regressed to the position of a maiden, fearful of speaking because of her modesty. Her description of being unable to satisfy his requests, which fluctuate, recalls an essential feature of Petrarch's Laura: through a pun on her name, she is also the wind (l'aura). Petrarch's seven sonnets beginning with "L'aura" create an analogy between the female beloved and a constant wind of poetic inspiration, most noted in the opening verses of *RVF* 196: "L'aura serena che fra verdi fronde / mormorando …" (vv 1–2; "The calm breeze that comes murmuring through the green leaves …").[39] The Laura/l'aura pun functions in a similar manner to that of Laura-lauro by equating the beloved with poetic inspiration and immortality. Cereta plays with this trope when she claims that, "Ego quo scopulo iste ventus erumpat parum assequor" ("I too seldom reach the heights where that wind of yours gusts forth"). Cereta blames herself for not performing as she should, referring to herself as "iste ventus" ("that wind of yours") which has not always reached the "scopulus" (literally a cliff, but here "heights"). She creates a dual-language pun with "ventus" and her name, Laura, admitting to her frequent failures as his beloved. Her compromise is to whisper to him "insusurrem," with the Latin verb "susurro" synonymous with Petrarch's "mormorare" in *RVF* 196. Cereta counters her failures as Serina's beloved by taking on the persona of the Petrarchan poet-lover battling the rocky sea of love when she accuses Serina of inventing these accusations against her. She writes: "Censultò haec à te forte ad inventa sunt, ut dubio velo dubiores undas inter Scyllam Charybdimque sub remigem" ("Perhaps you invent these things on purpose so that I will row the unsteady seas under an unsteady sail between Scylla and Charbydis").[40] The Petrarchan imagery in this phrase recalls the opening quatrain of *RVF* 189:

> Passa la nave mia colma d'oblio
> per aspro mare a mezza notte il verno
> enfra Scilla et Caribdi, et al governo
> siede 'l signore anzi 'l nimico.

> My ship laden with forgetfulness passes through a harsh sea, at midnight, in winter, between Scylla and Charbydis, and at the tiller sits my lord, rather my enemy.[41]

Cereta borrows Petrarch's nautical metaphors – the perilous sea as love's fluctuations; Scylla and Charbydis, the obstacles to sailors; and the image of a helmsman – to describe the seemingly impossible state in which she finds herself. Serina's accusations create rocky waters for her, and set her on an unknown and perilous journey. She replaces Petrarch's "signore-nemico" with herself, as a "remigem" (oarsman) taking on the responsibility of navigating the difficulties in their marriage and not leaving things up to chance – or a supernatural being, as in Petrarch's poem. As we see in this letter, Petrarch's tropes concerning unrequited love, inspiration, silence, and amatory travails are repurposed to express the highs and lows of marital relations. Cereta's humanist Petrarchism here bridges the divide between her identity as a humanist and a wife, as she oscillates between the figures of the Petrarchan poet-lover and beloved to express the mundane frustrations of marriage.

As a final example, I would like to turn to a consolatory letter written by Cereta to Serina after his brother's death.[42] Cereta's tone throughout the letter is compassionate yet firm. She chides her husband for seemingly acting too feminine in his mourning, reminding him of his gender and the way he should act. While Cicero examined the issue of male bereavement in *De amicitia*,[43] what Cereta describes in her letter is more reminiscent of the Bacchae than of Laelius's more restrained expressions of grief:

> Funestam orbitatem tuam super immatura morte Nicolai adeo prae te fers; ut inter obortas lacrymas, quasi te perditum eas, & iam vivendi spes omnis videatur animo depulsa. Num memoratissimum te, & fortissimum forte praeterit, quod mori omnibus ita natura defiant, ut boni soli bona morte fungantur? An etia[m] si mala forte vixisset, capillos ne tu scindere, & clamare, aut tundere pectus alieno in funere conduceris?

> You bear your bereavement over the untimely death of Nicolai with unending tears, as though you yourself had died, and in such a way that you seem to have banished all hope of living from your mind. Have you forgotten, most celebrated and brave among men, that nature has so ordained dying for all men that only the good die well? And even if he had survived vile death, would you not be induced to tear your hair, cry out, and beat your breast at another man's funeral? (translation amended)[44]

Cereta's opening remarks echo Petrarch's *RVF* 91, the consolatory poem to his brother Gherardo: "La bella donna che cotanto amavi / subitamente s'è da noi partita … peso terren non sia più t'aggravi" (vv 1–2; "The beautiful lady whom you so much loved has suddenly departed from us … let there be no further earthly weight to hold you down").[45] In both Petrarch and Cereta, grief for the dead is misspent since it is a natural part of life. Cereta reminds her husband that nature has, indeed, ordained death for all men, a message reminiscent of Petrarch's explanation to his brother that, "ben vedi omai sì come a morte corre / ogni cosa creata" (vv 12–13; "you see how every created things runs to death"). Cereta amplifies her lesson to Serina by reminding him of his masculinity and chiding him for his feminine behaviour. Her hypermasculine address to him as "memoratissimum … fortissimum" ("most celebrated … brave") draws more attention to his feminine disposition in mourning, which is described in terms classically associated with the Bacchae: the tearing of hair, crying (mentioned twice in the passage), and beating of the breast.[46] Cereta intimates that Serina has been feminized by his bereavement, and attempts to call him back to his rightful self by appealing to his masculine identity.

The Petrarchan subtext courses through the letter, as Cereta next appeals to his status as her husband, repurposing Petrarchan rhetoric to express a new paradigm of desire and marital obligation:

> Velim ipsa iam, atque oro, quia tempus est, ut restituaste tibi, qui maiore officio obstringeris mihi, quam mortuo. Vir enim atque uxor catenus mutuo se amant, ut nullo aevo ab amore declinent. Erve igitur te tandem his fletibus, quibus tam acerbe, tam acriter tangeris, ne aut indicere bellum tibi, aut lego Iulia, in Deos, animarum fures, repetundarum agere videaris.

> I myself would like you, and I do beg you now because it is time, to return to your former self, since you have a greater duty towards me than towards the dead: for a man and his wife must so mutually love one another that they will not turn aside from that love at any time. Get a hold of yourself, then, and control this weeping of yours that has affected you so bitterly and harshly, lest you seem either to be at war with yourself, or, by the Julian law, to have launched a campaign against the gods who steal men's souls.

Just as Petrarch instructed Gherardo, "tempo è da ricovrare ambe la chiavi / del tuo cor" (vv 5–6; "It is time to recover both the keys of your heart"), in a similar fashion Cereta instructs her husband that "tempus est, ut restituaste tibi" ("it is time to return to your former self"). While in Petrarch's poem the emphasis is on controlling one's destiny, Cereta emphasizes Serina's greater obligation ("maiore officio") to her over his deceased brother. She recalls the trope of enchainment from *RVF* 266, addressed to Cardinal Giovanni Colonna, previously examined in chapter 1, removing, however, any obstacle to their marital bond. In that poem, Petrarch claims a dual obligation to his patron and beloved: "Carità di signore, amor di donna / son le catene ove con molti affanni / legato son, perch'io stesso mi strinsi" (vv 9–11; "Devotion to my lord, love of my lady are the chains where with much labor I am bound, and I myself took them on!"). Cereta's rewriting of the trope removes the male obstacle (Serina's brother) by applying the "catena" (chain) between man and wife: "Vir enim atque uxor catenus mutuo se amant, ut nullo aevo ab amore declinent" ("for a man and his wife must so mutually love one another that they will not turn aside from that love at any time"). Here, the terms "vir" (man) and "uxor" (wife) are chained to each other through the marital bond and mutual love. Cereta's choice of the general term "vir" over the more specific "conjux" or "maritus" ties this obligation to Serina's sex (gender), making it not only his spousal duty but indeed his masculine duty to devote himself to her. This is further supported near the end of the passage, where Cereta again commands him to control himself and his tears – an instruction that harks back to the analogy with the Bacchae.

In this letter of consolation, we see Cereta engaging with the more politically motivated poems of Petrarch's collection, wherein Petrarch explores the dynamics of obligation and control. Cereta attempts to recall Serina from his emotional, feminized state of bereavement to his regular self by appealing to his rational mind. The Petrarchan subtexts enable her to evoke Petrarch's masculine intellect, which she directs towards Serina's marital obligations. The stark contrasts, between prescriptive male and female behaviour, emotion and reason, brother and wife, lead to an idealized, Neoplatonic image in the closing of the letter, where Cereta affirms their relationship as unique: "Reminisci debes, quòd etiam si Nicolao te fata donarent, esses tamen carior multo mihi, quàm illi, velut qui iam sumus, erimusque semper unius animae Duo" ("You ought to remember that even if the fates were to give you to Nicolai, you would still be far more precious to me than to him, since we are now, and always will be, two souls belonging to a single being"). What is most striking about these Petrarch-inspired love letters is the way in which Cereta's relationship to her lyrical predecessor is markedly different from that in her autobiographical letter to Nazaria Olympica. As a female humanist, she distances herself from the figure of Laura, intent on making their shared name now signify female erudition. As a wife, however, she uses the lyrical figure and tradition to her advantage: she oscillates between playing the roles of Petrarch's Laura and of Petrarch himself to express requited love. As Petrarch's Laura, she channels the submissiveness of the lyric beloved to reassure her husband of her singular love and devotion to him. As Petrarch, she plays the more dominant role, advising her husband on matters of the heart and expressing her frustration at his absence.

What did Petrarchan poetry have to offer these women writers that the work of Cicero, Ovid, and other classical writers did not? Laura Cereta begins to answer this question in a letter to Alberto degli Alberti, written on 7 May 1487 after the death of her dear husband.[47] She writes,

> Proposueram summo studio deusum hoc, atque asperum dicendi genus ad lucis Tullianae fastigia provehere, nec praetermittere scientiâ quenquam ornatum, ad quem trepidula, & debito cum honore non scriberem: sed accidit heu subitarius certe nimium, & tolleratu difficilis casus; unde sementis illa jacta est, quae mihi funebres planctus obligamento viduitatis accumulat. Nuper enim evita, non ex corde peroptatus ille mihi maritus, immo vix agnitus sponsus sub aspecto meo periit: hunc misero luctu miserum eque pectus immugit.

> I had most enthusiastically planned to take this strange and unpolished manner of speaking to the heights of Ciceronian brilliance and I set out not to neglect any distinguished scholar, even if, trembling with apprehension, I might not write to him with the honor that was his due. But misfortune occurred, alas, which was unexpected and hard to bear; and thus the seeds were sown that heaped up a harvest of funerary lamentation for me, in accord with the obligation of widowhood. For recently my beloved husband, whom I scarcely knew, perished under my gaze, leaving my life though not my heart.

Ciceronian Latin failed her in this moment in her life. Polished Ciceronian prose would have masked the inner turmoil and grief that had overcome her. While Ciceronian Latin might have failed her, Petrarch's trope of the image of the beloved in the heart (*RVF* 96) consoles her. Even before her husband's death, however, her letters are laced with Petrarchan conceits and topoi, with nary a Ciceronian phrase to be found. Her emotionally charged letters are, perhaps, the most interesting case study of female humanist Petrarchism, because there was a Ciceronian model she could have imitated. In 58–7 BCE, while in exile, Cicero wrote four letters to his wife, Terentia. Sabine Grebe has shown how these letters provide a rare glimpse into marital love alongside evidence of shifting gender roles and female independence when Terentia had to take over some of Cicero's public duties in his absence.[48] Because Terentia's letters are not extant, the Ciceronian model of marital love is incomplete – one-sided; nevertheless, his letters provide a style guide one could conceivably imitate. Thus, Cereta's engagement in humanist Petrarchism is starkly different from that witnessed in the previous chapter. She rejected the Ciceronian model and instead embraced that of Petrarch, all the while ridding his topoi, rhetoric, and conceits of the unequal male-female binary that characterizes his poetry.

The cases of Costanza Varano and Cassandra Fedele are more similar to those of their male peers: they found themselves trying to establish a form of female friendship and *amicitia* that had no precedent in either Cicero's letters or *De amicitia*'s depiction of the friendship between Scipio Africanus and Gaius Laelius. Ciceronian *amicitia* is based on a sense of equality and loyalty and is an extension of the state. Petrarch's poetry was more easily adaptable to different social and political contexts, as evidenced by Petrarch's oscillation between the poetic (aesthetic) and the political in his own poetic collection. The *RVF* provided a cornucopia of tropes that could be lifted from their original contexts to recall either Petrarch's paradigms of desire and/or power or something entirely new. Hence, we see how the very same Petrarchan conceit – such as the image of a female humanist imprinted in the heart of a peer – could convey very different messages depending on the gender of the letter writer. Humanist Petrarchism came about from necessity, as a humanist social discourse that filled a gap within Ciceronian imitation: that of intellectual friendship between men and women and between two women. It better expressed marital love in a way that Cicero's letters from exile could not convey. And it granted the female humanist a sense of independence when mourning, to take up the pen again rather than suffer the fate of the women of the *Heroides* and *De mulieribus claris.* The second part of this book focuses on how the gendered politics of humanist Petrarchism continued into the next century and formed the foundation for Renaissance Petrarchism.

PART II

Pietro Bembo and the Legacy of Humanist Petrarchism

4 Theorizing Gender: Nation Building and Female Mythology in the Ciceronian Quarrel

Sed ut bene currere non potest qui pedem
ponere studet in alienis tantum vestigiis,
ita nec bene scribere qui tamquam
da praescripto non audet egredi.

But as you cannot run well if you strain
to put your feet in other people's tracks,
neither can you write well unless you dare depart
from what has been prescribed as it were.[1]

Angelo Poliziano to Paolo Cortesi, 1480s

Solo e pensoso i più deserti campi
vo mesurando a passi tardi et lenti,
et gli occhi porto per fuggire intenti
ove vestigio human la rena stampi.

Alone and filled with care,
I go measuring the most deserted fields with steps delaying and slow,
and I keep my eyes alert so as to flee
from where any human footprint marks the sand.[2]

Petrarca, *RVF* 35, 1–4

In the mid-1480s, Paolo Cortesi (1465–1510) sent Angelo Poliziano a compilation of letters he believed exemplified Ciceronian imitation. He had hoped to prove to him that major model imitation greatly surpassed the eclectic style supported and practised by Poliziano.[3] Rather than concede to Cortesi's position, or even admit to the high quality of his letters, Poliziano replies with a Petrarch-inspired anecdote that recalls Petrarch's own grappling with imitation. In the epigraph we see the image of the writer running alongside the tracks of his predecessors, a subtle echo of Petrarch's self-identification with Bellerophon in *RVF* 35 – a poem examined at length in previous chapters. When Petrarch writes that his gait in the desert is "tardi" and "lenti," it is supported by a sound reason: "et gli occhi porto per fuggire intenti / ove vestigio human la rena stampi" (vv 3–4; "and I keep my eyes alert so to as to flee from where any human footprint marks the sand").[4] As already noted, Petrarch's avoidance of other human footsteps is a rejection of apish imitation, in line with the poet's theories of poetic imitation outlined in *Familiares* 23.19.[5] There, Petrarch explains his preference for the Senecan-Horatian 'innutrition' model of imitation whereby the poet is figured as a bee who culls pollen from various sources in order to produce something original (honey/poetry). Thus, the relationship between the source texts and the new one should be modelled on that between a father and his son: a subtle resemblance, but not an exact replica. The poet's purported avoidance of any *vestigio human* in *RVF* 35 further supports this theory of imitation since the poet scans the landscape for other poets' footsteps, attempting not to step in them, but to follow their course.

Poliziano's choice of Petrarch in his reply is thus telling: although Petrarch often praised Cicero's style as unsurpassable in his genre, the poet's own writings on imitation testify to his more eclectic approach to imitation (inherent in the poet-bee analogy), one that he put into practice in both his Latin and his vernacular works. In the letter to Cortesi, Poliziano literalizes the metaphor of the footsteps of the ancients – one cannot easily run if confined to stepping in the footsteps of previous runners.[6] Poliziano thus exposes the Ciceronians' model of imitation as stifling to the creative process. Furthermore, by illustrating the age-old problem of writing in the shadow of one's predecessors through a recent, vernacular example, Poliziano alludes to the larger and more important issue at the heart of the debate: the relationship between *usus* (usage) and *norma loquendi* (linguistic standards). By translating a vernacular Petrarchan echo into neoclassical Latin, Poliziano provides a concrete example of eclectic imitation and, perhaps unwittingly, begins to dictate a new linguistic standard, not unlike that seen in the previous two chapters on the importation of Petrarch's vernacular poetry in neo-Latin humanist letters. In his debate with Cortesi, it would seem, Poliziano provides the theory behind his own eclectic imitation in his Latin letters and Greek epigrams to female humanists, examined in chapter 2.

Although Cortesi and Poliziano represent opposite sides of the debate over imitation models, Cortesi's discursive reaction to the running metaphor also gestures at the creation of a new linguistic standard. Recalling the same Senecan-Horatian 'innutrition' model of imitation as Petrarch did in *Familiares* 23.19, he writes, "Corrupti stomachi et intemperantis aegri esse putabam deteriorem cibum seligere, salutarem et optimum aspenari" ("I considered it a sign of a ruined digestion and a sickness born of intemperance to choose inferior food but spurn the healthy and best").[7] As a response to Poliziano's veiled accusation that he and his fellow Ciceronians practise apish imitation (i.e., they attempt to walk within the footsteps of Cicero), he links intemperance to the consumption of inferior food/texts. This presents Poliziano and his fellow eclectic imitators as gluttons consuming all things laid before them, to the detriment of their health. Thus, what is at issue is not a question of apish versus productive imitation, as implied in Poliziano's running analogy, but what authors/food will provide the best fuel for the new, emerging creative body. Cortesi essentially creates an analogy between the humanists and the body politic: if a humanist education is meant to train and prepare the elite class to rule, then the health of the state is dependent upon what is consumed. For Cortesi, then, eclectic imitation represents excess and gluttony, while a strict adherence to Ciceronian imitation is the healthy choice.

What is at stake in the Cortesi-Poliziano debate on imitation is how *usus* (language use) could determine *norma loquendi* (linguistic standards). Although traces of this can be found in Petrarch's writings on imitation in the *Familiares* and *RVF*, he does not theorize it to the extent that we see in the Ciceronian Quarrel of the Quattro- and Cinquecento.[8] And with the exception of Poliziano in this debate with Cortesi, none of the other male or female humanists examined in chapters 2 and 3 truly theorized their practice of imitation. The Cortesi-Poliziano epistolary debate was the initial spark for what would become an almost century-long discussion of imitation practices, one that would eventually spread beyond the borders of the Italian peninsula: the so-called Ciceronian Quarrel.[9] At the beginning of the Cinquecento (1512–13), Gianfrancesco Pico della Mirandola (1469–1533) – nephew of the more famous Giovanni Pico della Mirandola – and Pietro Bembo (1470–1547) picked up where Cortesi and Poliziano left off, debating on the proper mode of Latin imitation at a time when Latin composition was already waning. In 1528 Dutch humanist Desiderius Erasmus published his *Ciceronianus,* a dialogic and satirical commentary on these first two debates – between Cortesi and Poliziano, and Pico and Bembo – that set off a series of responses not only in Italy but also in France, attesting to the importance and universal applicability of the key issues addressed in the Ciceronian Quarrel beyond the Italian peninsula.[10] Although in 1532 Giambattista Giraldi Cinzio (1504–73) and Celio Calcagnini (1479–1541) continued the debate on imitation – in what is generally considered the third phase of the Ciceronian Quarrel – their epistolary exchange was not published until 1537, nine years after Erasmus's *Ciceronianus*. The delayed timing of the publication put them at the tail end of the Latin imitation movement, when Bembo's call for Petrarchan and Boccaccian vernacular imitation was already sweeping across the peninsula, and Petrarchism had become the imitative standard. As JoAnn DellaNeva has noted, even today their contribution to the historic debate continues to receive scant critical attention.[11]

One of the most important facets of the theorization of language usage (*usus*) and linguistic standards (*norma loquendi*) is the viability of a single model to address contemporary Italian issues and new social realities. The Ciceronians claimed that within the vast corpus of Cicero's writings one could find every expression and example needed to discuss contemporary issues. The eclectics, however, argued that certain new situations were unique, so unprecedented that only a new Latin idiom, created from the combined styles of various authors, could adequately express them. The advent of a new class of educated and publicly visible women writers at the beginning of the Quattrocento was certainly an Italian social reality without precedent. Although these women writers predated and subsequently coincided with the initial Cortesi-Poliziano exchange, surprisingly, the issue of whether or not a woman could imitate male classical writings is not explicitly addressed. Indeed, none of the three debates within the Ciceronian Quarrel deal directly with women writers and imitation, though, as we shall explore in this chapter, the issue of gender inadvertently arises in the Gianfrancesco Pico-Bembo debate of 1512–13.

Within the more general debate on cross-genre imitation between Gianfrancesco Pico della Mirandola (eclectic) and Pietro Bembo (Ciceronian), the female body, female mythology, and female learning become the exemplary sites upon which the two humanists' theories of imitation differ.[12] In Gianfrancesco Pico's adaptation of Boccaccio's Carmenta myth in a letter to Bembo, the female intellectual is figured as an active participant in both creating new linguistic norms and re-establishing Italian hegemony. The timing of this debate and its subject matter linking the female intellect to nation building make it particularly important for understanding the earliest stages of Bembo's intellectual history and founding of vernacular Petrarchism. First, it occurred in the decade after Bembo had edited the *tascabile* Aldine Petrarch (pub. 1501), while he was beginning to work on his *Prose della volgar lingua* (1525) in Urbino. Although the ambitious treatise that advocated replacing Vergil and Cicero as imitation models with the vernacular of Petrarch and Boccaccio, respectively, would not be published until 1525, the most intense years of its composition coincided with Bembo's debate with Gianfrancesco Pico. Thus, this letter exchange reveals the beginnings of Bembo's argument for creating a new, vernacular language that would unite the peninsula both linguistically and politically.[13] Second, the prominent place given to the female intellectual (Carmenta) in this debate on imitation reflects what had already been common practice in the treatment of the female humanists of the previous century: they were lauded as the crown jewels of Italy and evidence of Italy's intellectual dominance. Most importantly, however, the practice looks forward to Bembo's own Petrarch-inspired discursive engagement with Cinquecento women writers, some of whom had risen to prominence as patrons of the arts, further complicating the politics of gender examined in the preceding chapters. This chapter is thus a transition moment in the book and history of humanist Petrarchism: the Gianfrancesco-Pico debate on imitation both theorizes what we have seen in earlier chapters and sets the stage for the final chapter of this study on Bembo's initiation of vernacular Petrarchism as a poetic, social, and political discourse.

Lingua and *Pectus*: Neoplatonic Forms and Cross-Genre Imitation

Gianfrancesco Pico's first letter to Bembo in this phase of the debate was titled *Ad Petrum Bembum de imitatione libellus* (*A Little Book on Imitation, dedicated to Pietro Bembo*) and sent from Rome on 19 September 1512.[14] Within Gianfrancesco Pico's larger defence of eclectic imitation we find an interesting discussion of the issue of genre in imitation. As a proponent of eclectic imitation, it would seem reasonable that he support cross-genre imitation, since the main argument against Ciceronianism was that a single author could not provide enough material for any given social reality. If we look closely at Gianfrancesco Pico's examples of failed, apish imitations versus successful ones (emulation, as will be discussed shortly), we find a strictly adhered-to, if not implicitly defined, set of rules that govern the practice of cross-genre imitation. The first example of failed imitation is Homer:

> At imitatus dicitur Homerus Orpheum adeo ut carmen quod hic poemati de Cerere composito praestituit, in Iliade duobus tantum nominibus exceptis oculatissimus caecus ille transtulerit. Nullus tamen inde honor est Homero partus, sed quoniam sonora magis grandiorique tuba res Troianas cecinit, multa illum et undequaque est gloria consecuta.

> Yet it is said that Homer imitated Orpheus, so that in the *Iliad* that blind yet most visionary poet carefully copied a song that Orpheus included in his poem on Ceres, changing only two nouns. Well, Homer received no honor for that. But since he sang of the Trojan war with a more sonorous and grander trumpet, he won great glory from all quarters.[15]

Gianfrancesco Pico's critique of Homer in this passage is initially rather surprising, as he claims that Homer's hymn to Ceres (Demeter) is part of the *Iliad*. On the contrary, the so-called Homeric Hymn to Demeter is part of a separate collection of songs written in the Homeric verse characterized by the Ionic dialect and dactylic hexameter – the style of the *Iliad* and the *Odyssey*. Nevertheless, the critique is quite telling. Homer's failure as an imitator of Orpheus's Hymn to Ceres is based on two transgressions: that he attempted to translate one genre (the Orphic hymn) into a different style (the epic), and that he only changed two words – an accusation of apish imitation. This criticism is further strengthened by the praise he bestows upon the epic *Iliad* for telling the story of the Trojans in the proper literary mode, since the offending Orphic passage is easily identified and separated from the entire work. Thus, Homer is criticized for his attempt at cross-genre imitation but overall is praised for his accomplishments in the epic genre. For Gianfrancesco Pico, then, an author's identity is tied strictly to genre, as he explicitly states later in the treatise when he claims, "Sed ut in summa dicam: ut varii sunt auctores et in suo quique genere probati, varia quoque humani animi propensio" ("In short, I would say that, just as there are various authorities and each has won approval in his own genre, so too is the propensity of the human soul diverse").[16] The importance of genre is underscored by the comparison between the diversity of human souls and literary authorities and the single genre for which a writer is praised.

In cases where an author attempted to imitate a classical source within the same genre Gianfrancesco Pico presents two positive example of *aemulatio* over apish imitation practices while beginning to formulate the guidelines for successful imitation. First, Gianfrancesco Pico distinguishes between imitation and emulation in the example of Vergil, whom he rescues from the common Renaissance criticism that he borrowed too much from other poets:

> [...] a quo tamen vitio longe illum abfuisse censeo: neque enim omneis aliorum imitatus est partes. *Suos ipses habet numeros, propria tenet lineamenta, dispositionemque in primis peculiarem et maxime propriam* (ut alia taceam) quae non sunt ei communia cum ceteris; aemulator veterum verius quam imitator: et quamquam *mutuo si non furto* quaedam hinc inde quasi signa veterum atque toreumata carpsit ad ornanda suorum poematum aedificia: propriis tamen illa sunt ornamentis magis conspicua, atque omnino magis illustria.
>
> But in my opinion Virgil is completely free of that fault, for he did not imitate other poets in every aspect. *He has his own rhythms, his own features and above all an individual and distinctive arrangement* (to name only a few of his qualities), which he does not share with other poets. He is more truthfully an emulator than an imitator of the ancients. Although *he borrowed, if not stole,* certain things to decorate the edifices of his poems, as though appropriating images and reliefs from the ancients, those edifices are more remarkable for their own ornaments and in every way more brilliant. (emphasis mine)[17]

Unlike Homer in the previous example, Vergil appears to be a practitioner of the apian (innutrition) model of imitation since he borrowed or stole ("mutuo si non furto") from the ancients yet produced a new work characterized by his own "rhythms" ("numeros"), "features" ("lineamenta"), and "arrangements" ("dispositionem").[18] That Vergil is an emulator rather than an imitator is further supported by the analogy between writing and building: the building ("aedificia") that he has constructed contains embellishments from ancient writers, but they do not form the foundation. The use of the verb "ornare" to describe his use of ancient texts contrasts drastically with the previous accusation against Homer, that he merely changed two words in his imitation. Thus, the text produced by Vergil greatly surpasses his models.

The theory of imitation expounded in the Vergilian passage is further strengthened by the second, positive example of Livy, in whose case we encounter the running metaphor from Poliziano's letter to Paolo Cortesi at the end of the Quattrocento: "Titus Livius Sallustio clarissimo historiarum scriptori palmam vel aequam habuit vel praeripuit, diversam tamen cucurrit viam ipsius consequandae gratia" ("Titus Livy either won a palm equal to that of Sallust, the most famous of historians, or snatched it from him, yet he ran a different course in order to achieve it").[19] Rather than following in the footsteps of Sallust, Livy is figured as a competitor in a race, alongside his predecessor. The course is emphasized in this passage, rather than the prize, since Gianfrancesco Pico does not pass judgment on which of the historians is the better of the two. The metaphor of running or walking alongside the ancients' footsteps recurs later in the treatise when Gianfrancesco Pico literalizes the analogy in order to point out the flaws in a model of imitation that would have the modern writer retrace the precise footsteps of the ancients. His tone is playful, as he poses a series of rhetorical questions to Bembo:

> Nam nec cursu solum veteribus similes nec gressu vel esse vel videri volunt quidam, sed ita incedere, ut eorum in vestigiis ponant vestigia. At si veterum maiora vestigia fuerint ut etiam corpora, num in illis minor pes firmabitur an labascet si solum maxime subudum fuerit? Si vero illa nostris minora extiterint, num exludentur curiosi pedes et frustrabuntur voto? Aequum enim vestigium quod omni ex parte quadret quis invenerit? Ni calceorum fortassis officina quaepiam subministraverit. At quot veterum pedes tot calcei. Nec ambigas, Bembe, etiam si antiqua sandalia in absconditis thesauris inveneris et apraveris tibi, te umquam propterea posse a criticis impetrare ut antiqua credantur. Efficiet hoc invidia.

> For certain men wish neither to be nor to seem like the ancients either in the way they run or the way they walk alone, but to advance by stepping in their predecessors' tracks. If the ancients' steps are bigger, even as their bodies were, will the smaller foot step surely in those tracks or will it slip if the ground there is soaked? But if the ancients' steps turn out to be smaller than ours, will careful feet be kept out of them and be frustrated of their wish? For who will find a footprint of the same size that fits him exactly? That is, unless some shop is unearthed from the ruins of Rome to provide us with some shoemaker's lasts. But the ancients had as many shoes as they had feet. Don't think, Bembo, even if you discover ancient sandals among some hidden treasures and get them to fit, that you can ever get the critics to reckon them ancient. Envy will make sure of this.[20]

Gianfrancesco Pico's literal explanation of the metaphor further clarifies the Livian example by first appealing to logic – not every foot is the same size, therefore it is impossible to walk or run in someone else's footsteps – and then to pride (in this case, specifically Bembo's pride), since even if one were to actually manage to walk in his predecessor's steps, contemporary scholars would still not recognize the work as that of the ancients. Thus, the previous examples of Homer's failure as an imitator of Orpheus and Vergil's success in emulation are subtly recalled in the positive example of the historian Titus Livy who is praised for his ability to borrow from ancient writers and produce something uniquely his own. What becomes clear in these three successive examples is that, despite Gianfrancesco Pico's support of an eclectic method of imitation, he views successful imitations and emulations as those created by writers who imitated strictly within their specific genres, and condemns the appropriation of one genre's characteristics to another form of writing. Throughout the remainder of the *libellus,* in fact, we encounter several pairings of successful imitators and their subtexts, all working within the same genres: Cicero-Demosthenes (pp 18–19, par. 5), Tacitus-Curtius Rufus (pp 20–1, par. 5), Herodotus-Thucydides (pp 20–1, par. 6), to name but a few. In short, according to Pico's theory the content and form are inseparable and have historically been so, since he is able to recall major classical authors who adhered to the same rules he is outlining to Bembo. The inclusion of Cicero as a successful imitator of Demosthenes, whom the Roman orator claimed was the *exemplum* of perfect oratory, is a particularly poignant example to hold up to the Ciceronians and Bembo as an example of maintaining the line of genre in imitation, and of an eclectic style of imitation. That is, if Cicero himself imitated Demosthenes, shouldn't the Ciceronian imitator also study Cicero's source text in a Ciceronian imitation?[21] This, in itself, would constitute eclectic imitation.

Despite the necessity to maintain content and form, Gianfrancesco Pico is careful to point out that a good imitator must retain his own style (lest he be accused of being slavish or apish in his imitations). The issue of personal style is one of natural attribution and genius, something that cannot be learned or practised. This is a fundamental point in his theory of imitation, since it creates a distinction between natural genius and the practice of imitation:

> Et si enim homo omnium maxime vim obtinet imitandi, ut hinc et multa et varia discere possit, quod scribit Aristoteles in *Problematibus* (eaque de

> causa poeticam homini naturalem esse, primo quem ea de facultate libro scripsit, est aperte testatus) proprium tamen et congenitum instinctum et propensionem animi nactus est ab ipso ortu, quam frangere et aliorsum vertere est ipsam plane violare naturam.

> For even if man is the greatest of all in asserting his power of imitation in order to learn many different things, as Aristotle writes in the *Problems* (which is why he openly states that poetry is natural to man in Book I of his work on that ability), he has from birth his own hereditary instinct and intellectual propensity. To wreck this and twist it in another direction is clearly to violate one's very nature.[22]

His clear distinction between the art of imitation and the "congenitum instinctum" ("hereditary instinct") and "propensionem animi" ("intellectual propensity") begins to clarify what a writer's personal style constitutes. He underscores that personal style is innate and cannot be learned, since it is present in man at birth, and to go against it thus becomes a violation of nature ("violare naturam"). This further clarifies the difference between apish imitations and emulation since, in a successful imitation, the style of the original text must, obviously, be present in order to have the new text recognized as an imitation. Emulation, however, occurs when one's own style ameliorates the work and produces something new.

The innateness of one's genius and personal style leads to the aspect of Gianfrancesco Pico's theory of imitation that best reveals his Neoplatonism – one of the main points against which Bembo will argue in his response. Gianfrancesco Pico goes on to explain how going against one's own genius and style is against nature by applying the Neoplatonic notion of ideas and shadows to imitation and writing:

> Itaque cum nostro in animo idea quaedam et tamquam radix insit aliqua, cuius vi ad quodpiam muneris obeundum animamur, colere illam potius quam incidere, amplecti quam abalienare, operae pretium est. Nihil enim nostrae consulens felicitati aut a virtute alienum aut noxium nobis impertiit ipsa natura. *Ideam igitur ut aliarum virtutum ita et recte loquendi subministrat, eiusque pulchritudinis affingit animo simulacrum,* ad quod respicientes identidem et aliena iudicemus et nostra. Neque enim eam quisquam adhuc perfecte attigit, ut hac in re illud etiam possit dicier, nihil omni ex parte beatum.

> Since in our soul there is a certain idea and root, if you will, whose power inspires us to achieve any reward, leads us by the hand, and helps us avoid certain things, it is important to cultivate that root rather than sever it; to embrace it rather than cast it aside. For nothing that nature itself imparts for the sake of our happiness is foreign or injurious to us. *Thus it subserves the idea of correct speech, as it does our other virtues, and produces the likeness of its beauty in the soul.* By gazing on this likeness we may judge the works of others as well as our own. For certainly no one yet has perfectly grasped that idea, so one could even say that no one is entirely fortunate in that sense. (emphasis mine)[23]

Gianfrancesco Pico's description of the innate quality of one's own genius and personal style (read, language use) echoes Plato's theory of forms (or ideas)[24] and applies it to language. The Neoplatonic adaptation in this case, however, creates a conundrum that Gianfrancesco Pico is forced to recognize by the end of the passage. The notion of correct speech ("recte loquendi") as a Platonic form initially seems an apt analogy on two levels: first, since Gianfrancesco Pico has already claimed that genius and style are innate, and since the "idea" of correct speech is immutable and perfect within itself, then going against it would be unnatural; second, the relationship between the form (or idea) and its shadows in reality is analogous to the very nature of imitation, since shadows mimic forms. Thus, within this Platonic analogy, Gianfrancesco Pico suggests that man is born with a form of language/speech against which he is able to judge his language production and that of others – all distinct and separate shadows, which, however, bear some resemblance to the idea. Although this analogy works with regard to one's own use of language, and, to a certain extent, the most basic principles of imitation, it does not account for emulation. If the form of correct speech is inherently perfect, and man is to seek it out in the shadows of reality, how then could one emulate or surpass that perfect form through imitation?

Notwithstanding the fact that both Gianfrancesco Pico's perfect language and Plato's forms are innate and therefore not fully perceptible, the limitations of Gianfrancesco Pico's application of the theory of forms are not really addressed. He ultimately passes over them by recognizing Plato's conceit of infinite regress. Plato himself recognized the limitations of his theory in *Parmenides,* where the notion of one ideal form is contested since, if we are to understand forms as perfect universals, and shadows (particulars) as multiple, then the theory would necessitate multiple forms.[25] Thus, the world of forms would also be multiple, and would infinitely regress as shadows are linked to their forms. Gianfrancesco Pico will later give concrete examples of this precise philosophical problem as it relates to imitation when discussing the models imitated by the ancients: "Proposuerunt enim non unum quempiam, sed multos imitandos. Nec id satis: ad ipsam ideam filum esse dirigendum praeceperunt. Num igitur mihi quaeso licebit, num et expediet vim Demosthenis, quamquam eam expressisse Cicero dicitur, in ipso potius Demosthene, ubi inesse illam non ambigitur, et demirari et imitari?" ("For they [the ancients] proposed that we imitate not any one person but many. And if that was not enough, they taught that we should guide our style by the idea itself. Shall I not, if you please, be permitted to imitate, won't it be profitable to imitate the power of Demosthenes, when Cicero is said to have imitated it, when Cicero admired and modeled himself on Demosthenes, of whose power he had no doubt?").[26] What is a problem in Plato is a given in Gianfrancesco Pico's theory of perfect language; since each man is born with an innate and unique form of language, the circle of imitation is infinite and quickly becomes an issue of origins. Pico alludes to this in the first passage examined, when he states that the form of correct speech cannot be fully realized by human speech ("Neque enim eam quisquam adhuc perfecte attigit, ut hac in re illud etiam possit dicier, nihil omni ex parte beatum"; "For certainly no one yet has perfectly grasped that idea, so one could even say that no one is entirely fortunate in that sense").[27]

On 1 January 1513, Pietro Bembo replied to Gianfrancesco Pico's treatise on eclectic imitation with a defence of Ciceronian imitation that challenged the importation of Neoplatonism into the evolving debate concerning imitation – the foundation of Gianfrancesco Pico's argument.[28] Bembo did not entirely dismiss the applicability of the Platonic theory of forms (ideas); rather, he attempted to correct his friend's understanding of how it could be applied to the writing and imitation process. For Bembo, correct language comes only from practice, and is not innate as Gianfrancesco Pico claims:

> Nam de Ideis quod scribis, difficile quidem est tibi, homini doctissimo et in omnium philosophorum disciplinis et scholis multa cum laude atque gloria diu versato, aliquid affirmanti non credere. Sed quam tu esse in animo tuo insitam atque a natura traditam scribendi ideam atque

formam sentias, de eo ipse videris. De meo quidem animo tantum tibi affirmare possum nullam me in eo stili formam, nullum dictandi simulachrum, antea inspexisse quam mihi ipse mente et cogitatione legendis veterum libris multorum annorum spatio, multis laboribus ac longo usu exercitationeque confecerim.

It is difficult not to believe what you assert about the Ideas considering your great learning and what a long time you have spent with the teachings and schools of all the philosophers, to your great praise and glory. But it's your business if you see in your soul an idea and form of writing planted there and handed down by nature. I can speak to you only of my own soul. I saw no form of style in it, no pattern of discourse before I developed myself in mind and thought by reading the books of the ancients over the course of many years, by long labor, practice and exercise.[29]

Bembo's emphasis on *labor, usus,* and *exercitatio,* as well as the undefined long period of time spent reading, highlights the active process of writing in a way that Gianfrancesco Pico's adaptation of Neoplatonism does not. Bembo does not use this moment as an occasion to defend Ciceronian imitation over Gianfrancesco Pico's eclectic model; instead he lays the foundation for his argument about the nature of imitation and one's own personal style – something that could be applied to any preferred methodology. Rather than completely dismissing the practice of understanding the writing process through philosophy – indeed, he praises Gianfrancesco Pico for his philosophical studies – Bembo instead subtly corrects his colleague in the application of Plato's theory of forms (ideas) to writing:

Videoque quasi oculis, sic cogitatione, quae conficiendo scripto opus sunt, unde sumam. Ante quam in iis quas dico cogitationibus magnopere essem versatus, inspiciebam quidem in animum meum nihilo sane minus, quaerebamque tamquam a speculo effigiem aliquam, a qua mihi sumerem conficeremque quod volebam. Sed nulla inerat in eo effigies, nihil se mihi offerebat, nihil conspiciebam. Itaque si quid calamo uterer, si quid molirer, non lege, non iudicio quo volebam, sed temere inconstanterque ferebar; nulla me earum quas commemoras idea speciesque moderabatur. Neque vero sum nescius, te id cum diceres, de Platonicorum sententia dicere, qui quae prima quaeque praestantia in natura rerum sunt vel esse aliquo modo possunt ad divinas illas imagines speciesque referebant.

> I see by thought, as though with my eyes, from what source to take the highest example which I need to compose some piece of writing. Yet, before I engaged in the thoughts I mention, I too used to look no less into my soul and to seek, as in a mirror, some likeness I might use to compose what I wanted. But there was no likeness in my soul, nothing presented itself to me; I saw nothing. Therefore, if I used the pen at all, if I composed anything, I was taken where I wanted to go not by law or the faculty of judgment but randomly and inconsistently. None of these things that you mention – the Idea and form – guided me. I am aware that you were speaking here about the opinion of the Platonists who used to compare what is best and most excellent in nature (or can be in some way) with these divine images and types.[30]

Bembo describes two different processes by which he would look into his soul, one successful and the other not. The first example corrects Gianfrancesco Pico's process of introspection, which he will then mirror in his second example. Bembo's first description of his writing process emphasizes the eyes as a vehicle for thought and finding a source ("unde sumam" [from where to take]). He echoes Petrarch's vein of Neoplatonism and understanding of poetic inspiration, as previously examined in *RVF* 96: because he carries Laura's image in his heart, he is able to see her everywhere. In Bembo, inspiration comes from the object seen, and then remembered, in the soul (heart); but only through study, exercise, and practice is one able to translate that source of inspiration into discourse. Bembo presents this process as the correct application of Neoplatonism, particularly in light of the second example (Gianfrancesco Pico's process) that he introduces as a preliminary, unformed kind of introspection that sought out the form of language. The analogy with the mirror ("speculum") undermines Gianfrancesco Pico's assertion about the innate nature of writing, since Bembo claims he tried his friend's process and saw nothing in the mirror that guided his writing. The distinction that Bembo makes is an important one since it reaffirms the Platonic notion of form (idea), insofar as inspiration is concerned, but negates it as a model for writing and imitation.

To a certain extent, Bembo agrees with Gianfrancesco Pico in holding that there are specific authors to imitate depending on the genre imitated. Although a staunch Ciceronian, Bembo does include a certain kind of eclecticism in his model of imitation, since he adheres to a strict sense of genre. This is first noted in his initial response to Gianfrancesco Pico's discussion of cross-genre imitation:

> Venio igitur ad illam partem sermonis nostri in qua ea mea sententia fuit, ut dicerem eos mihi vehementer probari, qui prosa oratione scripturi Ciceronem sibi unum ad imitandum proponerent, heroicis carminibus Virgilium.
>
> Thus I come to that part of our discussion in which I gave my strong approval to those who, intending to write prose, resolve to imitate Cicero alone and who intend to imitate Virgil if they are going to write heroic verse.[31]

Bembo echoes Quattrocento imitative practices by proposing Cicero as a model for all "prosa," and Vergil for the subgenre of "carminibus heroicis" (heroic verse, or epic). Yet, despite Bembo's staunchly Ciceronian stance, he does recognize and support the need to adapt Ciceronian prose and imitation to various situations:

> Ac Ciceronis quidem imitatio omnibus, qui pedestri oratione scribere aliquid volent, opportuna esse poterit, quacumque illi de re atque materia sit scribendum; idem enim stilus aptari rebus innumerabilibus potest ... Neque enim in omnibus eius scriptis, cum idem sit stilus, eadem tamen amplitudo inesse, idem verborum apparatus conspicitur.
>
> The imitation of Cicero will be perfectly suitable for all those who wish to write in prose, whatever the subject or material they must address, for the same style can be adapted to countless subjects ... Although the style is the same in all Cicero's writings, neither the amplitude nor the verbal resources are conspicuously uniform in them.[32]

Bembo draws an important distinction between *stilus* and *res* – the logical end products of what he terms "amplitudo" (breadth) and "verborum apparatus" (vocabulary). This is an important point for his theory of imitation, since for Bembo it is the style that is consistent in Cicero's writing not the subject matter. Thus, a Ciceronian imitation does not necessarily have to follow a strict style-subject dyad, since Cicero himself did not maintain such a relationship. What we see is a much greater amount of flexibility given to prose imitators who, following the Ciceronian model, are able to adapt Ciceronian style freely to any given situation. The same cannot be said, however, of poets, who are confined by a much stricter process of imitation that maintains the style-subject relationship:

> De Virgilio vero non idem possumus dicere, ut idoneus sit, quem, qui carminibus delectantur, imitari omnes queant. Neque enim qui aut elogos aut lyricos conficiunt versus, quique vel comoediarum vel tragoediarum scribendarum studio detinentur, horum ullos Virgiliana carminum structura, numerus, ratio ipsa multum iuvabit. Sed imitentur ii quidem eos quos habent principes singulis in scriptorum generibus singulos atque illis assequendis superandisque sese dedant.

> We cannot say the same thing about Virgil, that he is a suitable model and that everyone who enjoys poetry should imitate him. For no one who composes either elegiac or lyric verse or is occupied in writing tragedy or comedy will profit much from Virgil's poetic structure, meter or general method. They should rather imitate whomever they consider the leading representative of each literary genre and should devote themselves to equaling or surpassing them.[33]

The universality of prose in the previous passage and its adaptability to different subject matters are at odds with the specificity of poetry based on structure, metre, and method – as stated in the passage – as well as subject matter. Vergil is specifically held up as a model of the epic genre, his *Aeneid* privileged as a model for imitation over any of his other works that had been in circulation among the Italian humanists for some time. When Bembo continues, "Heroicis autem conscribendis carminibus qui se dederit, huic certe erit Virgilius ediscendus, ebibendus et quam maxime fieri poterit exprimendus, quemadmodum coram tibi dixeram, mihi videri" ("But it seems to me that whoever dedicates himself to writing heroic verse will surely have to study, imbibe and copy Virgil as much as possible, as I explained to you in person"), he excludes Vergil as a model for any other poetic genre, supporting the idea that poetry as a general genre is not universal and that the poet, therefore, cannot divorce style (including metre and form) from the subject matter (love, tragedy, comedy, war, etc.). Although Cicero wrote various and divergent prose pieces – from the political orations *In Catilinam*, to rhetorical treatises like *De oratore* and *De re publica*, as well as the philosophical books *De finibus* and *De natura deorum*, and the widely known *Laelius de amicitia* and epistolary *Ad Atticum*, rediscovered by Petrarch in Verona in 1345 – Bembo insists that the style is consistently Ciceronian, despite the very different subject matters addressed by the great Roman orator.

If, however, we look closely at Bembo's argument for maintaining the style-subject relationship in poetry, while dismissing it in the case of prose, we see that although in theory the rules for style and subject are oppositional, in practice they are not. That is, imitation is not only about style but, just as importantly, about content:

> Atque hanc quidem cum Vergilii, tum Ciceronis, tum aliorum excellentium in suo cuiusque genere scriptorum expressionem non ita intellegi volo, ut praeter stilum et scribendi rationem (uti autem me iisdem saepius verbis non paenitebit), nihil omnino a quoquam sumendum existimem. Quis enim opus legitimum conficere potest ullum qui nihil mutuetur, nihil a quoquam sumat, quod scriptis inserat atque interspergat suis? Quis non aut sententias aut similitudines comparationesque aut alias scribendi figuras atque lumina? Quis non aut locorum aut temporum descriptiones aut ordinem aliquem ac seriem?
>
> Yet when I talk about copying Virgil, Cicero and the best writer of every literary genre, I don't mean that, apart from style and method of composition (I shall not regret using the same words too often), you should borrow nothing at all from anyone. For that of course always has been and will be permitted to all. Who can produce any decent work without borrowing, without appropriating something from someone to sow and sprinkle about in his own writings? Who does not borrow either maxims or similes and comparisons or other figures and ornaments of composition? Or descriptions of either places or times or some arrangement or sequence? Or examples either of war or peace, storms, wanderings, deliberations, love affairs or all sorts of other things? Who does not appropriate something from the authors in which he is deeply read, the authors he has long held in his hand, be they Latin, Greek, and even vernacular authors – as there are some excellent writers in that language?[34]

Within the argument of my larger study, what is most interesting about Bembo's position here is that he expands imitation to include the borrowing of topoi and tropes (*loci,* in the most general sense). In these cases, it is not the style that serves as a marker to alert the reader to which texts are informing the new text but the explicit borrowings that place the original and the new text in dialogue with each other. Thus, although Bembo has seemingly separated style from subject matter in his discussion of Ciceronian prose, he does recover their symbiotic relationship when discussing the specific mode of imitation that would have the modern writer cite phrases, images, places, themes, and so on, from a classical model. Though to the modern reader this might seem obvious, if not banal, within the great literary and cultural debate encompassed by the Ciceronian Quarrel it provides a loophole: despite his protestations, Bembo's model allows for cross-genre imitation, in a similar manner to what Gianfrancesco Pico advocates in his treatise.[35]

What is consistent in both Gianfrancesco Pico's and Bembo's approaches to this issue, in fact, is the difference between imitation (*imitatio*) and emulation (*aemulatio*), since Bembo claims that although invention is privileged over borrowing (i.e., explicit citation), "Maxime vero earum rerum ratio tum probatur laudabilisque est, si id perficimus ut quae mutuati sumus ipsi, ea splendidiora illustrioraque nostris in scriptis quam in eius a quo sumimus conspiciantur, ut non minor in exornando laus quam in inveniendo fuisse videatur" ("Our method in these matters will be most acceptable and praiseworthy if we make what we have borrowed more splendid and brilliant in our writings than they are in the author's from whom we take them, so that there seems to be no less praise in the embellishment than in the invention").[36] In Gianfrancesco Pico's final response to Bembo he brings up an important issue that will inform future iterations of the debate on imitation, particularly in the practice of imitation and Bembo's proto-nationalistic project, the *Prose*.[37] Taking a cue from Bembo's argument about "borrowing" from the ancients in order to surpass them, Gianfrancesco Pico reiterates his original Neoplatonic stance that Bembo had attempted to negate:

> An putas, Bembe, ullos nostri temporis Ciceroni fore in loquendo similes, nisi in intellegendo etiam similes fuerint? Sane Augustinus eos non probat qui linguam Ciceronis tantum, non autem pectus admirantur, ut qui probe noverit eruditam et ornatam linguam, nisi ab exculti pectoris imaginibus, prodire non potuisse. Hoc, quid est aliud quam cum forma convenire materiam, et elocutionem inventioni, atque dispositioni ad unguem iungi, et tamquam (ita dixerim) ferruminari oportere?

> Do you think, Bembo, that any men of our time will be similar to Cicero in speech, unless they will also be like him in understanding? Augustine surely does not approve of people who admire only Cicero's tongue and not his heart, for he knew very well that learned and ornate language could develop only from the images in a cultivated heart. Doesn't this

mean that the matter of one's speech should agree with its form, that its style should be precisely linked to its invention and arrangement, as if they were cemented together, as one might say?[38]

Gianfrancesco Pico attempts to repackage his Neoplatonic view of imitation, previously described through recourse to the theory of forms (ideas), by appealing to Bembo's admiration of Cicero: how could one imitate only Cicero's voice (*lingua;* literally, his tongue) when it is his soul (*pectus;* heart) that distinguished Cicero from other writers? For Gianfrancesco Pico, then, style is directly correlated to one's soul. In this newest incarnation of his position, he forgoes the previous claim that "correct speech" and style are innate, instead putting forward the hypothesis that Cicero's style has had such an effect on Bembo (and others) precisely because it was guided by his soul. If an imitator does not understand Cicero's point of view – his experiences, sentiments, world view, and so forth – then he cannot imitate his writing, since he would not understand his soul.

A second issue that arises pertains to linguistics, since Gianfrancesco Pico asserts that the subject matter is just as important as style in imitation, even in prose. Thus, limiting oneself to a single model of imitation limits the imitator to a strict and fixed set of expressions. At the very heart of Gianfrancesco Pico's argument against Ciceronian imitation are questions of current language use and the constraints on expression that limiting oneself to a single model would bring about. His point is an important one for this debate on imitation, for it holds true with any idiom posited as a contemporary model for imitation:

Oportet itaque gerere animo conceptus Ciceronis, esse praeterea instructos rerum multarum et magnarum doctrina et experimentis, eos qui se existimant vivam linguam Ciceronis esse consecutos, ne, si Tulliano careant spiritu, eos Cato nuncupet *mortuaria glossaria.* Dices fortasse te verba primum observaturum, inde numeros et lineamenta structuramque omnem, nihilque prorsus afferre quod non sit etiam allatum a Cicerone, nec aliis omnino loqui de rebus velle quam de iis de quibus ipse disseruit. Hoc furari erit, Bembe, non imitari.

So whoever supposes that they have acquired the living tongue of Cicero should bear in their mind Cicero's conceptions; they should have experience and knowledge, moreover, of a great many important affairs. Otherwise, if they lack the Tullian spirit, Cato may call them "Glossaries of the Dead."

> You will perhaps say that you will first observe his words, then his rhythms, features and entire structure, that you will employ no expression that Cicero did not use, and that you do not want to discuss any subject at all that he did not discuss. This will be stealing, Bembo, not imitation.[39]

Without eclectic imitation – a model that would allow for a much more expanded vocabulary and set of expressions – the Ciceronian imitator becomes a mere borrower, since he would be unable to discuss, in Ciceronian Latin, situations or ideas not found in Cicero's writings. The potential for emulation, thus, does not exist, since the strict Ciceronian imitator would not be able to invent new expressions in Ciceronian style, given Gianfrancesco Pico's argument that form and style cannot be separated. Since the "vivam linguam Ciceronis" (the living tongue of Cicero) does not exist, the imitator is very limited in his range of expression. Furthermore, if one is to imitate Ciceronian prose – the closed system of signs available from Cicero's writings – then he must understand "Tulliano … spiritu" (Cicero's soul, his motivations, desires, etc.) if he is to imitate his expressions.

Gianfrancesco Pico's and Bembo's discussion of cross-genre imitation within the larger debate over eclectic versus Ciceronian imitation sheds light on key issues faced by Quattrocento humanists in the previous century. With no classical model for male-female intellectual exchange, humanists resorted to the kind of eclectic imitation supported by Gianfrancesco Pico, though they did not theorize about it. Thus, the issues of literary "borrowing" (or stealing, according to Gianfrancesco Pico), of how to make Latin a living language, and of the letter versus the spirit in this phase of the Ciceronian Quarrel elucidate the imitation practices examined in chapters 2 and 3. In retrospect, the Gianfrancesco Pico-Bembo debate justifies the use of Petrarchan rhetoric beyond the vernacular lyric form if the writer understands the motivation behind the discourse. This goes back to Bembo's argument – there is a difference between "borrowing" and "imitation"; thus one cannot simply borrow discourse to ornament his own writing. The innovation, according to both Bembo's and Gianfrancesco Pico's arguments, comes from understanding the root of the discourse and imitating it in a new context or social reality. This is the kind of imitation we see deployed in Quattrocento letters between male and female humanists, female intellectuals, and a wife (Cereta) and her husband. In all of the cases examined, Petrarchan tropes were borrowed from their original contexts and co-opted to express a new reality that had no precedent in Cicero or his classical counterparts. Even in the most Ciceronian of Quattrocento letters, we find vernacular idioms filling in the gaps, so to speak. While neither Gianfrancesco Pico nor Bembo theorizes on whether or not the gender of the imitator affects his or her ability to properly imitate classical texts, they do not wholly ignore the figure of the intellectual woman. As we will see in the following section, the figure of the intellectual woman figures prominently in the connection between language (imitation) and nation building.

Carmenta: The Politics of Female Mythology and Nation Building

The Pico-Bembo debate, particularly the question of whether style and subject matter can be divorced in imitation, brings up a host of issues concerning gender and the advent of women writers. If, as Gianfrancesco Pico claims, one must understand the model author's heart, would it be possible for a woman writer to identify with and understand the social reality of classical male authors who did not engage intellectually with contemporary women? In accordance with Bembo's model, if the imitator were limited to using only expressions and vocabulary found in Cicero's writings, could a woman writer adopt the idiom of a male author writing from the position of a political orator entrenched in governmental politics, if the woman writer herself were not engaged in politics? The most basic issues brought about by the debate are further complicated when applied to women.

Although the contemporary issue of women's writing and imitation is not directly addressed in any of the three phases of the longer, historical Ciceronian Quarrel, there is a subtle female presence in the debate. In Gianfrancesco Pico's first letter to Bembo, he mobilizes metaphors about language acquisition and the female body that are reminiscent of earlier iterations of the longer debate on the *questione della lingua*.[40] Whereas Dante, for example, likens the acquisition of one's first language – the vernacular – with the nursing female body in *De vulgari eloquentia* I.1.2,[41] Gianfrancesco Pico employs pregnancy and childbearing metaphors when justifying eclectic imitation of Latin. In discussing what aspects of oratory can be studied and which ones are innate, Gianfrancesco Pico writes:

> Nam de memoria et pronuntiatione tacendum puto, quando earum neutra chartis mandetur, et alteram nulla ex imitatione tibi compares, sed ex matris (ut inquit Lucilius) bulga tecum feras. Ut autem haec exercitatione

perfici solet, ita exempla maiorum aliis partibus, quae referri litterarim monumentis queunt, opem ferre non mediocrem iure affirmaverim.

I don't think there is any need to talk about memory or pronunciation, since neither of these is set down on paper. You don't get the second of these from imitation; you bring it with you, as Lucilius says, from your mother's "pouch." But while one usually perfects this [last] part of rhetoric by practice, I have rightly claimed that the examples of our ancestors give no small aid to the other parts of rhetoric which can be preserved in literary form.[42]

Gianfrancesco Pico explains the acquisition of pronunciation by recalling Gaius Lucilius's *Satires* 26.623, where he actually claims that the acquisition occurs at conception.[43] Gianfrancesco Pico's change to physically locating it in the womb ("ex matris ... bulga") mimics and literalizes his application of the Platonic theory of forms (ideas) to "correct speech" as examined earlier. Just as each person holds inside himself/herself the form of correct speech, so too does a woman hold inside herself the first stages of pronunciation that she naturally passes on to her child in the womb. This creates a privileged and necessary place for women in male humanistic learning, attributing to them one of the first moments of learning. Gianfrancesco Pico's metaphor concerning Latin pronunciation in the womb precedes Dante's nursing metaphor for the vernacular – a subtle acknowledgment not only of the Italian literary tradition but also of a logical privileging of Latin over Italian. Furthermore, just as the innate form of "correct speech" is only perfected through seeking out its shadows in the writings of the ancients, and imitating those shadows, so too is the pronunciation acquired in the womb in need of perfection through practice. Within Gianfrancesco Pico's analogy, women play an integral and necessary part in the initial formation of the male acquisition of Latin, since they provide the building blocks of a humanist formation. This is where Pico's innovation is most clear, in his adaptation of a classical trope not only within a (fairly recent) Dantean tradition concerning vernacular language acquisition but also within the emerging tradition of Neoplatonism.

The metaphor of pregnancy continues in an example that counters the classical tradition of viewing nature as an old woman tired from too much childbearing. He writes,

Neque enim quasi vetula mulier suis est viribus parens effete natura, ut nostro scilicet hoc saeculo quasi nimio partu lassata defecerit. Nec deus optimus maximus nostrae aetati non est largitus ingenia. Utinam tam bene excolerentur quam bona sunt edita ...

Nature is not like a poor old woman, a mother exhausted of her powers, so that it has faded in this age of ours, weary from much childbearing, as it were. Nor has God Almighty ceased to bestow natural talent on our age. Would that those talents had been as well cultivated as they were bestowed![44]

In this passage Gianfrancesco Pico rejects the Lucretian theory that nature ages and grows weary (*De rerum natura* 5.1150 ff) by shifting the blame onto contemporary writers who do not cultivate what has been given to them by God. His version of nature is young and ever-fruitful; it is man that does not take advantage of his natural gifts. The regenerative potential that Gianfrancesco Pico attributes to nature is also an important point about the eclectic model of imitation because it counters the Ciceronian model's inflexibility with regard to language. As we saw in the previous section, although it is impossible to find a "vivam linguam Ciceronis," imitating multiple models generates a new, living language, one that has echoes of classical Latin but that cannot be traced to a single source.

Gianfrancesco Pico presents Bembo's adherence to a solitary Ciceronian model as unnatural, a privileging of one man over another because of the misguided belief that nature endowed only him with eloquence.[45] After making an initial point against this theory by claiming that no one will ever be like Cicero – not in diction or structure – he then takes his pregnancy metaphor to its logical conclusion:

Alterum est quod tacito videris existimare, ut ceteri auctores legitimi non sint naturae partus, sed tamquam abortivi, ac ut cum eis praeclare agatur veluti octimestris infantes habendi. Si ita reris, si ita censes, dabitur provocatio ad eloquentiae magistros antiquos illos quidem et probatissimos. Ipsum etiam appellabo Ciceronem. Proposuerunt enim non unum quempiam, sed multos imitandos.

The second reason is that you seem to assume tacitly that other authors are not nature's legitimate offspring, but are like premature infants, and that one may deal with them as if they were eight-month-old fetuses. If this is what you think, if this is your opinion, this will be a challenge to those ancient and excellent masters of eloquence. I shall even call Cicero himself to witness.[46]

If Gianfrancesco Pico's metaphor holds true, then even "premature" babies are endowed with the form of language and therefore should not be discounted. Not only is Bembo's approach to imitation, thus, unnatural, but he has failed to truly imitate Cicero since Cicero, too, practised a form of eclectic imitation. Bembo thus represents the kind of scholar Gianfrancesco Pico criticizes in the previous passage since he has failed to fully cultivate the natural talent he received from nature.

The next female-gendered example diverges from the earlier pregnancy and childbirth metaphors while retaining the notion of the generative power of women. Beyond the generative nature of women (figured as both nature and everywoman) in language and oratory, the connection between the female gender and learning presents itself again in the literary example of Carmenta, a sibyl who created the Latin alphabet by converting fifteen Greek letters. Although Carmenta invented the new alphabet, her son Evander ultimately introduced it into Latium. Gianfrancesco Pico explains that since all people are affected by different styles of writing, as well as different figures of speech, the ancient writers were forced to present lessons of eloquence in various forms. He compares this to the dressing habits of the ancients:

> Induebant animum illi variis habitibus, ceu ipsis quoque vestimentis induimus corpora. Atque ut in his, non secus in illis varia materies, variae figurae, variique colores et placebant olim et nunc etiam placent; sunt enim nostra tempestate plurimi qui panno vestiantur libenter qui sit contextus ex lato illo Ciceronis stamina et presso Plinii subtegmine; admittunt etiam tramam Celsi et Collumellae. Alii, quia frigus fortasse metuunt, conantur ut evolvant scrinia Carmentae, unde peplum surripiant aptandum sibi.

> They used to dress the soul with different habits just as we dress the body with clothes. And habits are no different from clothes in the sense that different material, different figures, different styles once gave pleasure and still do. Many people of our time willingly dress in garments woven from Cicero's broad warp and Pliny's tight woof. They even use the web of Celsus and Columella. Others, perhaps because they fear the cold, try to open up the writing-desk of Carmenta, when they pilfer a robe to suit themselves.[47]

Here, imitation is compared to draping oneself with the robes and woven fabrics of the ancients, depending on the inclinations of the soul.[48] The analogy between changing clothing and changing models of imitation is presented as a daily practice, yet Carmenta stands out from the other Latin authors named not only because of her gender but because she invented the language used by the authors listed in the example: Cicero, Pliny, Celsus, and Columella. Thus the "pilfering" of her robes from her writing desk is a return to the origins of the Latin language, rather than a cloaking of one's writing in another author's style.

Furthermore, what is most significant about the Carmenta example is that she provides Gianfrancesco Pico with a tangible example of his pregnancy metaphor while emphasizing the commonality of all Latin writers, regardless of style, thereby supporting his model of eclectic imitation. Although Ovid provides a brief biography of Carmenta in the *Fasti* (I.461–542),[49] it is in Boccaccio's *De mulieribus claris* that we find a more complete biography of her, one that emphasizes her contributions to humanist learning and, especially, Roman hegemony.[50] Boccaccio begins his biography with details similar to what we find in Ovid: she was the daughter of King Ionius of Arcadia, was learned in Greek, and bore Evander, who, based on his mother's prophecy, went on to found the Palatine Hill (and the city Pallenteum) where Rome would eventually be founded. Throughout the remainder of the biography, Carmenta is described as the mother of the Latin tongue and, by extension, its domination over other languages. Boccaccio initially describes her as being responsible for educating the native inhabitants of Pallenteum in letters:

> Sane Carmenta, cum indigenas fere silvestres comperisset homines, esto iamdudum, Saturni profugi munere, segetes didicissent serere, eosque nullo literarum usui, seu modico et hoc greco, assuetos, a longe divina mente prospiciens quanta loco regionique celebritas servaretur in posterum, indignum rata ut adminiculo exterarum literarum futuris seculis sua monstrarentur magnalia, in eum stadium ivit totis ingenii viribus, ut proprias et omnino a ceteris nationibus diversas literas exhiberet populis.

> Carmenta found that the native inhabitants were still very primitive. Although they had learned long ago how to plant seeds (thanks to Saturn who had come there as a fugitive), these people knew little or nothing of writing and what letters they did know were Greek. With divine farsightedness she perceived the fame lying in store for that place and region, and so she thought it unworthy that their great deeds should be told to future generations in a foreign tongue. Carmenta then used the full force of her genius to give them their own alphabet, completely different from that of other nations.[51]

The link Boccaccio makes between the origins of the Latin language for the documentation of future Roman exploits and victories (history) is an important one. By locating the invention of the Latin tongue in Carmenta's desire to educate her people, he also locates the origins of Roman history with her. Although her son is credited with the actual founding of the Palatine Hill and its inhabitants, his mother is credited with educating them and beginning the history of not only the Latin language but also the Latin peoples. This is in line with what Helena Sanson has noted in a 1535 visual depiction of Lady Grammar as Carmenta: "she is the gate-keeper who can physically unlock the portal to the Tower of learning for the very young student on his path to acquire knowledge."[52] Furthermore, Carmenta provides Gianfrancesco Pico with another example of innovation and emulation, since Boccaccio continues that "Quas nos in hodiernum usque latinas dicimus eiusque tenemus munere, dato aliquas, et opportune, quidam sapeintes addiderint, nulla ex veteribus amota" ("The Latin alphabet we use down to the present day consists of the original letters inherited from her as well as some others added by certain wise men for the sake of convenience").[53] Carmenta's founding of the Latin alphabet is presented as both fruitful – it gave a language to a new people – and generative, since after her initial invention other men added new letters to her alphabet. The generative nature of the expansion of Carmenta's original Latin alphabet is parallel to eclectic imitation and emulation, since those men did not limit themselves to the original alphabet. Instead, through invention they expanded what would have been a more limited and closed system of signs. Carmenta is thus associated not only with origins but with an ongoing generative fertility – where the expansions of the language by men could be considered as perpetual reconceptions of a fertile and significantly female ground.

Boccaccio also credits her with establishing Italian hegemony on the world stage by alluding to the debts owed to Carmenta by other nations when he writes,

> Verum, quomodocunque de ceteris nostro crimine a fortuna actum sit, nec germana rapacitas, nec gallicus furor, nec astutia anglica, nec hispana ferocitas, nec alicuius alterius nationis inculta barbaries vel insultus, hanc tam grandem, tam spectabilem, tam oportunam latino nomini gloriam surripuisse potuit unquam, ut sui scilicet iuris prima literarum possent aut auderent dicere elementa et longe minus suum compertum fuisse

> gramaticam; quas, uti comperimus ipsi, sic etiam dedimus ultro, nostro tamen semper insignita vocabulo.
>
> But regardless of the effects of fortune and our neglect on these other gifts, neither the rapacity of the Germans, nor the fury of the Gauls, nor the wiles of the English, nor the ferocity of the Spaniards, nor the rough barbarity and insolence of any other nation has been able to take away from the Latin name this great, marvelous, serviceable glory. These other nations could never say, or have ever dared to say, that the invention of the alphabet was rightfully theirs, much less the invention of grammar. We discovered these things, and we gave them freely to others, though always marked with our Latin name.[54]

For Boccaccio, regardless of the political losses suffered by Italy, it remains a politically dominant force because of Carmenta's creation of the Latin language, which she subsequently "gifted" to the other nations. Boccaccio's linking of language and hegemony looks forward to the major cultural movements of the civic humanists in the Quattrocento: the theory that reviving Republican Latin would usher in a revival of Republican political domination.[55] Thus, when Gianfrancesco Pico claims that writers often "pilfer robes" from Carmenta's writing desk, he underlines the commonality of Cicero, Pliny, Celsus, and Columella as all writing in the language created by Carmenta, urging a return to Latin's linguistic origins. By extension, if we consider closely the four male authors named as pilferers, we see a coupling of master texts and imitations that serve as a reminder of Italy's eclectic origins, since Cicero was imitated by Pliny, and Celsus by Columella. The example of Carmenta serves as a reminder of Latin's prowess before the cult of Cicero, of which Bembo is a member.

The figurations of the female body in Gianfrancesco Pico's "Little Book on Imitation, Dedicated to Pietro Bembo" are starkly different from the classical narratives to which we are generally accustomed. His pregnancy metaphors and reference to the Carmenta myth emphasize the generative power of women by mapping intellectual transmissions to the metaphor of a regenerative physical fertility. The inclusion here of a myth concerning the female intellect and its role in founding a nation occurs at an important moment in the history of women's writing. It reflects the previous generation's use of its neo-Latin female humanists as symbols of Italy's intellectual preeminence; Isotta Nogarola was often called "Decus Italiae," and Cassandra Fedele often gave public speeches for visiting dignitaries. In the sixteenth century, female vernacular poets' widespread publication, roles in establishing literary salons, and involvement in the various academies helped further Bembo's proto-nationalistic program of uniting the peninsula under a common, Petrarch-inspired language. The new social reality of the humanists in this moment includes a new class of educated, visible, and, most importantly, publishing women. We see this reflected in all three stages of the Ciceronian Quarrel, but especially in this letter by Gianfrancesco Pico della Mirandola, which bears the imprint of a growing recognition among lettered men that theories of language had to be conveyed through metaphors of female bodies, a perhaps implicit acknowledgment of the thick relation between language and gender; men were arguing with men about language, sure, but the trump card was woman.

5 Politicizing Gender: Bembo's Private and Public Petrarchism

Assai mi fia potervi poi dire quando che sia,
o forse quando io arò la neve alle tempie:
Tanti e tanti anni ha già rivolto il cielo,
Poi che 'n prima arsi e gia mai non mi spensi.[1]

I want so much to be able to then tell you when it might be,
or perhaps when I will have snowy temples;
For many, many years the sky has already turned,
since I was first set ablaze and was never extinguished.

Pietro Bembo to Maria Savorgnan, 20 July 1500

In Pietro Bembo's private correspondence with his lover Maria Griffoni Savorgnan between 1500 and 1501, he masterfully weaves Petrarchan conceits and verses into his love letters, in a manner reminiscent of Laura Cereta's letters to her husband, which were examined in chapter 3. Like Cereta, Bembo calls upon the Petrarchan lyric to describe requited love and as a testament to his faith. In the epigraph above, he partially adapts a Petrarchan anniversary poem (*RVF* 122) to memorialize their affair, saying that, "Tanti e tanti anni ha già rivolto il cielo, / Poi che 'n prima arsi e gia mai non mi spensi" (For many, many years the sky has already turned, / since I was first set ablaze and was never extinguished). In the *RVF,* Petrarch's anniversary poems mark the precise passing of time since his *innamoramento* with Laura, the dates contributing to the narrative cohesion of the poetic collections. In *RVF* 122 he celebrates the seventeenth anniversary of his *innamoramento*: "Dicesette anni à già rivolto il cielo / poi che 'mprima arsi, et già mai non mi spensi"

(1–2; "The heavens have already revolved seventeen years since I first caught fire, and still my fire is not extinguished").[2] Bembo maintains enough of the Petrarchan original for it to be easily identified, while changing the more specific details in order to make the verses an accurate reflection of his love affair with Savorgnan. Petrarch's specific "dicesette anni" (1) is replaced by the more vague "tanti e tanti anni." While this new phrasing is not entirely accurate – Bembo sends the letter in the early months of what would ultimately be a short-lived affair – the vagueness of the phrasing conveys the strong sense of devotion and passion that we find in Petrarch's original. Indeed, the expression projects their love into the future rather than describing their (brief) past, when we consider Bembo's play on the classical Petrarchan oxymoron of fire and ice as he describes his future self as having "la neve alle tempie" (grey hair; literally, snowy temples) while still being consumed by the fire that initially burned in him ("Poi che 'n prima arsi e già mai non mi spensi"). The use of "neve" (snow) alongside the verb "ardere" produces the same iconic Petrarchan oxymoron we find in *RVF* 134: "et ardo et son un ghiaccio" ("and [I] burn and am of ice").[3] Taken as a whole, the juxtaposition of the ice and fire imagery with Petrarch's anniversary poem projects the Bembo-Savorgnan affair into the future – "tanti e tanti anni" – monumentalizing their affair despite its brief lifespan thus far.

Though Bembo's relationship with Savorgnan lasted less than two years, they wrote to each other at a feverish pace: around seventy-seven letters from each of them, often including poems. Their epistolary correspondence documents the highs and lows of an early love, intertwining poetic proclamations of love with the mundane details of everyday life and the logistics of their correspondence by courier. Given the very Petrarchan nature of Bembo's letters to Savorgnan, the timing of their affair is significant: it coincides with the composition of *Gli Asolani* (1497–1504; pub. 1505), Bembo's book of pastoral dialogues, and his first public example of Petrarch-inspired literature. Indeed, as will be seen, alongside Petrarchan citations he often quotes from *Gli Asolani* in his letters to Savorgnan, holding up the Asolan discourses of love as a model for their own relationship. These letters thus connect him to an earlier history of humanist Petrarchism, where Petrarchan imitation mediated intellectual, and other, dialogues between men and women.[4] And, they represent a crucial step in the intellectual formation of Bembo's more ambitious socio-political project tied directly to Petrarchism.

The Bembo-Savorgnan letters have received scant critical attention compared to Bembo's other "major" works. One cannot help but attribute this to the carefully guarded history of the letters after Bembo's death in 1547. Beginning in 1548 with Giovanni Della Casa (1503–56), the question of whether or not to publish the correspondence became an issue of Bembo's legacy. In two letters to Carlo Gualteruzzi, Della Casa expresses hesitation about publishing them, claiming on 22 December that "temo che parer alla gente che l'haverle così conservate sia stato un poco di vanità" (I fear that it will seem to people that having conserved them [letters] might have stemmed from a bit of vanity) and following up on 29 December that "se si potesse trovar qualche forma che paresse che altri che noi le stampassimo, forse saria meglio" (if a way could be found to make it appear that people other than us published them [letters], maybe that would be better).[5] While the letters were ultimately published, Savorgnan's identity was concealed. Nearly four hundred years later, when Carlo Dionisotti was summoned to the Vatican to examine and verify the letter collection, he echoed Della Casa's hesitation in his modern, critical edition of the letters, asking himself, "come non restarne turbato pensando alla responsabilità della publicazione? Intendiamoci bene: qui trattasi di una corrispondenza che è l'esponente di sentimenti che intercedono tra due che hanno tra loro una relazione amorosa irregolare" (How could I not be worried, thinking about the responsibility of publishing them? Let's be clear: here we're talking about a correspondence that exhibits feelings between two people who shared an irregular love affair).[6] Yet it is precisely the very private and "irregular" nature of the relationship between Bembo and Savorgnan that makes Bembo's use of Petrarch in his letters such a fascinating object of study. It shows that, twenty-five years before the publication of his monumental *Prose della volgar lingua* (1525), Bembo had already begun testing the real-world applicability of Petrarchan rhetoric. And despite having taken a very strong position against cross-genre imitation in the Ciceronian Quarrel, we see that his earliest writings belie the imitation theory he had expounded. For these reasons, his letters to Savorgnan, while deeply personal, are crucial to an understanding of Bembo's intellectual history and that of Renaissance Petrarchism. His Petrarchan-infused letters provide us with a unique glimpse into the early stages of Bembo's experimentation with Petrarchism, beyond the lyric genre and in real-world sitatuations, something that would become fundamental to his *Prose della volgar lingua* and his championing of Petrarchism as a way both to unite the peninsula politically under a common, Petrarch-inspired language and to enable women to become active participants in the Italian literary scene.

This chapter examines the two stages of Bembo's Petrarchism: the private epistolary exchanges with Maria Savorgnan and, later, Lucrezia Borgia, a continuation of humanist Petrarchism, and the public works dedicated to them and other women, including *Gli Asolani* (1505) and various poems from the *Rime* (1530). Between the two stages of Bembo's Petrarchan practices we find a distinct change in tone, from the idealistic and lovelorn poet-lover of the Savorgnan letters and the more cautious and polished courtier-lover in the Borgia letters to a more sinister and self-aware Petrarchan poet in the *Rime* who demands inspiration from his beloveds. In the case of Borgia, Bembo synthesizes the figures of Petrarch's patron and beloved into one female figure who is taught to perform her gender and role as simultaneous lover-muse-patron according to Bembo's desires. The prescriptive nature of his Petrarch-inspired poetry thus blurs the lines between love, poetry, and politics, placing the politics of gender at the centre of both his socio-political project outlined in the *Prose della volgar lingua* and the birth of poetic Petrarchism in the sixteenth century.

An Example for Future Lovers: Bembo's Petrarchan Love Letters to Maria Savorgnan, 1500–1501

Mixed in among Petrarchan professions of love and desire, and promises of eternal love and devotion are the logistics of the letter exchange and love affair of Bembo and Savorgnan: Which trusted friend or servant will act as a courier at any given time? When will Bembo visit again, and to whom should he communicate this? Has anyone discovered their affair? The two subjects could easily appear paradoxical, the intrusion of one into another jarring, but, particularly in the case of Bembo's letters, his tendency to poeticize everyday events emblematizes their love in a way that makes it real rather than the subject of literature or fantasy. One such example is the letter exchange concerning Savorgnan's gift to him. On 22 July 1500, Savorgnan sends him a small portrait of herself that she had commissioned from the famous portrait artist Giovanni Bellini (1430–1516).[7] She writes in an accompanying letter that, "vi mando el retrato, che non sta bene; pur vi lo ricomando" (I am sending you the painting, which is not good; but I am still sending it to you). Savorgnan laments the quality of the painting, which she refers to as "el retrato," but sends it to Bembo anyway.

In Bembo's response to her, he draws upon two distinct Petrarchan poems to describe the effect of the portrait on him.[8] First, he echoes RVF 96 when he writes, "La vostra immagine, come che io l'abbia sempre nel cuore, pure ho io carissima sopra quanti doni ebbi giammai. Nè bisognava che voi la mi raccomandaste" (Your image, despite my always carrying it in my heart, I truly cherish more than any other gift I have ever received. It wasn't necessary to send it to me). Bembo changes Savorgnan's original "el retrato" (painting) to "immagine" (image), which serves as a double entendre throughout his letter – it is both the image in his heart and the portrait. As briefly discussed in the introduction to this book, Bembo thanks his lover for her portrait while also rendering it redundant. Like Petrarch before him, he already carries Savorgnan's image ("immagine") in his heart as a constant reminder of his love for her and an eternal source of inspiration. Bembo thus grounds Petrarch's metaphysical description – "'l bel viso leggiadro che depinto / porto nel petto, e veggio ove ch'io miri" ("that lovely smiling face, which I carry painted in my breast and see wherever I look")[9] – by emphasizing the mundane aspects of the trope in this particular situation. Since he already carries around the "immagine" (image) of Savorgnan in his heart, there was really no need for her to send a replica of it, even if it was painted by the great Bellini. The point is made explicit when he tells her, "nè bisognava che voi la mi raccomandaste."

Bembo is not entirely dismissive of the gift, however. He does refer to the "immagine" as the dearest gift he has ever received, though it is unclear whether or not he is referring to the actual portrait or to her love symbolized by her image in his heart. Nevertheless, he goes on to describe the unique properties of the actual portrait when it becomes a physical substitute for Savorgnan in her absence. Again, he calls upon Petrarch when he continues, telling her that "holla basciata mille volte in vece di voi, priegola di quello, che io volentieri pregherei, e veggo che ella *benignamente assai par che m'ascolte*, più che voi non fate, *se risponder sapesse a' detti miei*. Ma di questo, ragioneremo altra volta" (A thousand times I kissed it instead of you, I beg her for it, which I would gladly beg for, and I see that she very kindly seems to listen to me, more than you do, if only she knew how to respond to my words. But we will discuss this another time). Here, Bembo directly quotes from RVF 78, "Quando giunse a Simon l'alto concetto" ("When Simon received the high idea"), the sonnet about the now-lost Simone Martini portrait of Laura.[10] In Petrarch's poem, the poet-lover expresses jealousy over Pygmalion and his statue, creating an analogy with Petrarch-Pygmalion and Laura's portrait-Pygmalion's statue, writing that,

> Però che 'n vista ella si mostra umile,
> promettendomi pace ne l'aspetto,
>
> Ma poi ch'i' vengo a ragionar co·llei,
> benignamente assai *par che m'ascolte:*
> *se risponder savesse a' detti miei!*
>
> Pigmalïon, quanto lodar ti dêi
> de l'imagine tua, se mille volte
> n'avesti quel ch'i' sol una vorrei. (7–14; emphasis mine)

> For in appearance she seems humble, and her expression promises peace //; then, when I come to speak to her, *she seems to listen most kindly: if she could only reply to my words!* // Pygmalion, how glad you should be of your statue, since you receive a thousand times what I yearn to have just once![11]

In his letter, Bembo emulates both Petrarch and Pygmalion, surpassing them both in the realm of requited love. He explicitly cites from the first tercet, comparing the humility of Laura in her portrait to that of Savorgnan's, and claiming that in Savorgnan's portrait, as in Laura's, she appears to be actively listening to him. While in Petrarch's poem the excitement of her seeming to listen to the poet stems from their unrequited love, in Bembo's letter he comically feigns surprise, since he claims the portrait listens "più che voi non fate" (more than you do). The interjection of reality continues the lighthearted tone of the letter, while also gesturing at the real relationship between the two lovers. Two more details further emphasize his surpassing of Petrarch and Pygmalion. First, Bembo's use of "immagine" earlier in the letter as a substitute for Savorgnan echoes Petrarch's use of the word to describe Pygmalion's statue-beloved (v. 13, "imagine tua"). Second, that Bembo kisses Savorgnan's image "mille volte" (a thousand times) ties in directly to the figure of Pygmalion receiving affection from his statue-beloved (vv 13–14) . In *RVF* 78, Petrarch's jealousy stems from Pygmalion's ability to kiss his statue thousands of time while Petrarch yearns for just a single kiss. Not only does Bembo kiss his beloved's portrait a thousand times, like Pygmalion, but also in real life: something neither Pygmalion nor Petrarch succeeded in doing.

The Petrarchan conceit about the physically absent lover who is perpetually present in his heart recurs throughout several letter exchanges between Bembo and Savorgnan. In a letter dated 13 August 1500, Savorgnan laments that she had sent her errand boy F[rancesco] to Bembo's home, only to learn he was not there to receive her letter.[12] The frustration about the logistical complications of their affair is met by Bembo's appropriation of Petrarchan imagery to describe their requited love, and to reassure her of his devotion to her. He exclaims, "O quanto mi sarebbe dolce e caro, che a me fossero così aperti tutti i vostri pensieri, come io vorrei che a voi fossero tutti i miei, e così ora io potessi mirare nel vostro cuore, e voi nel mio, come io nel mio e voi nel vostro tuttavia possiamo!" (O how sweet and dear it would be to me, if all of your thoughts were open to me as I would like mine to be to you, and in this manner now I could look into your heart, and you into mine, as I in mine, and you in yours, as we are always able to do!). If only Savorgnan could see her image in his heart, she would be reassured of his devotion to her. In like manner, he desires to see his image in her heart – a definitive symbol of their mutual love. He adds to the Petrarchan trope by making requited love integral to his language: the chiasmic structure of his phrasing creates a mirroring of each clause, stylistically emphasizing their mutual affection. The reference to the heart and the mind makes their relationship equally amorous and intellectual, since their relationship is sustained also by their letter exchange and this tangible evidence of their love and thoughts. Thus, assuaging any doubts or fears about their commitment requires an understanding of the other's heart and mind.

One very striking aspect of Bembo's letter is his subsequent reference to *Gli Asolani* – which would have been in an early draft form at this time – as a model for increasing their love. Through the consummation of their love, they have already surpassed Petrarch's model of desire, so he offers up another one – his own writing,

> sappiate che il nostro amore non fia giunto dove egli ancora dee giugnere. E se questo mio dire, che il nostro amore non fia giunto dove egli ancora dee, vi nojerà, sì come colei che ogni perfezione gli disiderate, vedete quello che due perfetti amanti chiamati a ragionar de' loro diletti nel secondo degli Asolani ne parlano al proposito della nostra materia presente.

> know that our love has not arrived where it still needs to arrive. And if what I am saying, that our love has not arrived where it still needs to

arrive, bothers you, just as you desire every perfection for it, look at what the two perfect lovers, called upon to discuss their delights in the second [book] of the *Asolani*, say about it, when it comes to this matter.

Bembo's earlier desire for each of them to see into the other's mind takes on more meaning here, as he holds up the second dialogue of his unfinished work as a model. It is not just the Neoplatonic love described in the dialogues that is important but the discussion and reasoning about love. Bembo inverts the real life-fiction dyad when he claims that the dialogues in *Gli Asolani* will provide a model for his and Savorgnan's "materia presente."[13] The choice of the second book of dialogues is significant, since there Gismondo refutes Perottino's negative portrayal of love in Book 1 by expounding the positive aspects and effects of love. He thus holds up Gismondo's optimistic viewpoint to Savorgnan's epistolary laments about Bembo's absence. By replacing the Petrarchan subtext with his own, he presents himself as an authority on love, and the second book of *Gli Asolani* as a new model for their love.

The mixing of Petrarchan and Bembian references is not limited to the letter examined above. That same summer, near the end of June 1500, Bembo alludes to Petrarchan poems while explicitly citing one of his own *Rime*.[14] He opens the letter in a strongly Petrarchan fashion, writing,

> Bello e caro e dolce obietto de' miei pensieri, mando a quelle mani, che tengono oggimai l'una e l'altra chiave del cuor mio, il rimanente d'alquanta paja di guanti che io ebbi in Spagna più mesi sono … Volea pregargli che essi a tutti gli altri tenessero coperto quel bello avorio a cui coprire io gli mando … Avrete con essi il vostro *solingo augello*, la qual canzone mi sè incominciata a piacere, poi che io la veggo piacere a voi. State sana.

> Beautiful and dear and sweet object of my thoughts, I send to those hands, that now hold the one and the other keys to my heart, what is left of various pairs of gloves which I got in Spain a few months ago … I wanted to beg them to keep hidden from everyone else that beautiful ivory, which I send them to cover … You will have with them "your solitary bird," which song I am beginning to enjoy, since I see it pleases you. Be well.

While the opening cadence of the letter "bello e caro e dolce obietto" subtly recalls the famous incipit "chiare fresche et dolci acque" of *RVF* 126, the strongest echo is in the image of the gloves and his lover's ivory hands. The fetishistic aspect of Bembo's sending Savorgnan gloves in order to cover her ivory-white hands recalls Petrarch's triptych of sonnets devoted to Laura's hands covered by gloves: *RVF* 199, 200, 201. In Petrarch's poems, he cannot see Laura's hands, only the gloves, and thus fetishizes them, as we see in *RVF* 199: "candido leggiadretto et caro guanto / che copria netto avorio et fresche rose, / chi vide al mondo mai sì dolci spoglie?" (vv 9–11; "white, light, and dear glove, that covered clear ivory and fresh roses: who ever saw in the world such sweet spoils?").[15] The juxtaposition of ivory and rose is titillating, the glove becoming a symbol of Laura's chastity, much like the veil in his pastoral poem.[16] The glove is later replaced by Petrarch's sorrow in *RVF* 200 – the famous *effictio* poem describing Laura's beauty – and its golden embroidery fetishized by the poet-lover who thinks to himself "A chi fu quest'intorno!" ("who has worn this!") in *RVF* 201, 4. Bembo plays off Petrarch's poems by emphasizing the mundane: he has seen Savorgnan's ivory hands and thus sends along a pair of gloves to protect them from the elements and the prying eyes of others. The repetition of the verb coprire – "volea pregargli che essi a tutti gli altri *tenessero coperto* quel bello avorio a cui *coprire* io gli mando" (emphasis mine) – gestures at a lover's jealousy. Petrarch's fetish becomes Bembo's possessiveness, as he wants both to protect the delicate ivory of her hands and also to conceal it from the gaze of others.

A second Petrarchan reference is found in Bembo's initial description of Savorgnan's hands as "quelle mani, che tengono oggiamai l'una e l'altra chiave del cuor mio" – an echo of Petrarch's poem to Gherardo, *RVF* 91, which was examined in chapter 1. When Bembo tells her that she now ("oggimai") holds both keys to his heart, he recalls the paradigm of desire that Petrarch seemingly criticizes in his poem: a complete surrendering of the self for love, even after the beloved's death. But the use of "oggimai" complements the Petrarchan poem by emphasizing the terrestrial over the other-worldly. In the Petrarchan original, the poet tells his brother, "tempo e da ricovrare ambe la chiave / del tuo cor ch'ella possedeva in vita" (vv 5–6), urging him to take control of his life now that the beloved has died; she only held the keys to his heart in this life. Bembo's appropriation of this phrase is thus positive, a sign to Savorgnan that he is completely hers. She possesses the keys to his heart, and he, in turn, hopes to possess her ivory hands.

While the Petrarchan allusions in the beginning of this passage serve to reinforce the bond between Bembo and Savorgnan, the final lines include a citation from his own poetry, putting his art in competition with

Petrarch's. He tells Savorgnan that, "Avrete con essi il vostro solingo augello, la qual canzone mi sè incominciata a piacere, poi che io la veggo piacere a voi" (You will have with them "your solitary bird," which song I am beginning to enjoy, since I see it pleases you.). The relative pronoun "la qual [canzone]" prefigures the second gift Bembo sends to Savorgnan: the poem "Solingo augello, se piangendo vai." Thus, "il vostro solingo augello" both refers to Bembo, the lover whose keys she holds, and the poem written for her, which she now literally possesses. The poem is a song originally performed by Perottino in the earliest draft of Book 1 of *Gli Asolani*, and would eventually become *Rime* 48 in Bembo's 1530 collection of poems.[17] While the poem contains several Petrarchan echoes, Bembo's identification with the "solingo augello" in the letter changes the perspective of the poem:

Solingo augello, se piangendo vai
la tua perduta dolce compagnia,
meco ne ven, che piango anco la mia:
insem potrem fare i nostri lai.
   Ma tu la tua forse troverai;
io la mia quando? e tu pur tuttavia
ti stai nel verde; i' fuggo indi, ove sia
che mi conforte ad altro, ch'a trar guai. (1–8)

Solitary bird, if you go about crying for
your sweet, lost companion,
come with me, since I'm also crying for mine:
together we can create our songs.
   But you will probably find yours;
when will I find mine? and nevertheless you surely
find solace in the green; I flee, instead, to anyplace
that will bring me anything but tears.

In the poem, Bembo identifies with the anguish of the "solingo augello" – they become companions in their search for their lost loves – but the outcomes of their respective searches are different. While Bembo believes that the bird will find his lover, he questions his ability to do so. By citing the poem's incipit in his letter to Savorgnan, he repositions himself as the solitary bird, who, while separated from his lover now, will eventually reunite with her. Bembo thus distances himself from his unrequited, lyrical persona in the poem by instead aligning himself with the bird whose search for his lover will end in success. Citing his own poetry provides a model of requited love lacking in Petrarch's poetry. While the references to the *RVF* throughout the letter idealize and mythologize his relationship with Savorgnan, his own *Rime* and *Gli Asolani* ground their love. In his absence, the gloves become a substitute for his physical presence, his poem a new and original testament to their love and eventual reunion.

In these letters, Bembo's auto-citation can be seen as a kind of poetic rivalry with Petrarch over the extent to which poetry can express real-world situations. When the Petrarchan model fails to adequately reflect the situation at hand, Bembo resorts to his own writing to fill in the gaps, so to speak. This is most evident in a lively exchange between the two lovers, beginning on 21 July 1500, when Savorgnan writes a short letter to Bembo accusing him of offending her and not addressing the offence in his written reply.[18] She threatens punishment for his error, claiming, "Io non resterò de amarvi, chè, si ben altra mente far volese, non potrei. E voi farete quello potrete. Non crediate perhò che con voi mi adiri, ma ben con la mia avara sorte" (I will not stop loving you, even if I wanted to do otherwise, I could not. And you will do what you can. Don't think, however, that I am angry with you, but really with my avaricious fate). Bembo's reply is playful and picks up the vague judicial theme of accusations, judgment, and punishment that characterizes Savorgnan's letter. He writes, "Voi m'accusate, e io son contento che voi medesima, che sete accusatrice, siate ancora giudice, pure che m'ascoltiate innanzi che io in questi dolori perda il natural vigore e sentimento: ciò sarebbe per aventura non meno vostro danno che mio" (You accuse me, and I am happy that you yourself, who are the accuser, and who are also the judge, would still listen to me before I lose my natural vigour and feelings in these pains: that would be, if it were to happen, no less your loss than mine).[19] Bembo's reply, replete with references to courtroom procedures, echoes the exchange between Laura Cereta and her husband that was previously examined in chapter 3. But here he places his beloved in the position of accuser (emphasized by the repetition of "m'accusate" and "accusatrice") as well as judge. His reply is sexually tinged when he tells her that he is happy she is accusing him now and listening to his defence, before he loses his "natural vigore" (natural vigour) and "sentimento" (feeling). The waning of his youthful virility would be a great loss to them both ("non meno vostro danno che mio"), he claims, so while she might play the role of both accuser and judge, she has as much to lose as he does from her accusations and punishment.

The judicial repartee between the two lovers gives way to Bembo's loftier, Petrarchan reaffirmations of his feelings for Savorgnan. Drawing now from the *Triumphi* and *RVF*, he presents himself as proof of the truth in poetry when he writes, "Fu già tempo che io approvai in me quel verso: Vivace amor, che negli affanni cresce. Ora sono in altro termine, e tengo per fermo che sia vero, Che ben muor, chi morendo esce di doglia" (It has been a long time since I personally proved [the validity of] that verse: "Intense love increases from challenges." Now I am in a new mood, and I strongly believe to be true the verse "He dies well, the one who by dying put a stop to his sorrow"). Bembo claims to be living proof of the the first citation, a passage from Petrarch's *Triumphus Cupidinis III* where constancy in love is praised in Jacob:

> Volgi in qua gli occhi al gran padre schernito,
> che non si muta, e d'aver non gli 'ncresce
> sette e sette anni per Rachel servito:
> *vivace amor che negli affanni cresce!* (34–7; emphasis mine)[20]

> Turn your eyes here, towards the mocked patriarch,
> who does not change, and who is not sorry for seven years
> to have served Rachel, and then for seven more:
> *Intense love increases from challenges!*

The Petrarchan passage retells Genesis 29, the story of how Jacob laboured for seven years in order to gain Rachael as his wife. Bembo aligns himself with Jacob, emphasizing his continual devotion to Savorgnan regardless of the travails of their relationship. Nevertheless, his hardship – defending himself against her accusations in this letter – is emblematized in v. 37 of Petrarch's poem. There, Petrarch provides an exegetical reading of the biblical story: true love grows, rather than withers, in the face of a challenge. In citing this verse in his letter to Savorgnan, Bembo claims to prove the validity of Petrarch's claim that hardship cannot extinguish love. He validates Petrarch's poetry while using it to prove his love for, and devotion to serving, Savorgnan despite any obstacle.

The same double use of Petrarchan poetry is at play in the second example from the *RVF* when Bembo says, "Ora sono in altro termine, e tengo per fermo che sia vero, *Che ben muor, chi morendo esce di doglia*" (It has been a long time since I personally proved [the validity of] that verse: "Intense love increases from challenges"). Again, Bembo attests to the veracity of Petrarch's poetry, though from the finite perspective of death. Here he quotes from *RVF* 207, "Ben mi credea passar mio tempo omai" ("I believed that by now I could live"):

> Aspett'io pur che scocchi
> l'ultimo colpo chi mi diede 'l primo;
> et fia, s'i' dritto extimo,
> un modo di pietate occider tosto,
> non essendo ei disposto
> a far altro di me che quel che soglia:
> *ché ben muor chi morendo esce di doglia.* (85–91; emphasis mine)

> I am waiting for him to loose the last arrow who shot the first: and, if I judge aright, it will be a kind of pity to kill quickly, since he is not disposed to make of me anything but what he usually does; *he dies well who escapes from sorrow.*[21]

Petrarch's canzone is a lengthy lament about his love for Laura, and a sustained expression of his desire for the end of the poet-lover's sorrows. He welcomes death, hoping for a fatal arrow to end the suffering brought about in *RVF* 2 where he was attacked, unsuspectingly, by Amor. Bembo uses the Petrarchan verse and broader context of the canzone to describe the other expression and stage ("altro termine") of love, from mythic, biblical devotion to profound suffering. However, this time he does not present himself as a living example of this Petrarchan conceit; rather, he merely claims to believe it to be true ("tengo per fermo che sia vero"). The use of the subjunctive here is in stark contrast to the earlier use of the passato remoto – "fu già tempo che io approvai in me" – making Bembo living proof of his earlier statement concerning devotion. While he holds himself up as a new incarnation of Jacob, the living example merely described by Petrarch but never lived, he distances himself from the figure of the poet-lover who exchanges his sorrow for a good death. The message to Savorgnan is that, despite the trials and tribulations she is putting him through, he will remain constant in his love.

Bembo's final proof of devotion to Savorgnan, and his surpassing of Petrarch as an authority on love, comes in the form of a *strambotto*,[22] which he includes with his letter. By including a poem with this particular letter, he moves from the position of a reader of Petrarchan poetry and example of and testament to its veracity to the creator of a new poetry grounded in lived experiences. As poet-lover he translates his desire for Savorgnan into rhyme:

Chi rompe ne l'Egeo, se poi vi riede,
  È gran ragion che senza pro si doglia.
Chi torna al ceppo, che gli offese il piede,
  Conviensi ch'indi mai non si discioglia.
Chi prova Amor un tempo, e poi li crede,
  Altro che pianto è ben che non ne coglia.
O miei pensieri imaginati e folli,
  Voi che speraste? o pur io che ne volli?

Whoever sinks into the Aegean, and then returns there,
  Should rightly suffer without benefit.
Whoever returns to the chains that wounded his foot,
  should never free himself from them.
Whoever experiences Love once, and then believes in it,
  beyond crying it is right that he take nothing from it.
O my imagined and crazy thoughts,
  what did you hope for? rather, what did I hope to gain?

Bembo's choice of the *strambotto* signals a return to the origins of the sonnet, Petrarch's preferred medium.[23] One of the earliest poetic forms in Italy, the *strambotto* is a single stanza of six to eight verses written in hendecasyllables and believed to be an early iteration of what would become the sonnet's octave.[24] Bembo's rhyme scheme follows the conventions of the *strambotto toscano* – abababcc – rather than the Sicilian *ottava* (abababab), a choice that emphasizes his return to Petrarch's poetic origins. Despite the form, Bembo maintains an important Petrarchan conceit in his *strambotto*: he figures the poet-lover trapped in a paradoxical state. Even after having been injured, he must return to the original site of offence, which will in turn make him wise. Bembo's examples are far removed from the metaphysical or otherworldly states of contradiction we find throughout the *RVF*, however. Here Bembo provides two mundane examples – the turbulent Aegean Sea, and enslavement – to introduce the pain of love. Man's encounter with human events like being chained or nearly drowning in the turbulent sea makes love an earthly, rather than spiritual, occurrence. The overall message to Savorgnan is that, despite her accusations against him – her persecution of him – he will continue to return to her, the source of his pain.

Bembo's emphasis on crying ("pianto") as an expected outcome of love contains a metapoetic tenor that elucidates both the accompanying letter and his developing poetics. "Oltre a pianto" (v. 6) looks forward to the opening poem of the 1530 *Rime*, "Piansi e cantai lo strazio e l'aspra guerra," which links crying (piangere) to poeticizing (cantare) rather than the more introspective Petrarchan "piango et ragiono" (I cry and reason) of *RVF* 1, 5. Indeed, Bembo dismisses Petrarchan introspection in the final two verses of the *strambotto*, where he rhetorically questions what he expected to gain from his "pensieri imaginati e folli" (imagined and crazy thoughts). Thus, while Bembo's accompanying letter to Savorgnan includes Petrarchan citations that simultaneously mythologize and ground their love affair, the composition of a *strambotto* that engages with Petrarchan conceits shows Bembo's early attempt at finding his own authorial voice beyond the confines of the Petrarchan sonnet form. The poetic medium predates his Petrarchan subtext, and his requited love affair with Savorgnan, documented in both letters and poetry, surpasses Petrarch's model of desire. Thus, his attempts to prove his love to Savorgnan are also attempts at proving his worth as a poet able to translate his reality into art.

The frequency with which Bembo cites Petrarch in his letters to Savorgnan points to a deliberate experimentation with language, genre, and form that runs contrary to the very strong public position he will take on the subject in the Ciceronian Quarrel with Gianfrancesco Pico della Mirandola only a few years later, which was examined in the previous chapter. While he occasionally accompanies his letters with original poems, he more frequently weaves into his letters prose citations of the *RVF* and *Triumphi* alongside references to his own poetry and *Gli Asolani*. And this habit seemingly did not go unnoticed by Savorgnan. On 24 August 2015 she expresses her frustration with his epistolary practice, even accusing him of being inauthentic and a fraud.[25] She opens the letter telling Bembo not to expect any more letters from her for now, and then moves on to a series of rhetorical questions, challenging his authenticity:

> Come ho io bastante lima da emendare e pulire vostri versi? Certo debo credere asai a tante altre vostre parole. Dhe, simulatore! E come? Che son io con voi? (h)o basa: a viva voce mi riservo.
>
> As though I have enough file to correct and polish your verses? Of course I must really believe all your other words. Please, you phony! And how? What I am to you? Enough: I'll restrain myself until we speak.

Virginia Cox has already noted the leitmotif of the "dolce lima" (sweet file) in the Bembo-Savorgnan epistolary correspondence, which points to a collaborative effort in their letter writing.[26] This is supported by the earlier examples in this section where both Bembo and Savorgnan present their relationship as one founded on both love and the intellect. Here, however, Savorgnan refers only to her "lima" – excising "dolce" from the recurrent symbol – emphasizing labour over any pleasure she derives from it, or might expect as a reward. The distinction between genres – the "versi" she polishes for him, and the "tante altre parole" he writes to her – collapses the divide between poetry and epistolary prose that we see occurring in his letters to her. The accusation that he is a "simulator" (a phony, or liar) has a double resonance within the broader context of their epistolary exchange. From the point of view of a lover, Bembo's professions of love are overshadowed by his expectation that she continually edit and polish his poetry. Given that he is an intellectual correspondent, the accusation could concern his practice of weaving Petrarchan verse into his letters, given the etymological link between "simulator" and the verb "simulare" – to copy, or reproduce artificially. Thus, Savorgnan's accusation cuts both ways: he is inauthentic both as lover and writer. This leads to her questioning her own worth, and whether she is valued more as an editor or a lover.

While Savorgnan's frustrations with Bembo in the preceding letter emphasize the uniqueness of their situation at this time – two lovers at the beginning of the Cinquecento corresponding in both prose and verse, and editing each other's work – it also points to the very experimental nature of Bembo's writing in this early stage of his career, and his approach to female interlocuters. There is a deliberate engagement with Petrarchan poetry and imitation that at times amplifies Bembo's professions of love and devotion and at other times reveals the failure of the Petrarchan model in real-world relationships. In these moments of failure, he cites himself, or composes a poem, in order to convey the real, requited love he shares with Savorgnan. This practice, noted throughout his correspondence, presents Bembo as a poet-lover whose love and artistic output rival – if not surpass – Petrarch's. For him, their love is unique and exemplary; it is a new paradigm of love. He makes this explicit in a letter of 18 to 20 September 1500, when he places himself and Savorgnan upon a pedestal, as an exemplum for future lovers:

> Tutta questa mattina sono stato con voi, e tutto oggi con voi starò e tutta questa notte. Non so di tutta l'altra. Il mio fuoco si fa ogni dì più bello e maggiore, in tanto che non è cosa grande alcuna, alla quale esso non ardisca di giugnere con la sua alta fiamma. E se da voi non rimarrà, veggo che ancora potremo essere essempio agli amanti, che doppo noi verranno.[27]

> I have spent this entire morning with you, and I will stay with you all day and all night. I don't know about the rest. My fire grows more beautiful and greater each day, so much that there is not any great thing that it cannot reach with its high flame. And if the fire will not stay in you, I see that we will still be able to serve as an example to other lovers who will come after us.

What is remarkable about this passage to Savorgnan is the paradoxical symbol of flames ("fuoco," "fiamma"), and the balance between Bembo's current passion and his uncertainty about the future. He projects the bliss of a morning spent together into the coming day and evening. His description of their time together is realistic rather than idealistic: the future tense "starò" looks forward to the coming hours but does not imply eternity. Indeed, Bembo claims not to know what is to come ("non so di tutta l'altra"). While his desire ("fuoco") for her grows daily, he is not concerned if it does not reach its high flame ("fiamma") – her. For, as he remarks in the final lines, even if the "flame" of their love ceases to burn in Savorgnan, nevertheless they – and, I would like to suggest, their epistolary correspondence – will be an example to future lovers. Despite the very private nature of their letter exchange, or Bembo's surprisingly candid acknowledgment that their relationship might not last forever, what he is certain of is the emblematic nature of their love.

Bembo's remark about being an example to future lovers ("essempio agli amanti, che dopo noi verranno") belies the very private nature of his epistolary exchange with Savorgnan, and the lengths to which they went to conceal their affair. Throughout their correspondence, several of their servants are mentioned (by their initials) in their roles as as couriers, and at one point Savorgnan reminds Bembo not to talk about their affair in town.[28] While scholars have argued that Bembo never intended to publish his correspondence, what has been left unresolved is why, then, he edited some of his letters, and added dates to several of Savorgnan's letters decades after their relationship had ended. We can never know his motives, but we can answer the question as to precisely what kind of "essempio agli amanti" emerges from Bembo's letter exchange with Savorgnan. Their relationship, correspondence, and especially collaborative efforts in poetry point to a new paradigm of love and desire rooted in an intellectual kinship. And as is outlined in the next section, this epistolary correspondence replete with Petrarchan and Bembian citations will, indeed, become a model for future lovers – in Bembo's love affair with Lucrezia Borgia.

"O me felice sopra gli altri amanti": The Case of Lucrezia Borgia

In November of 1502, about one year after his relationship with Maria Savorgnan had ended, Bembo went to the Este court at Ferrara where he met Lucrezia Borgia (1480–1519) – illegitimate daughter of Pope Alessandro VI (Rodrigo Borgia), sister to Cesare Borgia, and, as of February of that very year, new wife of Alfonso D'Este.[29] While it is largely believed that Alessandro VI arranged the marriage in order to expand his and especially his illegitimate son Cesare's territory and influence into the Appenines and Po valley, nonetheless Lucrezia Borgia soon became an influential cultural force in her own right. Almost immediately after her arrival, she filled the Este court with poets like Antonio Tebaldeo, Lodovico Ariosto, and Ercole Strozzi, making Ferrara a vibrant cultural and literary centre. In only a short matter of months, she had established herself as a great patron of the arts whose court rivalled her sister-in-law Isabella d'Este's court in Mantua.[30] It is within this courtly context that she met Bembo and began a well-known love affair and epistolary correspondence that would last almost until her death in 1519.

Between 1503 and 1517, Bembo and Borgia exchanged letters and poems, mainly in Italian, though Borgia often wrote in her native Spanish.[31] There are several similarities between Bembo's letters to Savorgnan and those addressed to Borgia. In the early years of their affair, his letters are rife with Petrarchan allusions and accompanying poems, with Bembo repurposing some of the same tropes to address his new love. Major life events are also documented, particularly the death of Alessandro VI in 1503,[32] as well as the more mundane details of his day. Perhaps because of Lucrezia Borgia's higher station, her position as both his lover and his patron, and the more public role he had in her court, Bembo's writing is stylistically much more formal and polished than that in his letters to Savorgnan. Considering the length of their affair, the number of letters is quite surprising: forty letters written by Bembo, and only nine by Borgia, numbering significantly less than the Bembo-Savorgnan correspondence.

Their correspondence begins on 25 May 1503, when Borgia sends a love poem by the Aragonese poet Lope de Estúniga (1415–65), copied by her hand.[33] Bembo's first letter to Borgia is a response to the poem, and though it opens with a topos of modesty, it quickly turns into a metapoetic comparison of Spanish versus Tuscan, and his virtue as a poet. He writes,

> Vergognansi due sonetti, questi dì partoritimi dal mio pensiero, di venire a V.S. innanzi, sì come rustichetti secondo il luogo dove essi nati sono, e mal vestiti; ma io ho dato loro ardire, accertandogli che nessuna altra cosa è bisogno di portare a voi che fede, della quale essi dicono che sono pieni. Vengono adunque a V.S. rassicurati, e seco arrecano una canzonina pur oggi nata a gara del vostro *Yo pienso si me muriesse*. Ma tuttavia essa gli fa riverenza, e conosce chiaro che le vezzose dolcezze degli spagnuoli ritrovamenti nella grave purità della toscana lingua non hanno luogo, e se portate vi sono non vere e natie paiono, ma finte e straniere.

> Two sonnets born to me these last days, being somewhat countrified on account of their place of birth and poorly clothed, were abashed at my proposal that they should enter your Ladyship's presence; but I have given them my heart by assuring them that to you they need bring nothing but fidelity, which they tell me they have in abundance. Thus emboldened they come to you, bearing a little song born this very day as rival to your own, *Yo pienso se me muriese*; and nonetheless it kneels to yours and freely concedes that the engaging tenderness of Spanish compositions have no home in the grave purity of the Tuscan tongue and if set therein appear neither native nor true, but false and foreign.[34]

Bembo is apologetic about the apparent unpolished nature of his poems, which he describes as "rustichetti" (countrified) and "mal vestiti" (poorly clothed). These humble descriptors stand in contrast to the formality and reverence of his address to Borgia as V.S. (Vostra Signoria; your Ladyship). He places himself – and his poems – below her, as a courtier presenting his patron with a gift. Bembo's conversation with the poems further emphasizes the courtier-patron relationship he stages when he assures the poems that their main objective is to communicate "fede" (fidelity, faith) to Borgia, despite their lowly status. With the poems, Bembo therefore pledges his faith to Borgia as a poet-lover-courtier.

The modesty with which Bembo opens the letter belies his subsequent explanation that the poetry was "nata a gara" (literally, born into competition with) the Spanish poem she had sent him, "Yo pienso se me muriese" ("I think were I to die").[35] Although we unfortunately do not know which sonnets Bembo sent to her,[36] and thus cannot compare them to the Spanish poem, the sense of rivalry seems to come from the poetic languages themselves, rather than the style or content of the actual poems.[37] Bembo compares the two languages, attributing a "vezzose dolcezze" (engaging tenderness) to Spanish, and a "grave purità" (grave purity) to Tuscan Italian. Bembo's emphasis on the purity of Italian is strengthened by his claim that one cannot include Spanish verses in Italian poems lest they appear "finte e straniere" (false and foreign) compared to the "vere e natie" (true and native) use of Italian. Yet Bembo's choice of the adjective "grave" in describing the purity of Italian connotes a sense of gravitas and authority that is in stark contrast to the emotional tenor of Spanish. This is an important distinction, since he specifically mentions "la toscana lingua" (the Tuscan tongue), which is not Bembo's native dialect (Venetian) but the literary language he would later hold up as exemplary in his *Prose della volgar lingua* (1525) – Petrarch's idiom. Despite his argument about the rivalry between Spanish and Tuscan, and his evidence of Tuscan Italian's preeminence, he tells Borgia that his poetry kneels before hers ("essa gli fa riverenza"), providing another instance of his "fede" to her, and reverence for her station. He, like his poetry, kneels before her, and he closes the letter with a third gift and example of his poetic abilities: "Mando a V.S. il primo degli *Asolani*, che in questa ora ho riavuto" ("I am sending your Ladyship the first book of *Gli Asolani*, which I received this very hour").

While Bembo's first letter to Borgia more formally establishes what appears to be a patron-poet relationship, as their affair develops so too does the amorous tone in his letters to her and his adaptation of Petrarchan conceits, often replicated from his Savorgnan letters. On 19 June 1503, for example, Bembo repeats a paradigm that he used in a previous letter to Savorgnan: the desire for lovers to look into the hearts and minds of their partners. Here, however, the image of a crystal, rather than a heart, symbolizes an intellectual and amorous kinship:[38]

> Mirando questi dì nel mio cristallo – del quale si ragionò l'ultima sera che io a V.S. feci riverenza – ho nel mezzo di lui letti questi versi che fuori mi traluceano; i quali ora scritti vi mando in questo foglio. Dolcissimo mi sarebbe, e sopra ogni Tesoro caro, che V.S. a me facesse vedere allo 'ncontro alcuna cosa che essa avesse letta nel suo. Il che tuttavia non so bene se io mi debba sperare che facciate, considerando che voi l'altro ieri ancora di quelle cose mi taceste che proposto m'avevate di ragionarmi. Bascio a V.S. la mano.
>
> Gazing these past days into my crystal, of which we spoke during the last evening I paid my respects to your Ladyship, I have read therein, glowing at its centre, these lines I now send to you inscribed upon this paper. It would be the sweetest consolation to me and more prized than any treasure if in exchange your Ladyship might permit me to see something that she may have read in hers. And yet I cannot be sure that I may hope as much, when I recall that the day before yesterday you still kept silent regarding those things of which you had proposed to speak with me. I kiss your Ladyship's hand.[39]

The symbol of the "cristallo" serves a double function in this letter. One the one hand, it is like the heart, symbolizing the internal sentiments of the lover. By looking into his *cristallo-cuore* he is reminded of his love for Borgia. On the other hand, the "cristallo" takes on a prophetic and inspiratory function, since it displays to Bembo poetic verses in Borgia's honour. Bembo transcribes the words he sees in the "cristallo" and subsequently sends his lover the poem. Thus, both love and poetic inspiration reside in the crystal/heart, synthesizing the previous images of the heart and mind that Bembo had already used in letter 27 to Savorgnan, examined above. Just as in the Savorgnan letter(s), the "cristallo" symbolizes both an amorous and an intellectual relationship between the two. Indeed, he entreats Borgia to follow his lead by looking into her "cristallo" and telling him what verses she sees written therein. While his request is one of knowledge of her feelings, the emphasis on the written word equally prioritizes their intellectual exchanges. He hopes that, "V.S. a me facesse vedere allo 'ncontro alcuna cosa che essa avesse letta nel suo" ("if in exchange your Ladyship might permit me to see something that she may have read in hers"), highlighting the active role of reading and then relaying what was read. Borgia's written words attesting to her feelings are what Bembo most desires. He ends with a reminder that she had promised to discuss "quelle cose" (those things), a level of discreetness we do not find in the Savorgnan letters that is simultaneously playful and a sign of reverence for her social station.

The poem Bembo sends with the letter would eventually be included at the beginning of his poetic collection, as *Rime* 7. Here, the "cristallo" becomes a secret sign that can unlock the true meaning of the poem only for the two lovers:

Poi ch'ogni ardir mi circonscrisse Amore
quel dì ch'io posi nel suo campo il piede,
tanto ch'altrui non pur chieder mercede,
ma scoprir sol non oso il mio dolore,
avess'io almen d'un bel cristallo il core,
che, quel ch'io taccio e Madonna non vede
dell'interno mio mal, senza altra fede,
a' suoi begli occhi tralucesse fore;
ch'io crederei della pietate ancora
veder tinta la neve di quel volto,
che'l mio sì spesso bagna e discolora.
Or che questo non ho, quello m'è tolto,
temo non voglia il mio Signor ch'io mora,
ché la difesa è poca, e'l strazio è molto.

Since love forbade my zeal while she was near
The first day I set foot on His battlefield.
Whence each cry for her mercy I restrain
And dare not let my wretchedness appear,
Would that I had a heart as crystal clear,
Then what I hide, nor she can ascertain,
Without more proof of my least inward pain
Would shine for her fair eyes in faith sincere;
I should yet believe I will see that face divine
Tinged with pity that now is white as snow,
And much has moistened and discoloured mine.
My heart's no glass, and this I must forego,
And fear my Lord would wish to see me pine,
Because my defense is small, the battle great. (translation amended)[40]

In the poem, Bembo hypothetically gestures at possessing a "cristallo" clear enough to display his inner feelings to the beloved. The desire of the hortatory imperfect subjunctive in the second quatrain ("avess'io almen d'un bel cristallo il core" ["would that I had a heart as crystal clear"]) is dashed by the stark reality of the final tercet's declaration that "or che questo non ho" ("my heart's no glass"). While the poet-lover wishes he had a crystal clear enough to show his beloved his innermost feelings, he does not, and thus must continue his battle against Amor, figured in the incipit.

On the surface, *Rime* 7 seems to replay Petrarch's metaphysical battle against Amor in *RVF* 2, the war metaphors symbolizing the poet-lover's internal, psychomachic struggle. But Bembo creates a slight variation in the model: his outward appearance of struggle and conflict contradicts his true feelings for the beloved. Were his heart clear and transparent, she would see that. In his accompanying letter, however, his "cristallo" is clear, so clear, in fact, that he was able to read verses of poetry in it. Having been privy to Bembo's explication of the poem and its symbolism, Borgia is in a unique position to understand the poem in a way that an outside reader would not. In this manner, the letter and poem are reminiscent of Dante's prosimetric model in the *Vita nova,* though here Borgia plays the unique role of both beloved and "prima amica" who reads and responds to the correspondence.

Borgia's response of 24 June 1503 picks up on the leitmotif of the "cristallo," Bembo's discretion, and the metapoetic nature of their relationship. Indeed, she chooses her own *senhal,* creating a secret code between the two lovers:

> Miser Pietro mio, circha el desiderio tenite intender da me lo incontro del vostro e nostro cristallo, che cusì meritamente se po reputar e chiamare, non saperìa mai che altro posserne dire o trovarçe salvo una extrema conformità, forsi mai per nisum tempo igualata. E questo basti, e risti per evangelio perpetuo.
>
> Questo da qui avante serrà el mio nome: FF.

> Messer Pietro mio. Concerning the desire you have to hear from me regarding the counterpart of your and our crystal as it may rightly be reputed and termed, I cannot think what else to say or imagine save that it has an extreme affinity of which the like perhaps has never been equalled in any age. And may this suffice. And let it be a gospel everlasting.
>
> This henceforth shall be my name: *f.f.*[41]

Borgia's use of "vostro e nostro cristallo" ("your and our crystal") discreetly symbolizes requited love. While "vostro cristallo" clearly refers to Bembo's heart, "nostro" implies a shared heart between them.

The use of the first-personal plural in the possessive form "nostro" is in stark contrast to her use of the singular possessive with regards to her name ("mio nome"): FF. She takes control of her identity in their correspondence, but equally shares a heart with him. Although she does not wax poetic about her feelings, she does make a strong – if not vague – gesture at a deep love: the "conformità" of their love has never been matched. Seemingly self-aware of the high level of discretion she has employed in her letter, she tells Bembo that he will have to make do with her few words on the subject, pledging her faith to him by calling her letter and proclamation an "evangelio perpetuo" ("gospel everlasting").

In both the Savorgnan and Borgia letters, Bembo introduces symbols that represent requited love and a relationship based on sentiments and the intellect. The desire for the beloved is not just emotional or physical but is also grounded in poetic and intellectual exchange. Bembo's general practice of citing Petrarch in order to critique him in the Savorgnan letters continues in the early Borgia correspondence, though with much less frequency. In an undated letter addressed "AD FF" – as Borgia requested in the letter examined above – Bembo laments their upcoming separation, citing from Petrarch as a reassurance of their love:

> Io parto, o dolcissima vita mia, e pure non parto né partirò mai. Se allo 'ncontro voi rimanendo non rimarrete, non voglio dire di voi, ma certo *O me felice sopra gli altri amanti*. E quale più dolce miracolo far si può di questo: vivere in altrui e morire in sé? Oimè, come posso io ben giurare che io in voi mi vivo!

> I am leaving, oh my dearest life, and yet I do not leave and never shall. If likewise you who stay were not to stay, I dare not speak for you, but truly "Ah, of all who love none more blest than I!" And what sweeter miracle could be wrought than this: to live in another and die in oneself? And oh, how truthfully I can swear I live in you![42]

Although Bembo is leaving for a brief trip, his physical absence is tempered by their everlasting love, which resides in each of them. The play on life and death, departing and staying, elevates their love to a realm untouched or unaffected by the physical. Interestingly, Bembo ventriloquizes Borgia's voice when he cites a verse from *RVF* 70: "O me felice sopra gli altri amanti" ("Ah, of all who love none more blest than I!").[43] Though he claims he would never speak on her behalf, he does precisely that, making her citation of Petrarch evidence of her love for Bembo. While the Borgia persona quoting Petrarch is made to perform her desire, the episode also serves as a form of poetic rivalry. *RVF* 70 is one of Petrarch's most metapoetic poems in his vernacular collection of rhymes. Each stanza ends with a citation from a poetic predecessor (Arnaut Daniel, Guido Cavalcanti, Dante, Cino da Pistoia), with the final verse of the poem citing Petrarch's incipit, "Nel dolce tempo de la prima etade" (*RVF* 23; "In the sweet time of my first age"). Petrarch thus figures himself within the poem as closing out a poetic tradition. By citing *RVF* 70, Bembo includes himself in this great lineage of poets but also distinguishes himself from them through the figure of Borgia. That is, the Borgia persona in the letter expresses desire for Bembo that is unprecedented in the poems of his predecessors. The particular verse Bembo ventriloquizes through Borgia comes from the second stanza of Petrarch's poem, where he imagines that his poetry is pleasing to Laura, and cites Dante:

> Ragion è ben ch'alcuna volta io canti
> però ch' ò sospirato sì gran tempo
> che mai non incomincio assai per tempo
> per adequar col riso i dolor tanti.
> Et s'io potesse far ch'agli occhi santi
> porgesse alcun diletto
> qualche dolce mio detto,
> *o me beato sopra gli altri amanti!*
> Ma più quand'io dirò senza mentire:
> "Donna mi priegha, per ch' io voglio dire." (emphasis mine)

> It is just that at some time I sing, since I have sighed for so long a time that I shall never begin soon enough to make my smiling equal so many sorrows. And if I could make some sweet saying of mine give some delight to those holy eyes, *oh me blessed above other lovers!* But most when I can say without lying, "A lady begs me; therefore I wish to speak."[44] (emphasis mine)

Petrarch can only hope to write something that pleases the unattainable Laura and that would make him the living example of Dante's verse, "Donna mi priegha, per ch' io voglio dire" ("A lady begs; therefore I speak"). This would make the poet-lover feel more blessed than any other man. What is merely a pipe dream for Petrarch and their poetic predecessors is a reality for Bembo – his beloved Borgia speaks, writes, responds to, and loves and cherishes him. By ventriloquizing her voice in the letter, he provides proof of the veracity of Petrarch's verse, and makes the love between him and Borgia, as well as the poetry it inspires, a rival to the *RVF*.

As with the Savorgnan affair, Bembo holds up his relationship with Borgia as an example for other lovers. On 5 October 1503 Bembo writes an impassioned letter to Borgia in response to accusations she has made against him.[45] Bembo only gestures at the nature of the accusation, stating "Sospettate ora il falso quanto molto vi piace, e credete il vero quanto poco potete che, o vogliate o no, conoscierete un giorno avere male a questa volta giudicato" ("Now think me false as much as you will, believe the truth as little as you please, but like it or not the day shall come when you must acknowledge how far you have judged me wrong"). Bembo presents himself as having been falsely accused of a crime through a series of contrasts – "sospettare" (to suspect) versus "conoscere" (to know), "il falso" (the false) versus "il vero" (the truth) – which culminate in the verb "mal ... giudicare" (to judge wrongly). Although he does not explicitly repeat Borgia's accusation against him, the recurrent fire imagery and his emphasis on passion throughout his letter would seem to imply that she has accused him of unfaithfulness or not loving her ardently enough. In the first example, the image of fire is used both to reassure Borgia of his everlasting love and to elevate their love to the status of an exemplum:

> non potrà tanto la mia fiera disaventura che, se io averò vita, il fuoco nel quale FF e il mio destino m'han posto, non abbia ad essere il più alto e più chiaro che oggidì in cuore d'amante si senta appreso. Alto il farà la natura del luogo nel quale egli arde, chiaro la sua stessa fiamma, che ancora a tutto 'l mondo ne darà testimonio.

> as long as there is life in me my cruel fate will never prevent the fire in which f.f. and my destiny have placed me from being the highest and brightest blaze that in our time ever set a lover's heart alight. It will soar by virtue of the place where it burns, bright with the intensity of its own flame, and one day it will be a beacon to all the world.

Bembo's initial reference to his "fiera disaventura" (cruel fate) begins a series of Petrarchan conceits that transform him into a battle-wearied poet-lover at the mercy of destiny, Amor, and the cruel beloved. When he claims that Borgia and "il ... destino" (destiny) have actively placed a fire in his heart, he presents himself as passive and without blame, much like Petrarch in *RVF* 2 and 3. However, he distances himself from the archetypical defeated lover when he claims that neither can prevent this flame – which now resides in him – from reaching its pinnacle. Thus Borgia, even with her accusations, cannot prevent his fire/love for her from increasing to the point of becoming an exemplum to the world ("a tutto 'l mondo ne darà testimonio"). While she might have provided the initial spark, she does not control its lifespan or intensity.

As Bembo continues, he presents himself as a wise lover by distinguishing Borgia from his previous lovers. He does so by playing on both the mundane realities of love and spiritual allusions and numerology, claiming,

> Non merita la grazia alla quale, vostra gran mercé, mi chiamavate, che, o renduta o tolta che ella ora mi sia, io più ad altra donna pensi giamai; sì perché nessuna potrà essere di tanta eccellenza, e sì perché alle terze fiamme concedendomi, se io la vita ne lasciassi, ben mi sarebbe investito, quando tutti i terzi avenimenti delle cose, perciò che sono perigliosissimi, si sogliono benedire.

> The state of grace to which in your great charity you have raised me, whether extended still or now withheld, is such an honour that no other woman could ever again enter into my thoughts, for none could rival you in excellence; and were I to lose my life in thus consigning myself to the flames for the third time, it would still be well with me, since all third things being so perilous in the undertaking are wont to enjoy a special benediction.

Bembo elevates Borgia above all other women by making her an exemplum of female virtue: she has no rival in "grazia," "mercé," or overall excellence. While he repeats the fire imagery from above, here it is used to describe the reality of love. When he refers to throwing himself into the "terze fiamme" (third [set of] flames), he places Borgia within the chronology of his previous love affairs: first, with a woman known to us only as Madonna G.; second, with Maria Savorgnan; and third, with Lucrezia Borgia. Bembo figures himself as a phoenix who has died twice before in a fire (love affair) only to be reborn and to find a new flame/lover. While Petrarch identified with the figure of the phoenix to describe his unique and everlasting love for Laura,[46] here Bembo uses it to explain the finality of a love affair and his never-ending potential to love again.[47] This veiled warning is tempered, however, by his assertion that no other woman can rival her, and that, essentially, third time is a charm. His earlier attribution of classical (Christian) female virtues to Borgia is further emphasized by his play on medieval numerology and religious rhetoric: the *third* flame is more special than the previous two, because the number three (trinity) is blessed ("si sogliono benedire").

As we saw in the Savorgnan letters, and the phoenix example above, Bembo again presents himself as a living example of the veracity of Petrarch's poetry, only to overturn the Petrarchan conceit with his real, lived experiences. He writes,

> Potrei scrivere molte cose che non vi seppi dire ieri, quando poteste vedere che *Caritate accesa lega la lingua altrui, gli spiriti invola*. Ma se non sapete conoscermi dalla mia vita, o leggermi ne gli occhi e nella fronte, che debbo io pensare che nelle carte facciate?
>
> Now I feel that I could write so many things to you for which I could not find words yesterday, when you could see how "burning love binds one's tongue, steals away one's breath." And if it happens that you fail to perceive how I am from the way I live, or you cannot read my feelings in my eyes and upon my countenance, what use may I suppose you could have for letters? (translation amended) [48]

Bembo's inability to defend himself against Borgia's accusation in person the previous day makes him the living example of Petrarch's *RVF* 170, whose final tercet he partially cites to her when he says that "Caritate accesa lega la lingua altrui, gli spiriti invola" ("burning love binds one's tongue, steals away one's breath"). Borgia, indeed, bore witness to his proving the verse's veracity, since he claims that she was able to see it in him ("poteste vedere"). Bembo excuses his silence by claiming that love stole away his breath and tied his tongue, reinforcing his previous claims of love through fire imagery. But Bembo also diverges from the Petrarchan subtext in the mere act of writing to her the following day. In this passage we see the distinction between the previous and current days, and speaking versus writing, all of which make his identification with Petrarch as a poet-lover a momentary phase. If we consider the full sestet from which Bembo quotes, we see that in writing the letter, Bembo surpasses his Petrarchan model:

> Ond' io non pote' mai formar parola
> ch'altro che da me stesso fosse intesa
> così m'à fatto Amor tremante et fioco.

Et veggi' or ben che caritate accesa
lega la lingua altrui, gli spiriti invola;
chi pò dir com' egli arde è 'n picciol foco.

Wherefore I have never been able to form a word that was understood by any but myself, Love has made me so trembling and weak! And I see well how burning Love binds one's tongue, steals away one's breath: he who can say how he burns is in but a little fire.

Petrarch's silence is equated with his weakened and trembling physical state. The only words he is able to speak are introspective and unintelligible to others, he claims. It is, of course, a Petrarchan conceit, since Petrarch continually figures his poems as made of sighs, emblematized in *RVF* 1. Bembo moves beyond Petrarch's topos of ineffability to emphasize the written word (their letters) and his body language, through the verbs "conoscere" (to know) and "leggere" (to read), when he questions, rhetorically, "Ma se non sapete conoscermi dalla mia vita, o leggermi ne gli occhi e nella fronte, che debbo io pensare che nelle carte facciate?" ("And if it happens that you fail to perceive how I am from the way I live, or you cannot read my feelings in my eyes and upon my countenance, what use may I suppose you could have for letters?"). If Borgia cannot "read" him, then why do the lovers exchange letters?

As a final example, I turn to an exchange between Bembo and Borgia's lady-in-waiting Lisabetta da Siena,[49] who functions as a kind of Dantean *donna schermo*. Though Lisabetta's letter is not extant, we know from Bembo's reply during holy week of April 1504 that it had been some time since Borgia had written to him directly, and that she had thus instructed her lady-in-waiting to write to him and offer him an apology for her silence. Bembo's reply on "mercoledì santo"[50] twice draws upon the Petrarchan conceit of the beloved's image in the heart (*RVF* 96) while also playing on the iconic tension between sacred and profane love that characterizes one narrative thread in the *RVF*. In the opening of the letter, Bembo first thanks Lisabetta for her letter and then describes an image before his eyes:

Accetto ogni scusa che mi fate per nome di FF; e tutti quelli rispetti, che dite esser molti, al non scrivere ella secondo il disiderio che ella ha di piacermi, io da me ho imaginati continovo, e imaginava tuttavia, quando io voi pregai di due versi di sua mano. Non per tanto non posso tenermi di non disiderar sue lettere, poscia che e il vederla e il ragionar seco, che essere soleano due fermissimi e dolcissimi sostegni della mia vita, mi sono interrotti e tolti.

I accept every excuse which you offer on f.f.'s behalf; and all those reasons, which you say are many, for her not writing to me despite her desire to gratify me have been constantly before my eyes and I picture them to myself even while asking you for two lines from her hand. And yet I cannot help wishing for her letters now that seeing her and speaking with her, formerly two such strong and cherished pillars sustaining my life, have been dislodged and taken from me.[51]

Because Bembo is lamenting the recent absence and silence of his beloved, we would expect the repetition of the verb "imaginare" (to imagine, see) at the beginning of the letter to evoke the portrait of Borgia. Instead, he thrice emphasizes writing, with her letters substituting for her physical presence: first, the image before his eyes is the (written) excuse that Lisabetta has provided for her Lady's silence; second, Bembo desires and requests "due versi da sua mano" (two lines from her hand); and finally, since he cannot see or speak with her, he desires "sue lettere" (her letters). Bembo's insistence on the written word highlights their intellectual relationship and their longer epistolary exchange as a mediator of their shared desire.

Bembo then describes another image he holds dear: Borgia's "memoria." In describing her ever-present image in his heart, Bembo plays on a Petrarchan anniversary poem:

È rimaso in piè il terzo [sostegno], e rimarra sempre, che torlomi nessuna cosa potrà giammai, se non quella una che è di tutte le cose ultimo fine: il pensier dico, e la memoria di lei, che intorno al cuore ogni giorno, ogni notte, ogni ora, in ogni luogo, in ogni stato mi si gira.

The third [pillar] still stands and always shall, for nothing save that which is the extreme end of all things could deprive me of it: I mean the thought, the memory, of her who encircles my heart each day, each night, every hour, wheresoever I am, whatever condition.

Bembo had already listed the first two pillars – "il vederla" (seeing her) and "ragionar seco" (speaking with her) – and so here provides her image as the third. Since he claimed that her letters substitute for the first two pillars, we see here that her portrait in his heart is equal to her letters. His use of the verb "ragionare" connotes an intellectual discussion; thus, he places equal weight on the amorous and intellectual sides of their relationship, making her image almost synonymous with her letters. The motif and cadence of the second clause – "ogni giorno, ogni notte, ogni ora, in ogni luogo, in ogni stato" – strongly recalls the first quatrain of *RVF* 61:

> Benedetto sia 'l giorno, e 'l mese, et l'anno
> e la stagione, e 'l tempo, et l'ora e 'l punto
> e 'l bel paese, e 'l loco ov'io fui giunto
> da' duo begli occhi che legato m'ànno

> Blessed be the day and the month and the year and the season and the time and the hour and the instant and the beautiful countryside and the place where I was struck by the two lovely eyes that bound me.[52]

Whereas in his letters to Borgia he often explicitly cites Petrarch, here in his letter to the lady-in-waiting he merely alludes to Petrarchan poetry. The letter is brief, and considerably less intimate than the ones addressed directly to Borgia, but the Petrarchan resonances are still palpable and meaningful. Petrarch celebrates the day he saw Laura for the first time, from a distance as she left a church in Avignon; Bembo celebrates the beginning of an epistolary and amorous affair. What is celebrated and cherished in Bembo's letters is requited love, with an interactive muse.

Despite the overlapping Petrarch-inspired epistolary practices of Bembo in his correspondence with Maria Savorgnan and Lucrezia Borgia, and the roles of both women as his interactive muses, Borgia's situation is unique. She had been born into a powerful family, given in marriage to three powerful men whose families had something to offer her father, Pope Alessandro VI. As previously mentioned, she was an influential patron in the Ferrarese Este court, of which Bembo was a part. Thus, in Borgia we find that the two roles Petrarch kept separate – patron and beloved – are now conflated in a single, female person. In the letters, we find traces of this commingling of love and patronage, particularly in the first letter of the exchange, examined above. The clearest moment in which Bembo addresses her as his patron is in his dedication of the 1505 *editio princeps* of the *Asolani* to her. Before the work went to press in March 1505, Bembo had drafted the dedication in a letter sent to Borgia on 1 August 1504[53] – the date that Bembo retains in the printed edition. The printed dedication is an elaborated and polished version of the original letter, which was already far more formal than his previous letters to her: he addresses her as "La Duchessa di Ferrara," instead of with the more frequently used *senhal* "FF," and there are no references to their personal relationship or previous correspondence. The dedication to Borgia at the beginning of the first edition of the *Asolani* contains numerous references to promises and favours, establishing patronage and the notion of gift exchange as a major theme. In the opening lines of the letter, Bembo writes,

> E io non ho a V.S. più tosto quegli ragionamenti mandati, che essendo l'anno passato in Ferrara le promisi giunto che io fussi qui di mandare; iscusimi appo lei la morte del mio caro fratello Carlo; che io oltre ogni mia credĕza [credenza] ritrovai di questa vita passato: la qual morte si mi stordi; che a guisa di coloro, che dal fuoco delle saette tocchi rimangano lungo tempo sanza sentimento, non ho peranchora ad altro potuto rivolger l'animo, che alla sua insanabile e penetrevolissima ferita.

> If I have not already sent Your Highness those discourses which I promised, last year in Ferrara, that I would send you as soon as I reached here, the loss of my dear brother Carlo, whom, contrary to all expectation, I found to have passed from life, may serve as my apology. His death so stupefied me that, like those who remain without feeling long after they have been stricken by arrows, I have not yet been able to turn my mind to anything but my deep, incurable wound. [54]

The dedication begins with a reference to a broken promise: Bembo promised to send Borgia a copy of the *Asolani* but never did because of the death of his brother Carlo (1503). Bembo describes the effects of his brother's death using Petrarchan language and imagery normally reserved for descriptions of the *innamoramento.* He presents himself as dazed, like those who, when pierced by fiery arrows, lose all feeling and can only focus their thoughts on the "insanabile e penetrevolissima ferita" ("deep, incurable wound"). Bembo describes himself as the Petrarchan lover of *RVF* 2, penetrated by Love's arrows, stunned by the blow, and unable to think of anything else. He presents his broken promise as a result of his victimization by a force beyond his control.

Bembo's appropriation of Petrarchan language here shows its adaptability to different ends, as it can be used to describe both the love for a woman (which he employed in his letters to Borgia) and the effects of the death of a brother. The connection between the two different experiences continues to the second reference to patronage, where Bembo's loss leads to the recognition of the debt owed to Borgia:

> Hora poscia che altro fare non se ne può, et che in me per la tramissione di questo tempo volgare et commune medicina più tosto che per altro rimedio, il dolore et le lachrime hanno in parte dato luoco alla ragione et al diritto conoscimento della promessa fatta a V.S. e delo mi debito sovenutomi, tali, quali essi sono, ve gli mando; e tanto più anchora volentieri a questo tempo quanto nuovamente ho inteso V.S. havere maritata la sua gentile Nicola, istimandogli non disdicevole sono a così fatta stagione, a fine che poi che io hora per le mie occupationi essere a parte delle vostre feste non posso, essi con V.S. e con la sua cara e valarosa Madonna Angela Borgia e con la sposa favellino e tentionino in mia vece, forse non sanza gli miei molto e da me amati e dal mondo honorati, et di V.S. domestici e famigliari Messer Hercole Strozza e Messer Antonio Tebaldeo. Et averrà che quello, che altri giovani hanno con altre donne tra gli sollazzi d'altre nozze ragionato, voi nelle vostre con le vostre damigelle et cortigiani da me, che vostro sono, isscrittivi leggerete.
>
> Now, since I can do no otherwise and, through common, ordinary medicine afforded by this interval rather than by any other remedy, my grief and tears have partly given way to reason and clear thinking, I remember my debt and the promise made to Your Highness, and send these discourses, such as they are, to you, and all the more readily at this time as I have recently learned that Your Highness has married off your worthy Nicola. For I consider them no unseemly gift at such a season, when, although my employments now prevent me from taking part in your celebrations, these may speak and argue in my place with Your Highness, with your dear and worthy Lady Angela Borgia, and with the bride, perhaps not without assistance of Master Ercole Strozzi and Master Antonio Tebaldeo, the familiars and followers of Your Highness, much loved of me and honoured by the world. And it may well be that the very things which other young men have discussed with other ladies during festivities for another marriage, you in your festivities will read with your maids of honour and courtiers, as they have been written down by me, who am likewise yours.

The pain suffered and tears shed for the death of Carlo led to a moment of clarity and remembrance of Bembo's political obligations to Borgia. He presents his mourning as an excuse for his error, praising her status by again mentioning the promise he had made to her and acknowledging the debt ("debito") he owes her. By sending her the *Asolani* and, in particular, by dedicating the work to her, Bembo has fulfilled his obligations to her. It is important to note that the publication and dedication happen at the same time that Borgia is presiding over the marriage ceremony of Nicola, her lady-in-waiting. The dedication thus takes on a particularly didactic function as he continues to tell Borgia what she should do with it: use it as a substitute for him in the wedding guests' discussions of love. Bembo thus presents his work to her as a manual about love, to be performed – through a reading – by Borgia, her cousin Angela (1466–1520/22), Nicola – the bride, and the poets Ercole Strozzi (who had introduced Bembo to Borgia) and Antonio Tebaldeo. Since his "occupationi" will not allow him to be present at her courtly festivities, the *Asolani* will serve as his authoritative *portavoce* on the subject, allowing him to be present in spirit. Rather than provide an example of how to initiate a debate on the nature of love, Bembo instead insists that his dialogues be read as a replacement for whatever discourse they might have had, alluding to the authority of his work. Borgia's authority over her court and her active participation in the discourse of love are superseded by Bembo's *Asolani*, as are the poetic reputations of his fellow poets Strozzi and Tebaldeo.

At the end of the dedication, Bembo alludes to expecting something in return for the gift he has given Borgia, using the language of courtly love and patronage to request it:

> e io assai buon guiderdone mi terro havere di questa mia giovenile fatica ricevuto, pensando per la qualità delle ragionate cose in questi sermoni che possa essere, che di questo nostro medesimo così alto e così lodevole disio leggendo li diveniate anchora più vaga, Alla cui buona gratia e mercé inchinevolmente mi raccomando.
>
> And I shall consider myself to have received a very good countergift for this youthful toil of mine if I may believe that, when you read these words, by virtue of the things discussed in them you may become still more devoted to that so high and praiseworthy wish of yours. To whose good graces I commend myself most humbly. (translation amended)[55]

From Bembo's "giovanil fatica" (youthful toil) he expects an "assai buon guiderdone" (very good countergift). Bembo's choice of the word "guiderdone" is an important one, since it stems from the Old French *guerdon*[56] and thus puts his dedication in dialogue with the long tradition of *fin' amor* (or *amour courtois*, to use Gaston Paris's term).[57] As in the feudal setting of medieval France, Bembo expects that this gift will yield one in return. Within the courtly love tradition, the *guerdon* is both a political bond between vassal and lord, as well as a bond between lover and Lady. In Bembo's case, Borgia simultaneously plays both roles. He thus reminds Borgia of her obligation to him as both beloved and patron, grounding their public relationship in a courtly tradition that predates them both. On the political side, just as his *Asolani* are referred to as "sermoni" – a clear allusion to the didactic function of the work – so too does the dedication serve as a lesson to Borgia on how to be a good patron. The true gift to Borgia is, thus, Bembo himself: an authority on love and patronage who has much to teach her.

In Bembo's 1505 dedication to Borgia we see a different side of their relationship, the public one steeped in politics, where Borgia's position as patron overshadows her role as beloved. Alongside this privileging of her public over her private persona, we see a change in the way in which Bembo presents the dynamic between them. In the letters, Bembo presents their relationship as founded upon both love and an intellectual bond. Her handwritten letters are as present in his heart as her portait. Throughout, he uses the verb "ragionare" – to argue with reason – in order to describe their many conversations, both oral and written. From their epistolary correspondence we see as much of an intellectual kinship as we do a love affair. While he often competes with Petrarch through his engagement with the *RVF* in his letters and poems, he does not present himself as more authoritative than Borgia in any of the matters under discussion. In the dedication, however, he oscillates between humility – and recognition of his place below Borgia in the patron-poet hierarchy – and his authority as a writer. Ultimately, however, he positions himself as Borgia's teacher, in both love and politics. As will be examined in the next section, the key term "guiderdone" is one that will appear in several poems of the 1530 *Rime*, where Bembo will grapple with the issues of poetic agency and patronage in his poetry, recalling Petrarch's "masculine intellect" in order to teach his beloveds how to perform their gender.

Performing Gender: Love and Politics in Bembo's *Rime*[58]

The years following the Savorgnan and Borgia letters and the first publication of the *Asolani* would change the course of Bembo's career and legacy. Bembo began to focus on the issue of imitation and the so-called *questione della lingua.*[59] As was examined in the last chapter, his staunchly Ciceronian stance on Latin imitation was well-known from his epistolary exchange with Gianfrancesco Pico della Mirandola in 1512–13 and would continue to influence great thinkers of this century. The much-anticipated 1525 publication of his *Prose della volgar lingua* shifted the emphasis to the vernacular as he championed the Florentine idiom of Petrarch and Boccaccio over the classical Latin of Cicero and Vergil. Despite his shift from Latin to the vernacular, theoretically his stance in the *Prose* was similar to that of the Ciceronian Quarrel of 1512–13: he favoured major model imitation, retained imitative boundaries between genres, and believed in a latent political power within language. This last point is, indeed, the founding principle of the *Prose*: that political stability could occur in Italy if the people were united under a common, Petrarch-inspired language. The *Prose* provided the theory behind Bembo's socio-political project as well as the first Italian grammar book, based on the writings of Petrarch and his greatest disciple, Boccaccio. Five years later, the publication of Bembo's own collection of Petrarchan poetry provided the model of Petrarchan imitation, sparking the wildfire that would become known as Petrarchism.[60] As I examine in this final section, Bembo's discursive treatment of his patron-beloveds in the *Rime* of 1530 reveals the very political nature of his larger project theorized in the *Prose,* placing the politics of gender and patronage at the heart of his poetry.

Poem 121 of Bembo's *Rime* is in many ways emblematic of his most classically Petrarchan style. In the octave he presents his beloved in almost static Petrarchan terms, describing her beauty through *effictio* in a way that immediately recalls Laura. Yet in the sestet, he does something seemingly un-Petrarchan: he threatens his beloved. He tells her,

Se 'n dir la vostra angelica bellezza,
neve, or, perle, rubin, due stelle, un sole,
subietto abonda e mancano parole,
a chi sua fama e veritate apprezza,
quai versi agguaglieran l'alta dolcezza,
ch'ogni avaro intelletto appagar sòle
di chi v'ascolta, e l'altre tante e sole
doti de l'alma, e sua tanta ricchezza?

Colui, che nacque in su la riva d'Arno
e fece a Laura onor con la sua penna,

direbbe a sé: – tu qui giugner non pòi –
Perché se questo stile solo accenna,
non compie l'opre e ne fa pruova indarno,
il mio diffetto ven, Donna, da voi.

If in describing your angelic beauty,
snow, gold, pearls, rubies, two stars, one sun,
the subject is rich and words are lacking,
for he who appreciates fame and truth,
which verses equalled the high sweetness,
that usually satisfies the poor intellect
of whoever listens to you,
and the many other unique
virtues of the soul, and its great richness?

That man, who was born on the banks of the Arno
and brought honour to Laura with his pen
would say to himself: "You cannot reach this place."
Because if this style only hints [at greatness],
does not complete the work and tries to in vain,
my defect comes from you, Woman. (my translation)[61]

The quatrains recall *RVF* 157 where Petrarch describes Laura's beauty through a series of precious objects and natural phenomena: gold, pearls, roses, stars, snow, and so on. In both Petrarch's and Bembo's poems, female beauty is abstracted through these symbols directly tied to the beloved's virtue. Although Bembo initially presents his beloved as quintessentially Laura, in the first tercet he describes an imagined encounter with Petrarch, who tells him he will never reach the same poetic heights as him. Petrarch uses the informal "tu" with Bembo, creating a direct paternal lineage between the two poets. Despite this literary kinship, a defect in Bembo's poetry has prohibited him from reaching the same stature as Petrarch: Bembo's beloved. When Bembo addresses the beloved with the more formal "voi," he creates a distance between the two that further emphasizes that the "defect" of his poetry is not his style but his subject matter. In other words, the beloved is blamed for her failure to inspire him, to fully embody the Laura that she resembles. Bembo thus presents love as a socio-poetic contract: the beloved's duty is to inspire him; his duty is then to honour her in poetry.

The fraught relationship between Bembo's poet-lover and the beloved and Bembo's directness with the beloved about the role she is supposed to play characterize the majority of the *Rime.* Although Petrarch explicitly connects his love for Laura to poetic inspiration and fame, she never failed to inspire him. Bembo's example of Petrarchism privileges his role over that of the beloved, a paradigm not grounded in the *RVF.* In examining Bembo's theory of *imitatio* in the *Rime,* Dante Della Terza has noted that, "what really seems to be relevant is, together with the general conservative attitude predominant in Bembo's *Rime,* the local motivation which pushes Bembo to attain a verbal experience which could find no roots in the Petrarchan world."[62] Indeed, that is precisely what we see in *Rime* 121: the poet-lover demands inspiration from his beloved in a manner reminiscent of Petrarch's treatment of King Robert of Naples in the dedication of the *Africa,* examined in chapter 1. There, Petrarch excused his choice of Scipio Africanus over Robert as an epic hero based on the king's lack of political accomplishments. In short, he had not yet done anything to inspire Petrarch's poetry. Petrarch's approach to poetic inspiration in the dedication is echoed in Bembo's accusation that the beloved has not lived up to his expectations. He ties this in to the beloved's destiny

In *Rime* 29, "Bella guerriera mia" (My beautiful warrior), he uses his power to write history to threaten his beloved into fulfilling her duty to him:

Bella guerriera mia, perché sì spesso
v'armate incontro a me d'ira e d'orgoglio
che in atti et in parole a voi mi soglio
portar sì reverente e sì dimesso?
Se picciol pro del mio gran danno expresso
a voi torna o piacer del mio cordoglio,
né di languir né di morir mi doglio
ch'io vo solo per voi caro a mestesso. (1–8)

My beautiful warrior, why do you so often
arm yourself against me with anger and pride
when in acts and in words I always come
to you so reverent and humble?
If a small advantage from my evident great injury,
or pleasure from my sorrow comes to you,
I will lament neither languishing nor dying
since I am dear to myself only because of you.

The opening signal "bella guerriera" – a common name given to Laura – immediately recalls the dominant metaphysical relationship between Petrarch and his beloved in the *RVF*: she is a warrior armed with hate and pride against a reverent and humble poet-lover. Laura is always the "bella guerriera" who never shows the poet any sign of pity, and remains forever beyond his reach. Bembo's beloved, however, is only "sì spesso" (so often) cruel to him, already signalling a drastic divergence from the Petrarchan subtext. But what is most surprising is that the question is not simply "Why are you so cruel to me?" but more specifically, "Why are you often so cruel to me when I have done so much for you, physically" ("in atti"; with subtle sexual undertones) and poetically ("in parole")? The allusion is to favours – favours that Bembo wants reciprocated in the tercets:

> Ma se con l'opre, ond'io mai non mi sazio,
> esser vi pò d'onor questa mia vita,
> di lei vi caglia e non ne fate strazio.
> L'istoria vostra col mio stame ordita,
> se non mi si darà più lungo spazio,
> quasi nel cominciar sarà finita. (12–14)

> But if with these works, in which I am never satiated,
> this life of mine can provide you with honour,
> take care of it and do not tear it to pieces.
> Your history that is plotted by my thread [of destiny],
> if more space is not allotted me,
> will be ended almost as soon as it begins.

Bembo's choice of "mio stame" to describe his poetic pen is a direct reference to the classic Roman myth of the Parche (the Fates) – the three sisters in charge of spinning each person's life and fate.[63] The Parche control the beginning of the metaphoric "filo della vita" (thread of life) and its length. The classic trope of "filare" as both spinning and writing is prevalent throughout literature, as we see in the Ovidian story of Arachne, as well as Homer's Penelope in the *Odyssey*. In this case, however, Bembo specifically references the double act as linked to destiny, more reminiscent of the myth of Er in the last book of Plato's *Republic*, or Ezekiel of the scriptures. In recalling this figurative double entendre of "filare," Bembo is able to threaten the beloved with the power he claims to have over her history ("istoria"). This is most explicit in the final verse, where he warns that her history can be finished almost from its beginning. The threat is much more menacing than at first glance: he has power over the length of her life, and the way she will be remembered in history.

Thus the sonnet is framed as a warning: why do you treat me so cruelly when I am the one who controls your destiny? His reference to the "acts" and "words" he has provided to the beloved, but which have not produced his desired end, presents love as a patronage system. The message could not be clearer: either return my favours or suffer the eternal consequences of my pen. Bembo takes up the same theme in a poem written and sent to Lucrezia Borgia in 1503, *Rime* 38, "L'alta cagion" (The supreme cause), where he explicitly uses political terms associated with patronage:

L'alta cagion, che da principio diede
a le cose create ordine e stato,
dispose ch'io v'amassi e dielmi in fato,
per far di sé col mondo exempio e *fede.*
Che sì come virtù da lei procede,
che 'l tempra e regge, e come è sol beato
a cui per grazia il contemplarla è dato,
et essa è d'ogni affano ampia mercede,
così 'l sostegno mio da voi mi vene
od in *atti cortesi* od in *parole,*
e sol felice son, quand'io vi miro.
Né maggior *guiderdon* de le mie pene
posso aver di voi stessa, ond'io mi giro
pur sempre a voi, come elitropio al sole. (emphasis mine)

The Supreme Cause, who from the beginning gave
order and being to all things created,
commanded me to love you and entrusted this to me by fate
to make us an example and *faith* in the world.
Just as virtue stems from the Supreme Cause,
who tempers and rules it, and only He is blessed
to whom, by grace, is given the ability to comtemplate her,
and the Supreme Cause is full of pity for my labour,
thusly does my support from you come to me
either in *courteous acts* or *words,*
and I am only happy when I see you.
No greater *countergift* for my pain
could I receive than you yourself, hence I turn
to you always, like a heliotrope to the sun. (emphasis mine)[64]

Several words and phrases associated with patronage stand out: *fede, guiderdon, atti, parole.* Although he claims in the incipt that God ("l'alta cagion") willed him to love Borgia, Bembo's recourse to the language of patronage highlights Borgia's position as both patron and lover. He repeats the expression from *Rime* 29 concerning "atti e parole," but here attributes them to Borgia, who sustains him "od in atti cortesi od in parole" (10; either in courteous acts or in words). Thus, the "deeds" and "words" with which he served his beloved in *Rime* 29, and for which he expected recompense, are seen as having been reciprocated by Borgia in "courteous acts" and "words." She is praised in this poem for having reciprocated the "guiderdon," which he values above all other things, and about which he reminded her in the dedication to the *Asolani.* In the closing of the poem, we see that she has fulfilled her end of the bargain by continuing to be a source of inspiration to Bembo, who turns towards her like a heliotrope to the sun. Indeed, Bembo plays on the Greek root of the word – ἥλιος (*helios;* the sun) and τροπεῖν (*tropein;* to turn) – through the active use of the verb "mi giro" (I turn myself), showing that he, too, has fulfilled his duty by taking inspiration from her and putting it into a poem.

The idea that the beloved could fail in her role as source of inspiration connects the three poems just examined. This leads to the question of what would happen to a beloved who fails to inspire Bembo. That the poet controls his beloved's history and her destiny implies that she is dispensable and not unique. The Petrarchan ideal of one beloved who inspires poetry is destabilized by Bembo's *Rime* 51 where the replaceability of the beloved unfolds in Bembo's address to *Amor:*

Se vòi ch'io torni sotto 'l fascio antico,
che tu legasti, Amor, forza disciolse,
e sparso in parte un desir poi raccolse,
più di costanzia che di pace amico,
rendimi il ricco sguardo, onde mendico
fui gran tempo, e, qual pria ver me si volse
Madonna e 'l mio cor timido raccolse
in grembo al suo penser saggio e pudico. (1–8)

If you want me to go back to that ancient bundle
that you cemented, Love – and force cast loose,
and scattered in part, then pulled in by desire,
friend of perseverance rather than peace –
then show me again the rich glance, which made a beggar

of me for so long, and bring me back to the first time she turned towards me,
Madonna, and took my timid heart
into the lap of her wise and chaste thought.[65]

Bembo undoes the work of Petrarch's *RVF* 96 and its iconic trope of the beloved's image in the poet's heart, which Bembo had often evoked in his letters to both Savorgnan and Borgia. In this poem, he asks Amor, "rendimi lo sguardo" (show me the face), desiring to see the image of a former love that has since been obliterated from his heart. This gestures at a form of poetic inspiration that is as changeable as are his lovers. The exact image of a beloved is secondary to the act of literary production, since Bembo implies that Love wants him to return to "'l fascio antico" (the old book of poetry) that Love himself bound – an allusion to an earlier songbook, or collection of love poetry. Bembo's poems are intrinsically bound up with his love affairs, making the link between a book and love similar to Dante's calling the *Vita nova* "libro de la mia memoria" (book of my memory).[66] The image of a failed, uninspiring beloved gives way to a new one who the poet hopes will not fail to inspire him. Although Bembo initially tells Amor to recall the previous beloved's image, he ends the sonnet by refusing to change the images:

Ma non la.cange poi chiara od obscura
vista del ciel, ché 'n sofferir gran doglia
non sarei più, Signor, come già, forte. (12–14)

But then do not change the clear or obscure
view of heaven, because in undergoing that great pain,
I would no longer be strong, as I have been before, Master [Amor].

Changing beloveds back to the former would only weaken the poet, as she has already been implicitly exposed as a failed source of inspiration (she has, after all, been replaced). Bembo's fidelity to his beloved exists only as long as she continues to inspire his poetry, after which time she is replaced by another. As we saw in *Rime* 121, there is a veiled threat to the beloved in this poem: if she fails to inspire him, she will be replaced. Bembo presents the possibility at the beginning of the poem, but then figures himself as choosing not to replace her. The threat against the beloved is as veiled here as it was in the first poem examined in this section, where Bembo tells the beloved that the only defect in his poetry is the subject matter (her).

Bembo further explores the notion of an image in the heart by questioning the very nature of representation in *Rime 19*, "O imagine mia celeste e pura" (O my image, celestial and pure) – a poem originally written for Maria Savorgnan. The poem refers to the portrait Savorgnan had commissioned from Bellini and sent to Bembo, previously discussed in the context of their letter exchange.[67] Bembo opens the sonnet by addressing Savorgnan directly:

O imagine mia celeste e pura,
che splendi più che 'l sol agli occhi miei
e mi rassembri 'l volto di colei,
che scolpita ho nel cor con maggior cura,
credo che 'l mio Bellin con la figura
t'abbia dato il costume anco di lei,
che m'ardi, s'io ti miro, e per te sei
freddo smalto, a cui giunse alta ventura. (5–8)

O my image, celestial and pure,
you who shine in my eyes more than the sun
and resemble the face of that woman,
whom I carried into my heart engraved in every detail,
I believe that with her semblance my Bellini
also gave you her decorum,
since you burn me if I look at you, though you are essentially
cold-hearted, touched by good fortune.[68]

The vocative "O imagine mia" (O my image) is striking, since it sets up a conversation between Bembo and the Bellini portrait. He evokes the portrait of Savorgnan and compares it with the face of "colei" (the actual Savorgnan) that he had already meticulously carved into his heart. Bembo thus compares three different images of the beloved: her actual face, the sculpted image in his heart, and the painted portrait by Bellini. His use of the verb "scolpire" (v. 4; to engrave or sculpt) echoes Petrarch's ode to Horace (*Fam.* 24.10), where the poet is compared to a sculptor, and emphasizes Bembo's poetic agency in choosing and memorializing his beloved. The painting has replaced the image in his heart, since it sets him aflame when he looks at it, in a manner similar to what happens when he sees Savorgnan herself. The visual representation of the beloved has a stronger physiological effect on him than the imagined portrait in his heart. This is slightly different from his letter to

Savorgnan, where he told her she needn't have sent the portrait since he already had one of her in his heart.

As the poem continues we see that the Bellini painting surpasses his actual beloved since it seems to show him pity for his torments:

E come donna in vista dolce, umile,
ben mostri tu pietà del mio tormento;
poi, se mercé ten' prego, non rispondi.
In questo hai tu di lei men fero stile,
né spargi sì le mie speranze al vento,
ch'almen, quand'io ti cerco, non t'ascondi. (9–14)

And like a woman with a sweet, humble face
you really show pity for my torments;
then, if I ask mercy of you, you do not respond.
In this you have a less haughty style than her,
you don't scatter my hopes thus to the wind,
since at least, when I seek you out, you don't hide.

Bembo's newfound preference for the Bellini portrait over the actual beloved, as well as her image in his heart, is based on two factors: the portrait shows him pity, and it does not hide from him. The first point is a major theme in his earlier letter to Savorgnan, where the portrait becomes a more attentive substitute for the beloved: "holla basciata mille volte in vece di voi, priegola di quello, che io volentieri pregherei, e veggo che ella *benignamente assai par che m'ascolte*, più che voi non fate, *se risponder sapesse a' detti miei*" (A thousand times I kissed it instead of you, I beg her for it, which I would gladly beg for, and I see that she very kindly seems to listen to me, more than you do, if only she knew how to respond to my words). As in the letter, the portrait in the poem is silent but shows him pity. The second point about hiding can be applied to both Savorgnan and her image in Bembo's heart. That is, Bembo can look at the Bellini portrait when he pleases and can kiss it a thousand times at his leisure, as he describes in his letter. The portrait will never hide from him like Savorgnan or the image nestled in his heart. When he wants to see the portrait, he merely looks at it, unimpeded.

This chapter has examined two phases of Bembo's Petrarchism: the private epistolary correspondence with Maria Savorgnan and Lucrezia Borgia, and the public *Rime* of 1530. Privately, Bembo's experimentation with Petrarchan imitation in his letters mirrored humanist Petrarchism in the previous century. Bembo sought a way to express requited love to his interactive muses, educated women who not only reciprocated his love but also corresponded with him in letters and poems, and often edited his poetry. Thus, as well as creating an idiom to adequately represent his amorous affairs, his experimentation became a form of poetic rivalry with Petrarch. To adapt Petrarchan conceits to a reality unimaginable to Petrarch and not rooted in his *RVF* – but still recognizable as Petrarch's – was to surpass the master text. The real-world applicability of Petrarchan rhetoric in these early, personal letters was a micro-example of the larger question examined in the Ciceronian Quarrel: the relationship between *usus* (usage) and *norma loquendi* (linguistic standards). Bembo's letters show, almost two decades before the publication of the *Prose,* that his socio-linguistic theory could work. But as we have seen in his *Rime,* adapting Petrarchan rhetoric to new historical realities was not without consequences. If in his private letters Bembo rivalled Petrarch, in his poetry we see him engaging in a form of rivalry with the beloved. The poet-lover of Bembo's *Rime* threatens his beloveds into submission, treating love as a patronage system based on an economy of gift exchange. Petrarch's unwavering faithfulness to his beloved is substituted by a model of inspiration that is tied directly into the Bembian beloved's reciprocation of his "atti e parole," lest she be replaced by another woman. His warning to the beloved that he controls her destiny, and the way she will be remembered by history, is reminiscent of Petrarch's treatment of his male patrons, and his struggle with poetic versus political agency. In the case of Bembo, this struggle over agency is further complicated by the fact that Lucrezia Borgia is both his lover and his patron. Thus while the replaceability of a beloved is a more realistic approach to love, it is a politically fraught message when applied to patronage. His examination of poetic agency is simultaneously one about political power.[69]

In Bembo's discursive treatment of his female beloved-patron, we see the culmination and advancement of the issues previously discussed in the book: the emergence into the public sphere of the learned woman, the use of Petrarchan rhetoric both to forge and to negotiate an intellectual relationship between men and women, and the establishment of a new linguistic norm linked to political power and hegemony. What further complicates Bembo's position, however, is unique: he is both ardent supporter and literary friend of a new generation of female vernacular poets like Vittoria Colonna (1492–1547) and Veronica Gambara

(1485–1550),[70] and is also subject to the patronage of a new class of powerful female patrons of the arts, like Lucrezia Borgia.[71] Thus, his working out of the patron-poet relationship, grounded in the question of agency, highlights that gender and politics are inherent to the Petrarchan aesthetic. Through Petrarchism, Bembo prescribes gendered behaviour for his female beloved-patrons, expecting them to perform their gender according to his expectations, and thereby placing gender at the centre of his proto-nationalistic project to unite the Italian peninsula under a common, Petrarch-inspired language. Viewing the longer history of Petrarchism, beginning with humanist Petrarchism in the fifteenth century, and situating Bembo in the middle rather than at the beginning of the tradition enables us to better appreciate the impact on gender politics of his socio-political project, the *Prose della volgar lingua* (1525): the poetic tropes that gave a voice to women in the publishing world of sixteenth-century Italy were the same ones that men had used to render women's voices ineffectual in the previous century.

Afterword

This book started with a simple declaration of Petrarchan love: *I carry your image in my heart.* For Petrarch it symbolized an unattainable beloved, a source of poetic inspiration that relied on the inaccessibility of a fictional woman whose static image was her very essence. For the authors in this study, the Petrarchan conceit was adapted to express new social realities that had no precedent in the *RVF* or fourteenth-century Italy: female intellectuality, emblems of requited love, female sociality, and intellectual dialogue between the sexes. Tracing the afterlife of this Petrarchan conceit, and others like it, led to two fundamental questions that have guided this study: In what ways and for what reasons did Latin humanism incorporate Petrarch's vernacular lyricism? And how did the corollary importation of the lyric's embedded associations contribute to the formation of humanist Petrarchism?

In broaching answers to these questions, it is important to recall the unique historical circumstances described in each of the two parts of this book. First, the advent of the first generations of educated, writing women in the fifteenth century complicated the humanist curriculum. The five pillars of humanistic study – poetry, history, ethics (philosophy), rhetoric, and grammar – were meant to transform Italy's young aristocratic boys into great civic-minded and moral leaders. Women had no formal place in this idealized program of study, no end goal for which to strive. What was seen as a morally edifying education in men could potentially corrupt women and undermine their female virtues: "the woman of fluent tongue is never chaste," as it were. Yet women were trained as humanists, they published letterbooks, delivered public orations, and created intellectual friendships with their male and female colleagues. In this regard, the theory behind the humanist curriculum did not entirely match up with its practice. And the classical texts that formed the foundation of humanism could not account for the unique historical circumstances of the fifteenth century. Thus, in the absence of a classical model of intellectual dialogue between the sexes or between women, humanists found in Petrarch's poetry a model for praising women and their virtues. Petrarchan tropes could be lifted from the *RVF* and translated into Latin, remaining recognizable enough to bring along with them a host of associated conceits, paradigms, and values. As we saw in the early chapters of this book, however, the Petrarchan model was not exactly a perfect fit in each particular case. Often the associations risked undermining the very intellectual relationship humanists were attempting to forge through these adapted Petrarchan tropes.

By the sixteenth century, women were, among other things, publishing love poetry, hosting literary salons, joining literary academies, and serving as patrons for other artists. While the figure of the learned woman had already been around for nearly a century, the political capital gained by women in the sixteenth century was unprecedented. Petrarchism was the currency traded between poets of both sexes, a calling card for one's membership in the newest cultural movement that had quickly spread beyond Italy's borders. Bembo had hailed Petrarch-inspired language as a proto-national language that would make Italy a force to be reckoned with on the literary and political stages. Despite the advances made by women in the fifteenth and sixteenth centuries, the most important language debate of the two centuries did not account for their imitative practices. If the main concern of the debate was theorizing whether or not imitation of a singular author could adequately address contemporary issues, the question of gender would seem of the utmost importance. Could a woman successfully imitate a male author, expressing her social reality by imitating texts that did not account for her intellectuality? While there was no theorization about female literary imitation, in practice women had been adapting male-authored texts to their own voices.

The case of Bembo's private versus public Petrarchism showed the degree to which Petrarchan tropes could be recalled as necessary, depending on the situation. Privately, the Petrarchan tropes in his letters emblematized requited love and intellectual kinship, but at the same time they were also products of literary ambition, attempts to rival Petrarch. Bembo's private experimentation with Petrarchism as a social discourse was a prelude to his public, more political, uses of Petrarchan imitation. The threats lobbied against the female beloved-patron in his poetry had a political precedent in Petrarch's vernacular and Latin works. Yet his working out of the patron-poet relationship was more fraught because of the new social reality of women serving as patrons of the arts. As such, he could use Petrarchan tropes to teach the female beloveds how to perform their roles as lovers and patrons. These political poems were just as much about the politics of gender as they were about Italian courtly society. Bembo's self-conscious insistence on the power of the poet to write and affect the history of his beloveds, modelled on his courtly lovers and patrons, reveals an anxiety about the male poet-courtier's place in this new courtly system. This book shows how deeply related were poetics, politics, and gender, from Petrarch's own anxiety about his relationship to patrons, to the fifteenth-century humanists' reckoning with a public, female intellectuality, to Bembo's Petrarchan complex.

The consequences of this story may shed new light on other poet-female patron relationships throughout the early modern period. For example, the discursive engagement with questions of female patronage is revived in the French court of Caterina de' Medici (1519–89), through the poetry of her courtier Pierre de Ronsard (1524–85). Ronsard, like Bembo before him, often threatens the fate and reputation of his female beloved in the *Sonnets pour Hélène*. His beloved, Hélène de Surgères (1546–1618), was a member of the Queen Regent's court, making her a stand-in for her queen, much like Castiglione's female courtier, Emilia Pia, in the *Cortegiano* (1528). Where Bembo's anxiety is centred on the instability of the male poet-courtier in the emerging Italian courts, Ronsard's is the opposite: Hélène's sonnet cycle expresses anxiety over the impermanence and instability of the royal court itself. He closes the collection with two poems lamenting the death of Charles IX, without reference to Henry III, who represented the future of the royal line, its continuation, and a new chapter. The self-consciousness in this sonnet cycle concerns the instability of the Valois rule, and with it the instability of the poet-courtier. The case of Ronsard shows how Petrarch's lyrical tropes will continue to be adapted to political expression, as a reaction to changing norms and the writer's place in an evolving world.

What I have tried to show in this book is a more complicated narrative surrounding the emergence of women at benchmark moments in Italian history, and the role Petrarchan imitation played in mediating conversations about these changes. To deny that there was tension or anxiety related to changing social norms is to underestimate human nature. In each of the case studies in this book, Petrarchan rhetoric, taken out of its original context and imitated in unconventional texts, released the latent politics of gender embedded in its very core. Petrarch defined his intellect and art as decidedly "masculine" against his disempowered female beloved and feminized patrons. Thus, the conceits, paradigms, and tropes of the *RVF* played a role in defining his masculine identity against the abstracted essence of "woman." In times when the concept of woman did not meet the historical realities of women, linguistic experimentation was the only way to attempt to find a new linguistic standard to express these new realities. When Petrarchism, in Latin or the vernacular, was employed as a social discourse, however, it ran the risk of undermining female intellectuality and reifying the association between the male intellect and power and women's lack of agency or power. In recovering texts not traditionally associated with Petrarchism – letters to, about, and from women, treatises on language and imitation – and comparing them to poetry, we are in a position to better appreciate the gendered inflections of the longer and more expansive history of the movement. We can understand how humanist and poetic Petrarchism transmitted and reinforced prescriptive ideals about gendered identities and performance, while at the same time contesting these very ideals. In writing the female beloved, Petrarch supplied the instrument with which women themselves would begin to write.

Notes

Introduction

1 Nogarola, *Isotae Nogarolae,* ed. Abel, 2: 20, ll 15–18; translation from Nogarola, *Complete Writings,* ed. and trans. King and Robin, 112. Unless otherwise noted, all English translations from Nogarola's letterbook are from this edition. This citation is more closely examined in chapter 2.
2 Cereta, *Epistolae,* ed. Tomasini, Letter 59, 145–54; translation from Cereta, *Collected Letters of a Renaissance Feminist,* ed. and trans. Robin, 23–31. See chapter 3 for a close reading of this passage.
3 Bembo, *Carteggio d'amore (1500-1501),* ed. Dionisotti, Bembo letter 8, 52–3; English version my translation. This citation will be examined more fully in chapter 5.
4 *RVF* 96, 5–6; Petrarca, *Petrarch's Lyric Poems,* 199.
5 I borrow the term from Virginia Cox's groundbreaking study *Women's Writing in Italy, 1400–1650,* 104.
6 See chapters 4 and 5.
7 For the classic formulation of the concepts of gender performance and performativity see Judith Butler, *Gender Trouble.*
8 Jones, *The Currency of Eros.*
9 Shemek, *Ladies Errant.*
10 Roland Greene, *Unrequited Conquests.*
11 Kennedy, *The Site of Petrarchism.*
12 Eisenbichler, *The Sword and the Pen.*
13 Chiodo, "Un petrarchismo negletto," 2: 293–303.
14 Cremonini, "Una topica petrarchesca," 2: 329–47.
15 Robin, *Publishing Women.*
16 Ross, *The Birth of Feminism.*

17 Cox and Ferrari, eds, *Verso una storia di genere della letteratura italiana.*
18 Quaintance, *Textual Masculinity and the Exchange of Women in Renaissance Venice.*

1 Women of Stone: Gender and Politics in the Petrarchan World

1 A portion of this chapter was previously published in Feng "'Volto di Medusa': Monumentalizing the Self in Petrarch's *Rerum Vulgarium Fragmenta.*"
2 In *Familiares* 4.1, Gherardo, a Carthusian monk, is Petrarch's hiking companion on Mt Ventoux. For discussions of *Fam.*4.1, and in particular the representation of a crisis of allegory and Augustinian subtext, see Ascoli, *A Local Habitation and a Name*, chapter 1,"Petrarch's Middle Age: Memory, Imagination, History, and the Ascent of Mount Ventoux"; Billanovich, "Petrarca e il Ventoso"; Chiappelli, "The Motif of Confession in Petrarch's 'Mt. Ventoux'"; Durling, "The Ascent of Mt. Ventoux and the Crisis of Allegory"; Thomas Greene, *The Light in Troy*; Mazzotta, *The Worlds of Petrarch*, Appendix 2, "Ambivalences of Power."
3 All citations from Petrarch's vernacular poetry are taken from Petrarca, *Canzoniere*, ed. Santagata. English translations are from Petrarca, *Petrarch's Lyric Poems. The* Rime sparse *and Other Lyrics*, trans. Durling; this citation at 94.
4 Although this description is reminiscent of Laura's death, Petrarch seems to cast doubt on whether or not his brother's beloved has ascended to heaven: he *hopes* she has, whereas he is *certain* that Laura is among the blessed.
5 For Pier delle Vigne and politics in the *Commedia* see Ferrante, *The Political Vision of the 'Divine Comedy'*; Cassell, *Dante's Fearful Art of Justice*, chapter 3. For the problem of language and representation in this episode, see Biow, *Mirabile Dictu*, chapter 3; Stephany, "Pier della Vigna's Self-Fulfilling Prophecies"; Olschki, "Dante and Petrus de Vinea"; Spitzer, "Speech and Language in *Inferno* XIII."
6 *The Divine Comedy of Dante Alighieri. Volume 1: Inferno*, ed. and trans. Durling, 200–1.
7 For the relationship between Frederick II and courtly poets see especially De Stefano, *La cultura alla corte di Federico II imperatore*; Mallette, *The Kingdom of Sicily, 1100-1250*; Haskins, "Latin Literature under Frederick II." See also Abulafia, *Frederick II.*
8 On 18 July 1351 Boccaccio wrote a letter to Petrarch criticizing his decision to remain under the patronage of Giovanni Visconti rather than return to Florence to establish himself officially there, but also, and most

importantly, to receive the patrimony confiscated from Petrarch's father upon his exile. *Epistle V* in Boccaccio, *Opere in versi*, ed. Ricci.

9 See especially Ascoli, *A Local Habitation*, chapter 4, "Petrarch's Private Politics: *Familiares*, book 19"; Kirkham, "Petrarch the Courtier"; Simonetta, *Rinascimento segreto*; Wallace, *Chaucerian Polity*; Westwater, "The Uncollected Poet (*Lettere disperse*)"; Wilkins, *Petrarch's Eight Years in Milan* and *Life of Petrarch*; Wojciehowski, *Old Masters, New Subjects*.

10 Foster, "*Beatrice* or *Medusa*."

11 Namely, *RVF* 51, 179, and 197. Petrarch dedicates two verses to Laura-Medusa in *RVF* 366 (vv 111–12).

12 *Petrarch's Lyric Poems*, 582

13 Although beyond the scope of this chapter, Petrarch's portrayal of Laura as Medusa seems to echo certain aspects of the "stony woman" in Dante's *Rime petrose*, as has been well noted by Antoni, "Esperienze stilistiche petrose da Dante e al Petrarca"; *Petrarch's Lyric Poems*, ed. Durling, 29–33, and Durling, "'Io son venuto.'" To date, the most comprehensive study of Dante's so-called "minor" poetic collection is Durling and Martinez, *Time and the Crystal*. See also Fenzi, "Le rime per la donna Pietra." For Dante's appropriation of the figure of Medusa, see especially: Ascoli, *Ariosto's Bitter Harmony*, 67; Freccero, "Dante's Medusa: Allegory and Autobiography," and his "Medusa: the Letter and the Spirit"; Mazzotta, *Dante, Poet of the Desert*, 277–8.

14 For Petrarch's punning on his name, see especially Ceserani's seminal article, "Petrarca: Il nome come auto-reinvenzione poetica."

15 It is interesting to note the reversal in Petrarch's application of the idea that "names are the consequences of things." Whereas in *Vita nova* XIII, 4 Dante famously uses this phrase to explain why his beloved Beatrice was thusly named (*Beatrice*, she who blesses), Petrarch applies the maxim to himself, rather than Laura. References to Dante's *libello* are from Dante, *Vita nova*, ed. Colombo.

16 *Petrarch's Lyric Poems*, 342.

17 For the representation of Petrarchan subjectivity, see especially Thomas Greene, "The Flexibility of the Self in Renaissance Literature." See also Mazzotta, *The Worlds of Petrarch*, chapter 3; Scaglione, "Classical Heritage and Petrarchan Self-Consciousness in the Literary Emergence of the Interior 'I'"; Trinkaus, *In Our Image and Likeness*.

18 For the importance of the Daphne-Apollo myth in Petrarch's poetry, see: Sturm-Maddox, *Petrarch's Laurels* and "'La pianta più gradita in cielo'"; DellaNeva, "Poetry, Metamorphosis, and the Laurel." For general

discussions of Petrarch's appropriation of Ovid's Daphne see: Freccero, "Ovidian Subjectivities in Early Modern Lyric"; Hardie, "Ovid into Laura"; Enterline, "Embodied Voices."

19 This is the second of the three "l'aura" poems that present the beloved as the wind: *RVF* 196, 197, 198.

20 *Petrarch's Lyric Poems*, 342.

21 The Atlas episode is in *Metamorphoses* 4.621–63. All references and translations are taken from Ovid, *Metamorphoses*, Books 1–8, trans. Miller; this citation at 225.

22 *Petrarch's Lyric Poems*, 342.

23 Ovid, *Metamorphoses*, 232.

24 Although in this book Perseus uses Medusa's head to turn other warriors into marble – Thesceleus, ("utque manu iaculum fatale parabat mittere, in hoc haesit signum de marmore gestu"; 5.182–3), and Astyages ("naturam traxit eandem, marmoreoque manet vultus mirantis in ore"; 5.205–6) – Phineus is the only one set up as an *exemplum*, and a monument.

25 Ovid, *Metamorphoses*, 253, 255.

26 Ibid., 255.

27 All Latin citations from Petrarch's *Familiares* are taken from *Le Familiari*, ed. Rossi. Translations are by Aldo S. Bernardo, *Rerum familiarum libri*; this citation at 336.

28 *Petrarch's Lyric Poems*, 206.

29 Barkan, *The Gods Made Flesh*, 209.

30 For a full transcription of the poem by Gianfigliazzi, to which Petrarch responds with *RVF* 179, see Petrarca, *Canzoniere*, 790, and the English translation by Durling in *Petrarch's Lyric Poems*, Appendix 1, 608.

31 *Petrarch's Lyric Poems*, 608.

32 Durling translates *ragionate* as "you speak." The medieval uses of this verb include to speak (discutere di, parlare, conversare), but it also emphasizes the use of reason (sostenere con ragionamenti, con prove). Retrieved September 2015 from: http://www.garzantilinguistica.it/ricerca/?q=ragionare%201.

33 *Petrarch's Lyric Poems*, 324

34 4.779–85.

35 "Ma 'l bel viso leggiadro che depinto / porto nel petto, et veggio ove ch'io miri" (4–5; "But that lovely smiling face, which I carry painted in my breast / and see wherever I look" [*Petrarch's Lyric Poems*, 198]).

36 See William J. Kennedy's reading of this sonnet as a Horatian configuration of art as mechanical and technical skill, in line with medieval economic theories of labour and utility value ("Public Poems, Private Expenditures").

37 *Petrarch's Lyric Poems,* 324.
38 The letter, dated 18 July 1351, is Epistle V in Ricci's edition, *Opere in versi.*
39 Kirkham and Maggi, eds, *Petrarch. A Critical Guide to the Complete Works,* Editors' introduction, 10. See especially Kirkham's chapter, "Petrarch the Courtier," 141–50.
40 Ibid., 10–11.
41 For Petrarch's relationship to the Colonna family, see Cretoni, "Il Petrarca e i Colonna." For the shadowy presence of various Colonna members in poems not explicitly addressed to them, see Sturm-Maddox, *Petrarch's Laurels,* 143, n31.
42 John Osborne has found a Colonna coat of arms in a Roman church. See "A Possible Colonna Family 'Stemma' in the Church of Santa Prassede, Rome."
43 *Petrarch's Lyric Poems,* 44.
44 This is at odds with the way in which Petrarch will later describe his patrons. For example, Petrarch attacks the legitimacy of Colonna power by exposing them as foreign-born tyrants in *Variae* 48 of 1347, the hortatory letter sent to Cola di Rienzo and the Roman people after the former's coup (*The Revolution of Cola di Rienzo,* trans. Cosenza, chapter 2, 9–36). Although *RVF* 10 was written in the late 1330s, Santagata notes that it was re-ordered as the tenth poem in the collection in the early 1350s, which would coincide with the years immediately following Cola's fall.
45 See Ovid, *Metamorphoses* 1.452–566.
46 *Petrarch's Lyric Poems,* 44.
47 Ibid., 87.
48 For a discussion of the structure, manuscript tradition, publication history, and textual variants of Petrarch's *Collatio laureationis* see especially Feo, "Le 'due redazioni' della *Collatio laureationis.*" More recently, Dennis Looney has read the coronation speech as Petrarch's earliest theorizing of the revival of the poet as an integral part of an emerging modern city ("The Beginning of Humanistic Oratory: Petrarch's *Coronation Oration* [*Collatio laureationis*]."
49 Citations from the Latin *Collatio* are taken from *Scritti inediti di Francesco Petrarca,* ed. Hortis; this citation at 324. English translations are by Wilkins, *Studies in the Life and Works of Petrarch,* at 309–10.
50 Patterson, *Pastoral and Ideology*. See especially chapter 1, where Patterson discusses the ways in which later commentators and editors had to account for Servius's political allegorization of Tityrus as a figure of Vergil, and the ensuing debate over its legitimacy as an analogy.
51 The MS is held in Milan's Biblioteca Ambrosiana, Sala del Prefetto, Scaf. 10, no. 27, *olim* A. 49 *inf.* For descriptions of this manuscript, see Ratti,

"Ancora del celebre codice manoscritto della opera di Vergilio già di Francesco Petrarca ed ora alla Biblioteca Ambrosiana"; Nolhac, *Pétrarque et l'humanisme,* I: 140–61; and Lord, "Petrarch and Vergil's First Eclogue."

52 Wojciehowski, *Old Masters, New Subjects,* 52.

53 *Petrarch's Lyric Poems,* 438.

54 Ibid., 438.

55 Ibid., 434.

56 Ibid., 176.

57 Gur Zak has suggested to me that Petrarch's emphasis on his own will in this poetic enchainment can be read as Petrarch's blaming himself in Augustinian fashion for allowing himself to be imprisoned, much like the laments of "Franciscus" in the *Secretum.*

58 Wojciehowski, *Old Masters, New Subjects,* 76.

59 *RVF* 30, 50, 62, 79, 101, 107, 118, 122, 145, 212, 221, 266, 271, 278, 364. For an examination of how the number of anniversary poems increased from seven in the first form of the *Canzoniere* to fifteen in the final form, see Dutschke, "The Anniversary Poems in Petrarch's *Canzoniere.*"

60 Zak, *Petrarch's Humanism and the Care of the Self,* 29.

61 *Petrarch's Lyric Poems,* 606.

62 Although references to her are uncommon during Petrarch's lifetime, Laura will become the subject of many poems written by Petrarchists in sixteenth-century Italy and France, although almost always in jest. Most notably, Pierre de Ronsard exploits the tension surrounding her figure in Petrarch's poetry by chiding Petrarch for putting a whore upon a pedestal and turning her into an angel: "Et sa Muse, au giron d'une seule maitresse: / Ou bien il jouissoit de sa Laurette, ou bien / Il estoit un grand fat d'aymer sans avoir rien, / Ce que je ne puis croire, aussi n'est il croiable: / Non, il en jouissoit, puis l'a faitte admirable" ("A son livre," vv 48–52; Ronsard, *Les Amours,* eds. Weber and Weber). The basis of Ronsard's accusation is that Petrarch couldn't possibly have written such beautiful poetry about a woman he did not know, in the biblical sense.

63 *Petrarch's Lyric Poems,* 304.

64 Ibid., 50.

65 "Dopo questa tribulazione avenne, in quello tempo che molta gente va per vedere quella imagine benedetta la quale Iesu Cristo lasciò a noi per essemplo de la sua bellissima figura, la quale vede la mia donna gloriosamente, che alquanti peregrine passavano per una via la quale è quasi mezzo de la cittade ove nacque e vivette e morio la gentilissma donna" (*Vita nova,* 75, par. 1).

66 "Queste donne andaro presso di me così l'una appresso l'altra, e parve che Amore mi parlasse nel cuore, e dicesse: 'Quella prima è nominata Primavera

cola per questa venuta d'oggi; ché io mossi lo imponitore del nome a chiamarla così Primavera, cioè prima verrà lo die che Beatrice si mostrerà dopo la imaginazione del suo fedele. E se anche vogli considerare lo primo nome suo, tnato è quanto dire 'prima verrà', però che lo suo nome Giovanna è da quello Giovanni lo quale precedette la verace luce, dicendo: 'Ego vox clamantis in deserto: parate viam Domini'" (*Vita nova,* 126–7, pars 4–5).

67 Laura died on 6 April 1348, three months before Giovanni Colonna.

68 *Petrarch's Lyric Poems,* 442.

69 *Canzoniere,* 1092, n 2.

70 Durling, "Petrarch's 'Giovene donna sotto un verde lauro.'" Durling traces the association through the vernacular poetry and, especially, the *Triumphi* to show that the brilliant gems represent Laura's "beauty and of her virtue, permanent and unassailable" (3). Most importantly, Durling shows how Petrarch's sestina is in dialogue with Dante's "Al poco giorno" and how the designation of the gems as diamonds and topazes is an attempt at surpassing Dante's poem.

71 A particularly vivid example is the second half of the highly influential *Roman de la rose,* where the two jewels in the fountain have been interpreted as representing the eyes of the beloved. See especially: Harley, "Narcissus, Hermaphroditus, and Attis"; Hillman, "Another Look into the Mirror Perilous"; Hult, "The Allegorical Fountain." Interestingly, the fountain that mediates Amant's vision of the rose, and subsequent desire for her/it is the marble Fountain of Love, upon which is a plaque naming it the Fountain of Narcissus.

72 *Rerum familiarium libri,* 322.

73 Tylus, *Writing and Vulnerability in the Late Renaissance,* 3.

74 Scholarship devoted solely to Petrarch's *Africa* is scarce. Most recently, Simone Marchese has highlighted the work as the centrepiece of Petrarch's larger project of self-fashioning and self-promotion as the leading poet-historian of his age ("Petrarch's Philological Epic. *Africa*"), and Leah Whittington has examined Book 5 and the story of Massinissa and Sophonisba as a supplicatory erotic fiction (*Renaissance Suppliants,* ch. 3). See also: Bernardo, *Petrarch, Scipio, and the "Africa"*; Colilli, *Petrarch's Allegories of Writing,* esp. chapter 3; Fenzi, "Dall'*Africa* al *Secretum*"; Festa, *Saggio sull'Africa del Petrarca;* Fera, *La revisione petrarchesca dell'Africa;* Velli, "Il proemio dell'*Africa.*"

75 Dido historically could not have known Aeneas, and after Vergil's account she is associated with lust. Marchese, "Petrarch's Philological Epic," 120–1.

76 All Latin citations are taken from the *L'Africa,* ed. Festa. English translations are from *Petrarch's Africa,* trans. Bergin and Wilson; this citation at

83–4, vv 30–42. A new critical edition in rhymed French translation was recently published, and includes the marginal notes of Coluccio Salutati: *L'Afrique/Affrica*, ed. and trans. with introduction by Pierre Laurens.

77 *Petrarch's Africa*, 84, vv 47–55.
78 vv 80–105; *Petrarch's Africa*, 83–4, vv 107–45.
79 *Petrarch's Africa*, 86–7, vv 146–50.
80 Ibid., 89, vv 246–56.
81 Ibid., 95, vv 459–69.
82 *Petrarch's Lyric Poems*, 358.
83 I have summarized the Latin, but for a full English translation see *Petrarch's Africa*, 95, vv 470–4.
84 Ibid., 95, vv 474–84.
85 Ibid., 97, vv 529–31.
86 Ibid., 97, vv 547–52.
87 Ibid., 98, vv 566–73.
88 *Petrarch, Scipio and the "Africa,"* viii.
89 *Petrarch's Africa*, 2, vv 55–60.
90 Ibid., 3, vv 90–9.
91 It is important to remember that Petrarch's choice of Scipio as his epic hero is an odd one, since he had already been immortalized in Ennius's *Annales*.
92 "Nec cura future / Solicitet casus. Quoniam lux crastina campos / Sanguine Penorum Latio victore rigabit" (212–14; Be not moved / by thought of misadventures yet to come; / under the light of morn the fields will run / with Punic blood as Latium rules the day [*Petrarch's Africa*, 230]).
93 Ibid., 230.
94 Ibid., 231.
95 "The Latin Hexameter Works"; this citation at 72.
96 Samantha Kelly, *The New Solomon*, 25.
97 Ibid., 40.
98 See especially Santagata, *I frammenti nell'anima*, where he contextualizes Petrarch's autobiographical "io" within the poet's cultural and moral crises. See also Fenzi, *Saggi petrarcheschi*.
99 Ascoli, *Ariosto's Bitter Harmony*, 166.

2 In Laura's Shadow: Gendered Dialogues and Humanist Petrarchism in the Fifteenth Century

1 Parts of this chapter were previously published in Feng, "In Laura's Shadow: Casting Female Humanists as Petrarchan Beloveds in Quattrocento Letters," in Jeff Rider and Jamie Friedman, eds, *The Inner Life*

of *Women in Medieval Romance Literature: Grief, Guilt, and Hypocrisy*, 223–47. The chapter that follows is a revised, expanded version of the earlier conclusions made in the article.

2 My translation. My sincere thanks to David Lummus for our fruitful conversations about this poem, and for his help in deciphering and translating some of its more ambiguous verses.

3 Nogarola, *Isotae Nogarolae*, ed. Abel, 2: 388–9. All Latin citations are from Abel's edition, and will be cited by volume and page number(s). English translations of Nogarola's letters are from Nogarola, *Complete Writings*, ed. and trans. King and Robin.

4 Nogarola debated Ludovico Foscarini, a close confidante. For their relationship, see Gothein, "L'Amicizia fra Lodovico Foscarini e l'Umanista Isotta Nogarola." For opposing views on who won the debate, see: Allen, *The Concept of Woman*, 2: 945–55; King, "The Religious Retreat of Isotta Nogarola (1418–1466)."

5 The inscription on the *liber* provides the exact date of publication: "Veronae III° Nonas Octobris 1468 Marius Philelfus manu propria."

6 Scholarship on neo-Latin humanism is vast. See especially: Celenza, *The Lost Italian Renaissance*; Garin, *Italian Humanism*; King, *Renaissance Humanism*, General Introduction, ix–xii; Witt, *In the Footsteps of Ancients.*

7 Susan Gaylard has noted that Foresti uses the same masculine-posed portrait for both Angela and Isotta Nogarola. She notes that, "In this volume, a printed 'portrait' is a loose term for a representation that is not expected to convey specific information about physiognomy. Foresti's 'portraits' function more like heraldic devices than as depictions of facial features. Images like that of Isotta, depicting an individual in a pose specific to her biography rather than a narrative moment, combine elements of the narrative tradition with the new interest in portraiture and in fact resemble the contemporary genre of 'famous men' frescoes" ("*De mulieribus claris* and the Disappearance of Women from Illustrated Print Biographies," 300). For the reception of Boccaccio's famous women tradition during humanism, see especially: Benson, *The Invention of Renaissance Woman*; Kolsky, *The Ghost of Boccaccio*; Robin, "Space, Woman, and Renaissance Discourse."

8 The figure recurs in *RVF* 135, 185, 210, 321, 323.

9 Grafton and Jardine, *From Humanism to the Humanities*, 40. See especially chapter 2, "Women Humanists: Education for What?," 29–57. For a transcription of the *vituperatio* and the male humanist response to it, see Segarizzi, "Niccolo Barbo patrizio veneziano del sec. XV e le accuse contro Isotta Nogarola." For more current readings of the invective as part of more widespread, humanist practice see Ross, *The Birth of Feminism*, 38–9.

10 Ann Rosalind Jones has noted a similar connection between female literary production and chastity in the sixteenth century: "A first contradiction that these women [female poets] confronted was a mixed message about writing itself. Ideological pressures worked against their entry into the public world of print: female silence was equated with chastity, female eloquence with promiscuity." *The Currency of Eros*, 1.

11 De Lauretis, *Alice Doesn't*, 5–6.

12 On the fragmentary nature of both the *RVF* and Laura see Vickers, "Diana Described."

13 Cereta, *Epistolae*, ed. Tomasini, 19–21; *Collected Letters of a Renaissance Feminist*, ed. Robin, 49. All citations from Cereta's epistolary collection are taken from Tomasini's edition. A digital reproduction can be found at http://www.uni-mannheim.de/mateo/desbillons/cereta.html.

14 For socio-historical accounts of women in the Renaissance, see: Joan Kelly, *Women, History, and Theory*, 19–50; Klapisch-Zuber, *Women, Family, and Ritual in Renaissance Italy*, trans. Cochrane; King, *Women of the Renaissance*; and Wiesner-Hanks, *Women and Gender in Early Modern Europe*. For educational practices in the Middle Ages and Early Renaissance see: Garin, *L'educazione in Europa, 1400-1600*; Grafton, *Joseph Scaliger*; Grafton and Jardine, *From Humanism to the Humanities;* and Grendler, *Schooling in the Renaissance*. For the rise of the female intellectual through an "intellectual family" model, see Ross, *The Birth of Feminism*. For the conditions of women participating in humanism, see Parker, "Women and Humanism."

15 As Gordon Braden has noted, "Most of the poems in which she [Laura] actually speaks come after her death, in dreams or visions: what few exchanges we have before that are ambiguous" ("Love and Fame: The Petrarchan Career," 134). Dante's Beatrice also provides a fine example of the beloved as a prophetic speaker in a text. For example, in *Paradiso II* when Dante fixes his gaze upon Beatrice rather than on the Heaven of the Moon, the haughty beloved warns, "'Drizza la mente a Dio grata', mi disse, / 'che n'ha congiunti con la prima stella'" (29–30; "Direct your mind to God in gratefulness,"/ she said, "He has brought us to the first star"). Italian citation and English translation are from *The Divine Comedy of Dante Alighieri. Paradiso,* trans. Mandelbaum. The words spoken by Beatrice mirror Augustine's warning against worshiping the creature instead of the creator and the episode provides another example of the moral dilemma facing Dante-pilgrim concerning sacred and profane love. This is further reinforced by the apparent change in the figure of Beatrice from the *Vita nova* to the *Commedia:* she is silent in the earlier text, and only in death (in the *Commedia*) does she become talkative.

16 The evolving language of friendship between men and women in early modern France is the topic of Seifert and Wilkin, eds, *Men and Women Making Friends in Early Modern France.*

17 I will examine the Ciceronian Quarrel more closely in Chapter 4.

18 In her examination of the Stoics' treatment of women in their writing, Elizabeth Asmis has noted that, "Antipatur, Musonius, and Hierodes take into account the opportunities available to women, whereas Panaetius, Cicero, and Seneca tend to shut women out" ("The Stoics on Women," 88).

19 Abel, LIII, 2:21, l. 3–4; *Complete Writings*, 112.

20 "Εὕρηχ᾽ εὕρηχ᾽ ἣν θέλον, ἣν ἐζήτεον αἰεί, / ἣν ᾕτουν τὸν Ἔρωθ᾽, ἣν καὶ ὀνειροπόλουν: Epigram 30, vv 1–2. Poliziano, *Angeli Politiani liber epigrammatum Graecorum,* ed. Pontani (hereafter cited as *Ep. Gr.).* There are currently no published English translations of Poliziano's Greek poems. All translations in this chapter are by John Bauschatz, and are part of a collaborative, ongoing project: *Poliziano's Greek Epigrams,* Introduction and Notes by Aileen A. Feng. Translation by John Bauschatz.

21 King, "Book-lined Cells," 76.

22 In this sense, the redefining of social and "natural" norms can be seen as neo-Aristotelian. The influence of Aristotelian thought on the natural order was pervasive throughout the Quattrocento. Personhood was understood through the universal category *homo,* and women were seen as defective males. On this latter issue, see: Maclean, *The Renaissance Notion of Woman;* Benedeck, "Belief about Human Sexual Function in the Middle Ages and Renaissance"; and Laqueur, *Making Sex.* For more on the terms against which Renaissance feminists revolted, see Jordan, *Renaissance Feminism. Literary Texts and Political Models.*

23 Most noteworthy is Maclean, who has argued that André Tiraqueau's treatise on marriage law (*De legibus connubialibus*) and Castiglione's third book of the *Cortegiano* "demonstrate the use of authority and the currency of commonplaces; both reproduce synthetic views of woman which concord with the intellectual outlook of their day" (*The Renaissance Notion of Woman,* 5).

24 Cox, *Women's Writing in Italy, 1400–1650,* 8.

25 De Lauretis, *Alice Doesn't,* 109.

26 Ross, *The Birth of Feminism,* 2. For Ross's discussion of Nogarola's use of "domestic" and familial rhetoric in her initial letters to prominent male humanists see ibid., 30–40.

27 For the learned women born into the Nogorala family after Isotta and her sister Ginevra, see Ross, *The Birth of Feminism,* 40. To Ross's list I would also add the vernacular poet Veronica Gambara (1485–1550), the Nogarola

sisters' great-niece. For a more complete Nogarola lineage of educated women, see Stevenson, *Women Latin Poets*, 156–76.

28 Since the late 1990s, Holt Parker has been largely responsible for making the Latin and Greek poetry of female humanists available in the original alongside eloquent English translations. Even today, while their prose works are becoming better known, thanks to the *Other Voices* series, their poetry is still grossly under-studied. For Angela and Isotta Nogarola's Latin poetry, see Parker, "Latin and Greek Poetry by Five Renaissance Italian Women Humanists," and his "Angela Nogarola (ca. 1400) and Isotta Nogarola (1418–1466): Thieves of Language."

29 For more thorough biographical information on Isotta Nogarola, see the volume editors' introduction to *Complete Writings*, 1–19.

30 "quibus doctissimarum mulierum et ipsarum Musarum memoriam in vobis renovari concernam." Nogarola, *Isotae Nogarolae veronensis opera*, 1: 20, ll 16–18.

31 Ibid., ll 5–8.

32 For a list of the extensive classical and biblical sources cited by Nogarola in her letterbook, see *Complete Writings*, 205–9.

33 For information about Bevilacqua's humanist career in Venice, see King, *Venetian Humanism in an Age of Patrician Dominance*, 273, 326, 370, 396, 446.

34 St Jerome (c. 347–420) was best known for his teachings on the moral Christian life, particularly those aimed directly at women that exhorted them to chastity. In 1441 Nogarola began dedicating herself to "sacred studies," and in 1453 she delivered an oration on the life of St Jerome in Verona (*Complete Writings*, 167–74). King has argued that while the oration celebrates his "heroic and conventional qualities, Nogarola appears to resist the pale ideal of chastity" (*Complete Writings*, 8).

35 Nogarola, *Isotae Nogarolae veronensis opera*, 1: 37, ll 1–12; *Complete Writings*, 36. Robin translates "quantum me amares" as "how much you esteem me," which is certainly within the Ciceronian spirit of this letter. I have chosen to translate it literally, to emphasize the repetition of "amare" throughout the passage.

36 All references and English translations are taken from the Loeb edition: Cicero, *Letters to Friends*, vols I–III, ed. and trans. Shackleton Bailey; this citation Letter 207 (XV.21), 256–61.

37 For homoeroticism in Cicero see Stroup, *Catullus, Cicero, and a Society of Patrons*, 144–54.

38 King, "The Religious Retreat of Isotta Nogarola (1418–1466)."

39 Nogarola, *Isotae Nogarolae veronensis opera*, 1: 38, ll 3–7; *Complete Writings*, 37. I follow King's and Robin's correction of the text in line 3 from

"perfectionem" to "profectionem," based on the context of the sentence. See *Complete Writings*, 37, n32.

40 See note 9, above.

41 For Quirini's humanist career see Branca, ed., *Lauro Quirini umanista*, and King, *Venetian Humanism*.

42 Nogarola, *Isotae Nogarolae veronensis opera*, 2: 9–22 (letter LIII); *Complete Writings*, 107. The date of the letter is disputed. Abel places it either in 1445–8 or 1451/52.

43 Cicero, *Letters to Friends*, I: Letter 22 (V.12), 154–5.

44 "Ardeo cupiditate incredibili neque, ut ego arbitror, reprehenda nomen ut nostrum scriptis illutretur et celebretur tuis … ut cuperem quam celerrime res nostras monumentis commendari tuis" ("I have a burning desire, of a strength you will hardly credit but ought not, I think, to blame, that my name should gain lustre and celebrity through your works … I want to see my achievements enshrined in your compositions …"); ibid., 156–7.

45 Nogarola, *Isotae Nogarolae veronensis opera*, 2: 12, ll 6–13; *Complete Writings*, 108.

46 For studies on Hypatia see Wider, "Women Philosophers in the Ancient Greek World."

47 Cox, *Women's Writing in Italy*, 24–5.

48 Nogarola, *Isotae Nogarolae veronensis opera*, 2:20, ll 15–18; *Complete Writings*, 112.

49 *Petrarch's Lyric Poems*, 199.

50 My use of the term "metaphysical" to describe the relationship between Petrarch and Laura is in a general transcendental sense – that is, the relationship transcends the physical and is non-corporeal – rather than in reference to philosophical notions of being. Petrarch does not philosophize the poet-beloved relationship as do, say, Dante, and later Bembo.

51 *Antologia della poesia italiana. Duecento*, ed. Segre and Ossola, 49; my translation. Da Lentini's famous sonnet is part of a three-sonnet *tenzone* with Jacopo Mostacci and Pier delle Vigne concerning the nature of love. The emphasis on sight in both Da Lentini and Petrarch echoes Andreas Capellanus, who states that blind men cannot fall in love: "Blindness is a bar to love, because a blind man cannot see anything upon which his mind can reflect immoderately, and so love cannot arise in him, as I have already fully shown" (*The Art of Courtly Love*, trans. Parry, 33). There are, however, several literary examples in which a man falls in love with a woman through reputation (that is, having heard about her, but never seen her), as, for example, in the case of the Roman matron Lucretia and Boccaccio, *Decameron* 7.8 (ed. Branca, 2: 849–60).

52 Nogarola, *Isotae Nogarolae veronensis opera,* 2:21, l. 3–4; *Complete Writings,* 112.
53 Ibid., letter LIII, 2:21, ll 5–8; *Complete Writings,* 112.
54 Ibid. 2:22, l. 7; *Complete Writings,* 113.
55 Fedele's esteem for her teacher is noted in her undated letter to Prince Gaspare of Aragon, the grandson of King Ferrante I of Naples. See Cassandra Fedele, *Epistolae & orationes posthumae,* ed. Tomasini, letter 43, 65–6. All Latin citations from Fedele's letterbook are taken from this edition. A digital reproduction is available at: http://www.uni-mannheim.de/mateo/desbillons/fedele.html. All translations of Fedele's Latin letters are from Fedele, *Letters and Orations,* ed. and trans. Robin, unless otherwise noted. For biographical information on Fedele, see Robin's introduction to *Letters and Orations,* 3–15, and her book chapter "Cassandra Fedele's Epistolae (1488–1521): Biography as Effacement." See also the "Cenni biografici introduttivi" of the facing-pages Latin-Italian edition curated by Fedele's descendant Antonino Fedele, *Orazioni ed epistole,* 27–40.
56 Fedele's letters exchanged with Queen Isabella of Spain make reference to the possibility of Fedele's joining the Queen's court. The relationship between the two and Fedele's Petrarchan allusions to patronage in letters addressed to the Queen are explored in chapter 3.
57 Fedele, *Epistolae & orationes,* oration 1, 193–201; *Letters and Orations,* 155–9. This is the first of three orations recorded in Tomasini's edition.
58 Cereta, *Letters and Orations,* Editor's Introduction, 9.
59 In 1374 Boccaccio published the *De mulieribus claris* (*Famous Women*), the first collection of Latin biographies of famous women of antiquity (and a small number of contemporary women). The 106 biographies are composed of both "virtuous" women meant to be imitated and "wicked" ones who served as anti-exemplary women. Composed around the same time as his *De casibus virorum illustrium* (*On the Fates of Famous Men),* the *De mulieribus claris* would become the model for later biographies of women and treatises on the dignity of women. For more on the history of the *De mulieribus claris,* see especially Virginia Brown's introduction to her translation of the text (*Famous Women,* xi–xxv).
60 Fedele, *Epistolae & orationes,* letter 100, 149–51; *Letters and Orations,* 67–8. Robin translates "carmina" as "hymns." I have chosen the alternative translation "poems" based on the ensuing discussion of Petrarchan intertext, and the fact that with his letter Tancredi will include a Latin poem written by Negri for/about Fedele.
61 *Petrarch's Lyric Poems,* 36.
62 See especially: Barchiesi, *Speaking Volumes,* 113; Hinds, "Medea in Ovid," 41–3; and Heslin, *The Transvestite Achilles,* 296.

63 Fedele, *Epistolae & orationes*, letter 100, 149–51; *Letters and Orations*, 67–8
64 Vergil, *Eclogues. Georgics. Aeneid*, I-VI, trans. Fairclough, 284–5.
65 Petrarch continues this theme in *RVF* 159.
66 Fedele, *Epistolae & orationes*, letter 114, 174–6; *Letters and Orations*, 82–3. The ellipses are present in the 1635 edition. As Robin notes (100, n79), we do not have any biographical information about Girolamo Broianico beyond knowing that he was part of the humanist circle that included Bosso, Panfilo Sasso, and others.
67 The third reference, to the daughters of Pisistratus, is unclear to me. Pisistatrus is known to have had four sons by two wives, as well as an illegitimate son, but there is no historical record of his having had daughters.
68 For a more detailed review of this encounter and its aftermath (including Fedele's relationship to Alessandra Scala, discussed below), see Allen, *The Concept of Women*, 936–42.
69 Fedele, *Epistolae & orationes*, letter CIV, 160–1. This particular epistle is incomplete in Tomasini's edition, and is not included in the Robin translation. The full letter, with the ending to be discussed shortly, was discovered by Giovanni Pesenti in a humanist codex, MS Ricc 974, and edited in his "Lettere inedite del Poliziano." English translations are mine.
70 Pesenti, "Lettere inedite," 300; my translation.
71 Jardine, "'O decus Italiae virgo', or the Myth of the Learned Lady in the Renaissance," 809.
72 De Lauretis, *Alice Doesn't*, 141.
73 Pesenti, "Lettere inedite," 300; my translation.
74 Ibid.
75 Ibid.
76 Poliziano, *Ep. Gr.* 28, 129; trans. Bauschatz.
77 In addition, Pontani notes that, in the performance witnessed by Poliziano, the role of Electra's brother Oreste was played by Alessandra's actual brother Giuliano (Poliziano, *Ep. Gr.*, 134–5, unnumbered note to verse 12).
78 *Petrarch's Lyric Poems*, 178.
79 Giuseppe Mazzotta has read this series of sonnets as a collapsing of the analogies made between the failure of Polycletus in *RVF* 77 and the success of Simone Martini in *RVF* 78, and the failure of Petrarch and the success of Pygmalion in *RVF* 78 in order to suggest, first, the "otherworldly uniqueness of Laura's beauty and, second, the anguish of the forever unrequited lover. It also suggests, more generally, Petrarch's disjunctive consciousness dramatized over the two sonnets" (*The Worlds of Petrarch*, 29). Mazzotta's discussion centres on his reading of vision as an aesthetic construction (27–31). For Petrarch's relationship to Martini see Rowlands,

"Simone Martini and Petrarch." For the portrait/beloved relationship, see also Rabin, "Speaking to Silent Ladies." For the role of Pygmalion in Petrarch's poetics see Migraine-George, "Specular Desires."

80 Susan Schibanoff has made an interesting case for the relationship between the female humanists of the Quattrocento and Botticelli's *Magnificat* – the first visual representation of a woman (the Virgin Mary) writing. Schibanoff claims that the depiction of the Madonna as a woman writer, whose hand is guided by baby Jesus to write scripture, is a visual representation of the "rhetoric of impossibility." That is, the painting implies that a woman cannot write without divine intervention ("Botticelli's *Madonna del Magnificat:* Constructing the Woman Writer in Early Humanist Italy").

81 Interestingly, in some scholarship available on Scala, she is depicted as Poliziano's actual beloved and object of desire. See especially Pesenti, "Alessandra Scala." In his edition of Poliziano's Greek epigrams, Pontani likewise refers to her as Poliziano's "great love of his final years" (grande amore degli ultimi anni) because she was "beautiful and learned" (bella e dotta); 130.

82 Poliziano, *Ep. Gr.* 30, 138; trans. Bauschatz.

83 *RVF* 15, v. 1; vv 9–11; *Petrarch's Lyric Poems*, 50.

84 *RVF* 248, vv 1–2; *Petrarch's Lyric Poems*, 410.

85 Alessandra's response is found in Poliziano, *Ep. Gr.* 30b, 141; trans. Bauschatz.

86 *Ep. Gr.* 48, 200; trans. Bauschatz.

87 Lakoff, *Language and Woman's Place*, 47–8.

88 The Petrarchism in the Latin epistolary exchanges in Italy represents the precise danger against which Christine de Pizan argued in the *Débat sur le Roman de la rose* (1401–3). For Christine de Pizan and female authority see Quilligan, *The Allegory of Female Authority*.

89 See chapter 2, "Did Women Have a Renaissance?," in Joan Kelly, *Women, History, and Theory*, 19–50; citation at 38. Although I agree with the conclusions drawn by Kelly in her close examination of eleventh- and twelfth-century France and fourteenth- and sixteenth-century Italy, and their respective forms of courtly love, she seems to dismiss the fifteenth century and does not give it much critical attention.

90 Although it is beyond the scope of this chapter, we should also question the use of Petrarchan rhetoric in Galeazzo Capella's *Della eccellenza delle donne* (1525), the first vernacular treatise on the dignity of women, which sparked a literary tradition of encomia in praise of women's intelligence. By writing in the vernacular, Capella was able to reach a much larger audience than the neo-Latin humanists.

91 It is generally believed that the addressee of the letter is fictitious. Diana Robin has noted that the comical name provides Laura with a "vehicle for her polemic" (Cereta, *Collected Letters*, ed. Robin, 74, n35).
92 Cereta, *Epistolae*, letter 65, 187–95; *Collected Letters*, 78.

3 Laura Speaks: Sisterhood, *Amicitia*, and Marital Love in the Female Latin Petrarchist Writings of the Fifteenth Century

1 Cereta, *Epistolae*, letter 59, 145–54; *Collected Letters*, 23–31.
2 See Robin's introduction to this letter: *Collected Letters*, 20–3. Janet L. Smarr has noted a similarity between Cereta's letter and Olympia Morata's (1526–55) Renaissance dialogue. See Smarr, *Joining the Conversation*, 261–2, n64.
3 *Petrarch's Lyric Poems*, 198.
4 In her 1486 letter to Sigismondo da Bucci, Cereta compares herself to two famous weavers: Arachne and Pamphile: *Epistolae*, letter 2, 12–17; *Collected Letters*, 31–5. Boccaccio often connects weaving with the female intellect. See especially his biography of Proba in *De mulieribus claris*. See *Famous Women*, ed. and trans. Brown, 410–16. For an analysis of the relationship between spinning, weaving, and embroidery and women's writing see especially Jones and Stallybrass, *Renaissance Clothing and the Materials of Memory*, part II, "Gendered Habits."
5 For more information on Battista Malatesta, and her writings, see especially: King and Rabil, eds, *Her Immaculate Hand*, 35–8; Woodford, *Vittorino da Feltro and Other Humanist Educators*, 199–201. Virginia Cox has argued that Bruni's choice of a female addressee for his treatise underlines the satirical nature of his claim that women should not study rhetoric – a core component of the humanist curriculum. Her provocative analysis challenges traditional interpretations of Bruni as equating female eloquence with sexual deviance. See Cox, "Leonardo Bruni on Women and Rhetoric."
6 For the life and works of Varano see especially: Feliciangeli, "Notizie sulla vita e sugli scritti di Costanza Varano-Sforza (1426–1447)"; and more recently Parker, "Costanza Varano (1426–1447)," 3: 31–53; King, "Book-lined Cells," 75, 83; King and Rabil, *Her Immaculate Hand*, 18, 39–44.
7 Although there is currently no modern edition of Varano's complete Latin orations, letters, or poems, Holt Parker has edited and translated nine works in his article "Costanza Varano" (see note 6, above). All Latin references and English translations are taken from his article.
8 Parker, "Costanza Varano," 35–6, 43–5.

9 The specific texts Varano cites are Lactantius, *De ira dei,* 19.1; Cicero, *De officiis,* 1.18; Quintilian 1.1.1.

10 This reference is unknown to me.

11 *Life of Pericles* 24.1–7, in Plutarch, *Lives,* trans. Perrin.

12 Petrarch began working on his collection of Latin biographies of men – *De viris illustribus* (*On the Lives of Illustrious Men*) – in 1337–9, with the last version produced in 1371–4 before his death. In the opening line of the preface to his *De mulieribus claris,* Boccaccio credits Petrarch's *De viris illustribus* with inspiring him to create a collection of female biographies for posterity (*Famous Women,* 9)

13 While the topic of female friendship in early modern Italy is still relatively uncharted territory, the last few years have seen a significant rise in criticism on the subject in other disciplines. For female homosociality in early modern Spain, see Vollendorf, "The Value of Female Friendship in Seventeenth-Century Spain." For recent studies in English literature, see especially: Anderson, "The Absent Female Friend," and *Friendship's Shadows*; Andreadis, "Re-configuring Early Modern Friendship"; Larson, *Early Modern Women in Conversation.*

14 *Petrarch's Lyric Poems,* 94.

15 Despite his insistence on avoiding the precise footsteps of the ancients, as Ronald Witt has shown, Petrarch believed in the link between eloquence and a virtuous life, and that only through concentrated study and imitation of certain ancient authors could the modern author impart virtue to his readers (Witt, *In the Footsteps of Ancients,* chapter 6, "Petrarch, Father of Humanism?," 230–91).

16 See especially *RVF* 70 and 287.

17 In a way, this looks forward to the virtual communities of women writers created by Cinquecento editors and anthologists, as examined by Diana Robin in *Publishing Women.*

18 "Così, lasso, talor vo' cercando io, / Donna, quanto è possibile in altrui / la disiata vostra forma vera" (vv 12–14; "Thus, alas, at times I go searching in others, Lady, as much as is possible, for your longed-for true form" [*Petrarch's Lyric Poems,* 50]).

19 Sandra M. Gilbert and Susan Gubar have noted that early women writers were empowered (rather than tortured) by examples of other female writers, and in fact worked to situate themselves within such lineages, to stave off the more primary anxiety of not being able or meant to create. Gilbert and Gubar, *The Madwoman in the Attic.*

20 Fedele, *Letters and Orations,* Editor's Introduction, 5.

21 Fedele, *Epistolae & Orationes,* letter 13, 20–2; *Letters and Orations,* 19–20. The letter is dated Kalends, November 1487.

22 *Petrarch's Lyric Poems,* 194.
23 Throughout the letter, Isabella I's deeds are characterized through martial rhetoric and imagery of the Crusades. Fedele credits her with leading armies against the infidels, savage nations of barbarians, and laying siege to numerous cities, all in the name of the Christian faith.
24 Fedele, *Letters and Orations,* 20.
25 Fedele, *Epistolae & orationes,* letter 12, 19; *Letters and Orations,* 20.
26 *Epistolae & orationes,* letter 11, 16–18; *Letters and Orations,* 21–2.
27 Lehfeldt, "Ruling Sexuality"; see especially 37–47.
28 Casas, "The Artistic Patronage of Isabel the Catholic."
29 Fedele, *Epistolae & orationes,* letter 60, 87–9; *Letters and Orations,* 22
30 Fedele, *Epistolae & orations,* letter 66, 93–4; *Letters and Orations,* 23.
31 This is the final letter to the queen contained in Fedele's letterbook.
32 This letter is not included in Tomasini's 1640 edition. Diana Robin has translated it from the Vatican manuscript Vat. Lat. 3176. Cart. 3. XVI (fol. 16v) and the Venetian manuscript Marc. Cod. Lat. XI, 28 [4186] mbr. XV (fols. 32–3). *Collected Letters,* 91.
33 Cereta, *Epistolae,* letter 8, 23–4; *Collected Letters,* 88–9.
34 Cereta, *Collected Letters,* 87–8
35 Cereta's letter points to a common difficulty for female humanists – the question of marriage versus a humanist career – which is prevalent in the letterbooks of several female humanists. For example, Cassandra Fedele and Alessandra Scala exchanged letters on the topic, with Scala asking Fedele for advice on whether or not to marry, in *Epistolae & orationes,* letter 111, 167; *Letters and Orations,* 31.
36 Durling translates "laccio" as "noose." I have chosen to translate it as "net," since Laura's hair functions as a net to trap Petrarch.
37 Gill, "Fraught Relations in the Letters of Laura Cereta."
38 Cereta, *Epistolae,* letter 10, 26–7; *Collected Letters,* 89–90.
39 *RVF* 194, 196, 197, 198, 246, 327, 356.
40 Cereta, *Epistolae,* letter 10, 27; *Collected Letters,* 90.
41 *Petrarch's Lyric Poems,* 334.
42 Cereta, *Epistolae,* letter 6, 21–2; *Collected Letters,* 92.
43 See especially *De amicitia* book III, where Laelius discusses Scipio's death; Cicero, *On Old Age. On Friendship. On Divination,* trans. Falconer, 118–21.
44 I have translated "memoratissimum" as "most celebrated" in place of Robin's "most mindful."
45 *Petrarch's Lyric Poems,* 194.
46 See especially Euripides' play of the same name.
47 Cereta, *Epistolae,* letter 29, 61; *Collected Letters,* 99–100.
48 Grebe, "Marriage and Exile."

4 Theorizing Gender: Nation Building and Female Mythology in the Ciceronian Quarrel

1 All citations of the letters exchanged in the various phases of the Ciceronian Quarrel, in both Latin and English translation, are taken from *Ciceronian Controversies,* ed. DellaNeva, trans. Duvick; this citation at 4–5.

2 *Petrarch's Lyric Poems,* 94

3 For the history of Ciceronianism in early modern Italy see the classic study by Sabbadini, *Storia del Ciceronianism,* and Izora, *Controversies over the Imitation of Cicero.* For Poliziano's eclecticism in imitation see Shafer, "The Eclectic Style in Theory and Practice in Angelo Poliziano's Ep. VIII.16." For Paolo Cortesi's style, see especially D'Amico, "Paolo Cortesi's Rehabilitation of Giovanni Pico della Mirandola."

4 *Petrarch's Lyric Poems,* 35.

5 *Letters on Familiar Matters (Rerum familiarum libri),* 3: books XVII–XXIV, trans. Bernardo; citation at 300–2.

6 The analogy between running and imitation-writing recurs in several letters by Isotta Nogarola, earlier in the century. In a January 1439 letter to Eusebio dal Borgo, she writes, "For our Ennius called the poets holy men because they seemed to have been entrusted to us as though by some gift from the gods. Along the same lines, Cicero has said that the poets derive their power from nature itself, whereas men in all other pursuits rely on skill and perseverance. Because of this, I beg you not to stop writing, but as he [Cicero] himself said, it is not those who watch, but those who run, who win the crown" (*Complete Writings,* 93). As Robin notes in note 37 to this passage, although Nogarola attributes the race metaphor to Cicero ("ut inquit ille, nec spectantibus coronae sed certantibus parantur"), the saying is not found anywhere in Cicero's writing.

7 *Ciceronian Controversies,* 8–9.

8 Petrarch's theory of imitation is the starting point for JoAnn DellaNeva's study of a related and under-studied debate between major and minor model imitation, which is not addressed in the Ciceronian Quarrel but has much to offer for a broader understanding of early modern theorizations of imitation. See DellaNeva, "Reflecting Lesser Lights." See also Pigman's foundational article, "Versions of Imitation in the Renaissance."

9 For the longer historical debate on imitation and language, see: Grayson, *A Renaissance Controversy*; Thomas Greene, *The Light in Troy*; Marzocco, *Linguistic Theories in Dante and the Humanists*; McLaughlin, *Literary Imitation in the Italian Renaissance*; Murphy, *Renaissance Eloquence*; and Vitale, *La questione della lingua.*

10 For studies of Erasmus's *Ciceronianus* see especially: D'Ascia, *Erasmo e l'umanesimo romano*; Pigman, "Imitation and the Renaissance Sense of the Past"; Pomilio, "Una fonte italiana del *Ciceronianus* di Erasmo."
11 As JoAnn DellaNeva notes in her introduction, the third stage of the debate – the polemical letters between Cinzio and Calcagnini – was not widely known until 1537, nine years after the publication of Erasmus's *Ciceronianus*. As a result, this set of polemical letters has received considerably less critical attention than the other texts and authors involved in the Quarrel (*Ciceronian Controversies,* viii).
12 A total of three letters on imitation were exchanged between Gianfrancesco Pico and Bembo in 1512–13. Compared to other epistolary exchanges concerning the issue of Ciceronian versus eclectic imitation, these letters are significantly lengthier.
13 As was seen in the previous chapter, the imitation of Petrarchan rhetoric beyond the lyric genre has political ramifications, particularly in the case of gender politics. The final chapter of this book examines how Bembo's attempt at creating a Petrarch-inspired national language is reminiscent of the Quattrocento letters exchanges between male and female humanists, and brings the issues of gender, power, and politics more explicitly to the public stage.
14 *Ciceronian Controversies,* 16–43.
15 Ibid., 18–19, par. 3.
16 Ibid., 40–1, par. 27.
17 Ibid., 18–19, par. 4.
18 As DellaNeva notes, the first of these attributes (rhythm) is praised by Cicero in *De oratore* 3.44.173, *Orator* 20.67, 50.169, 52.175, and 53.179; and Quintilian, 9.4.45–57.
19 *Ciceronian Controversies,* 18–21, par. 5.
20 Ibid., 30–3, par. 19.
21 *Brutus,* 35; *De oratore,* II.6.
22 *Ciceronian Controversies,* 22–3, par. 8.
23 Ibid., 22–3, par. 9.
24 All references to Plato are from *Complete Works,* edited with introduction and notes by Cooper and Hutchinson. Plato's theory of forms (or ideas) is discussed in various dialogues, including the *Phaedo, Republic,* and *Phaedrus.* The Allegory of the Cave – *Republic* VIII. 514, 532b, 539e – is perhaps the most well-known discussion (ibid., *Republic,* trans. Grube and rev. Reeve, 971–1223).
25 Ibid., *Parmenides,* trans. Gill and Ryan, 359–97.
26 *Ciceronian Controversies,* 36–7, par. 25.

27 Ibid., 22–3, par 9.
28 Ibid., 44–89.
29 Ibid., 50–1, par. 5.
30 Ibid., 50–1, par. 6.
31 Ibid., 66–7, par. 19.
32 Ibid., 80–3, par. 29.
33 Ibid., 82–3, par. 30.
34 Ibid., 82–5, par. 31.
35 Indeed, later in the letter, Bembo warns Gianfrancesco Pico that, "sunt quidam qui non solum ea puae ad stilum scriptionemque pertinent, sed illa etiam quae dico quaeque de genere alio sunt cum sumuntur, uno imitationis nomine includant" ("certain people include under the one term 'imitation' not only techniques pertaining to style and composition, but even those that I am now talking about and borrowings from other genres" [ibid., 84–5, par. 32]).
36 Ibid., 84–5, par. 31.
37 Ibid., 91–125.
38 Ibid., 112–15, pars 20–1.
39 Ibid., 116–19, par. 22.
40 Ibid., 16–43. The prologue to Helena Sanson's commendable book *Women, Language and Grammar* analyses iconographic depictions of Lady Grammar nursing and relates it to later historical relationships between women and language.
41 Dante Alighieri, *De vulgaria eloquentia,* trans. Botterill, 2–3. Scholarship on the nursing metaphor in Dante is vast, so I will highlight two outstanding works: Cornish, *Vernacular Translation in Dante's Italy*, chapter 5; Cestaro, *Dante and the Grammar of the Nursing Body*.
42 *Ciceronian Controversies*, 28–9, par. 16.
43 See also the elder Pico's use of the expression in the *Oration on the Dignity of Man.*
44 *Ciceronian Controversies*, 28–9, par. 17.
45 "Hunc igitur unum dices imitandum quem natura produxerit ut in eo suas vires omnis experitur eloquentia" ("You will then say that we should imitate this one man, whom nature produced so that all eloquence might test its power on him" [ibid., 36–7, par. 24]).
46 Ibid., 36–7, par. 25.
47 Ibid., 38–9, par. 26.
48 In *Fam.* 22.2, par. 16, Petrarch take the opposite approach to the clothing metaphor, preferring his own style over that of the ancients: "multo malim meus michi stilis sit, incultus licet atque horridus, sed in morem toge habilies, ad mensuram mei ingenii factus" ("I would much prefer that my

style be my own, no matter how uncouth and inelegant, just like a well-worn toga, made to measure to suit my own intellect"). This, perhaps, has to do with Petrarch's understanding of the Senecan apian metaphor that would have the poet-bee collect pollen from various sources in order to create something new that unifies all the sources. In this light, the toga would be a new fabric made from the threads of various sources, but unique to Petrarch.

49 Ovid, *Fasti,* trans. Frazer.

50 All Latin references and English translations of Boccaccio's *De mulieribus claris* are taken from *Famous Women,* ed. and trans. Brown; this citation, biography XXVII, 104–13.

51 Ibid., 106–7, par. 5.

52 Sanson, *Women, Language, and Grammar,* 2. See her longer argument and accompanying figure on 1–3.

53 Boccaccio, *Famous Women,* 108–9, par. 6.

54 Ibid., 110–12, par. 16.

55 For studies on the often contested place of Ciceronianism in Quattrocento civic humanism, see: Baron, *The Crisis of the Early Italian Renaissance;* Hankins, "The 'Baron Thesis' after Forty Years and some Recent Studies of Leonardo Bruni"; Rabil, Jr, "The Significance of 'Civic Humanism' in theInterpretation of the Italian Renaissance"; Seigel, "'Civic Humanism' or Ciceronian Rhetoric?"; Skinner, *The Foundations of Modern Political Thought,* 1: 69–112; Witt, *In the Footsteps of the Ancients,* 419–31.

5 Politicizing Gender: Bembo's Private and Public Petrarchism

1 All citations from the Bembo-Savorgnan epistolary exchange are from *Carteggio d'amore (1500–1501),* ed. Dionisotti; Bembo letter 38, 74–6. References will be made to author, letter number, and page(s). English translations are mine, unless otherwise noted.

2 *Petrarch's Lyric Poems,* 236–7.

3 Ibid., 272–3.

4 Very little is known about Maria Griffoni Savorgnan other than that she was originally from Urbino, married to a condottiere of Venice, and widowed in 1498. For Savorgnan's biography, see: Zappi, "Chi era Maria Savorgnan?"; and Kidwell, *Pietro Bembo,* chapter 2, "Maria Savorgnan," 24–70. Kidwell attempts to reconstruct the Bembo-Savorgnan love affair from their letter exchange by focusing on their overarching narrative elements, and ignoring the literary. As has been noted by scholars like Fabio Fionotti, Kidwell's approach to Bembo's works is flawed, but nevertheless

her biography of Savorgnan is well researched. See Fionotti's review of Kidwell's book, in *Renaissance Quarterly* 58.4 (Winter 2005): 1294–6. For an analysis of Savorgnan's letters, see especially: Pozzi, "Andrem di pari all'amorosa face"; Quaglio, "Intorno a Maria Savorgnan. I. Per una riedizione delle lettere," and "Intorno a Maria Savorgnan. II. Un 'sidio' d'amore." For an interesting study on Boccaccio's influence on Bembo, see Curti, "'Le sue lacrime con le mie mescolando.'" See also Zancan, "L'intellettualità femminile nel primo Cinquecento."

5 Quoted by Dionisotti in *Carteggio d'amore,* xxvii; my translation.
6 Ibid., xi; my translation.
7 Ibid, Savorgnan letter 9, 8. For the now lost Bellini portrait of Savorgnan see Humfrey, "The Portrait in Fifteenth-Century Venice," esp. 62–3. For a description and history of the only surviving female portrait by Bellini, see Richter, "A Portrait of a Lady by Giovanni Bellini."
8 *Carteggio d'amore,* Bembo letter 8, 52–3. All English translations of the Bembo-Savorgnan letters are mine.
9 *RVF* 96, 5–6; *Petrarch's Lyric Poems,* 199.
10 *RVF* 77 also concerns Martini's portrait.
11 *Petrarch's Lyric Poems,* 178.
12 *Carteggio d'amore,* Savorgnan letter 30, 17; Bembo letter 27, 64–5.
13 For Savorgnan and *Gli Asolani,* see Dilemmi, "'Andrem di pari.'"
14 *Carteggio d'amore,* Bembo letter 33, 69.
15 *Petrarch's Lyric Poems,* 344.
16 See especially his erotic pastoral poem *RVF* 52, "Non al suo amante più piacque Diana."
17 *Rime,* 545–6. Bembo's poem is an imitation of Perarch's *RVF* 353, "Vago augelletto che cantando vai," where Petrarch laments the death of Laura to a wandering bird. All references to Bembo's prose and poetry are taken from *Prose e rime,* ed. Dionisotti.
18 *Carteggio d'amore,* Savorgnan letter 5, 5. The alleged offence is not made explicit.
19 Ibid., Bembo letter 39, 76–7.
20 Petrarch, *Triumphi,* ed. Ariani.
21 *Petrarch's Lyric Poems,* 360.
22 This poem is included with other *Rime rifiutate,* poem 10, 682–3.
23 This poem is the second of only three *strambotti* Bembo composed over the course of his career, all early compositions that were ultimately excluded from his 1530 *Rime* (later published by Dionisotti with the *Rime rifiutate*). Stefania Signorini has argued that the three poems' initial inclusion in letters and the *editio princeps* of *Gli Asolani* point to a phase of Bembo's

experimentation with Dantean form (*Vita nova*), as well as contemporary Ferrarese poetry, that made them incompatible with the 1530 Petrarchan-inspired *Rime*. See Signorini, "Da Maria a Lucrezia."

24 For a resurgence of the *strambotto*'s popularity in the Quattro- and Cinquecento, see especially: Bianconi and Rossi, "Sulla diffusione del repertorio strambottistico di fine Quattro- inizio Cinquecento"; Galli, "Strambotti anonimi quattrocenteschi da un codice della Colombina di Siviglia."

25 *Carteggio d'amore*, Savorgnan letter 40 [44], 23–4.

26 Cox, *Women's Writing in Italy*, 60 and 287, n94.

27 *Carteggio d'amore*, Bembo letter 4, 49. Dionisotti notes that Bembo dated the letter 3 March 1500 ex post facto, but has postdated it to 18–20 September 1500, given the context of the letter.

28 See especially Savorgnan's letter 52 [58] of 18 September 1500 where she explains that since "F" had been bitten by a dog, she has sent "B" to Bembo with her letters, and urges Bembo to be careful about what he says in town (*Carteggio d'amore*, 30–1).

29 Alfonso d'Este was Borgia's third husband. Her first marriage to Giovanni Sforza (1466–1510) was annulled in 1497, and her second husband, Alfonso d'Aragona (1481–1500), was killed, with rumours attributing his assassination to her brother Cesare. Historically, there has been a fascination with Lucrezia Borgia, making the scholarship devoted solely to her biography vast. I would highlight the following: Bellonci, *Lucrezia Borgia la sua vita e i suoi tempi*; Catalano, *Lucrezia Borgia Duchessa di Ferrara*; Kidwell *Pietro Bembo,* chapter 3, "Pietro and Lucrezia," 71–98; Nicolai Rubenstein, *Lucrezia Borgia*.

30 For an interesting comparison of the women's respective patronage styles, see Prizer, "Isabella d'Este and Lucrezia Borgia as Patrons of Music." For the overlap in artists who frequented both courts, see Fenzi, "Tra Isabella e Lucrezia," and Russo, *Letterati a corte*, chapter 2. For Borgia's approach to patronage, see especially: Ghirardo, "Lucrezia Borgia as Entrepreneur"; Benvenuti, "L'Arrivo di Lucrezia a Ferrara."

31 All citations of the Bembo-Borgia correspondence are taken from Bembo and Borgia, *La grande fiamma*, ed. Raboni. I refer to both author and letter number. English translations are from *The Prettiest Love Letters in the World: Letters between Lucrezia Borgia and Pietro Bembo, 1503 to 1519*, trans. Shankland, and will be labelled only by letter number, since Shankland does not include pagination for the letters. The preface (7–45) provides a succinct description of the letters, and also includes helpful biographical information about Bembo and Borgia.

32 Bembo and Borgia, *La grande fiamma,* Bembo letter 11, 51–3. The letter is dated 22 August 1503, four days after the death of Alessandro VI. The style is very rigid and formal, with no hint of their affair or previous correspondence.
33 For the Spanish poem and English translation, see *The Prettiest Love Letters,* page before letter I.
34 Bembo and Borgia, *La grande fiamma,* Bembo letter 1, 33–5; *The Prettiest Love Letters,* letter I.
35 "Yo pienso se me muriese / y con mis males finase / desear, / tan grande amore fenesciese / que todo el mundo quedase / sin amar. / Mas esto considerando, / mi tarde morir es luego / tanto Bueno, / que devo razon usando / gloria sentire en el fuego / donde peno" ("I think were I to die / And with my wealth of pain / Cease longing, / Such great love to deny, / Could make the world remain / Unloving. / When I consider this, / Death's long delay is all / I must desire, / Since reason tells me bliss / Is felt by one in thrall / To such a fire" [*The Prettiest Love Letters,* introductory poem to Letter I]).
36 In his translation, Shankland includes a poem possibly written about Borgia's famous golden hair ("Di que' bei crin, che tanto più sempre amo") as representative of the types of poems Bembo wrote for her, but there is no evidence that this was one of the two poems that accompanied the letter.
37 While Bembo tried his hand at Spanish versification, the poems were ultimately excluded from his official letter collection. For an analysis and discussion of the original Spanish poems exchanged between Bembo and Borgia, see especially Rajna, "I versi spagnoli di mano di Pietro Bembo e di Lucrezia Borgia serbati da un codice Ambrosiano."
38 Lina Bolzoni takes this image as a starting point for her analysis of male friendship and the *Asolani.* See Bolzoni, *Il cuore di cristallo.*
39 Bembo and Borgia, *La grande fiamma,* Bembo letter 3, 37–8; *The Prettiest Love Letters,* letter IV.
40 In *The Prettiest Love Letters,* Shankland transcribes and translates the final, published version of this poem – *Rime* 7 – which contains variants from the original. The changes from the original poem that accompanies Bembo's letter to *Rime* 7 are: v. 2, "campo" becomes "regno"; v. 9, "crederei" becomes "spererei"; v. 14, "ché la difesa è poca, e'l strazio è molto" becomes "La medicina e poca, il languir molto." I have adjusted the translation to reflect the original poem.
41 Bembo and Borgia, *La grande fiamma,* Borgia letter 2, 123–4; *The Prettiest Love Letters,* letter V.
42 Ibid., Bembo letter 8, 45–6; *The Prettiest Love Letters,* letter X.

43 For a fascinating study of the male ventriloquization of women's voices in sixteenth- and seventeenth-century vernacular letter collections, see Ray, *Writing Gender in Women's Letters Collections of the Italian Renaissance.*
44 *Petrarch's Lyric Poems,* 150–1.
45 *La grande fiamma,* Bembo letter 13, 56–8; *The Prettiest Love Letters,* letter XV.
46 *RVF* 135, 185, 210, 321, 323
47 As Veronica Andreani has recently discussed, Gaspara Stampa will later repurpose the figure of Petrarch's phoenix to poetically justify taking on a new lover after her affair with Collaltino di Collalto ends ("Gaspara Stampa as Salamander and Phoenix: Reshaping the Tradition of the Abandoned Woman," in Falkeid and Feng, eds, *Rethinking Gaspara Stampa in the Canon of Renaissance Poetry.*
48 I have replaced Shankland's translation "pure love inflamed / Ties the tongue and bears the spirit away" with Durling's (*Petrarch's Lyric Poems, RVF* 170, 316–17).
49 We have no biographical information for Lisabetta da Siena.
50 *La grande fiamma,* Bembo letter 20, pp. 71–72; *The Prettiest Love Letters,* letter XXIII.
51 *La grande fiamma,* Bembo letter 20; 71–2; *The Prettiest Love letters,* letter XXIII
52 *Petrarch's Lyric Poems,* 138–9
53 *La grande fiamma,* Bembo letter 23, 77–80.
54 I have transcribed the letter from the facsimile of the 1505 Manuzio publication, found in Dionisotti's critical edition (Bembo, *Prose e rime*), between 352–3. Although I have retained the spelling from the original, I have added accent marks and separated words to facilitate comprehension. English translations are taken from *Gli Asolani,* trans. Gottfreid, 1–3. For studies of the 1505 *Asolani* see especially Clough, "Pietro Bembo's *Gli Asolani* of 1505," and "The printing of the first edition of Pietro Bembo's *Gli Asolani*"; Fortini, "Itinerari di scrittura"; Scarpa, "Qualche proposta (e qualche ipotesi) per i primi *Asolani.*"
55 I have changed Gottfreid's translation of "guiderdone" from "reward" to "countergift" to better reflect the meaning of the Old French root "guerdon," discussed below. I have also changed "assai buon" to "very good."
56 Sharon Kinoshita and Peggy McCracken provide a succinct explanation of the use of the term "guerdon" in medieval French literature in their book *Marie de France,* 54.
57 See Paris, "Etudes sur les romans de la Table Ronde."
58 For Bembo's *Rime* see: Clough, "The Problem of Pietro Bembo's *Rime*"; Richardson, "From Scribal Publication to Print Publication"; Zanato, "Indagini sulle rime di Pietro Bembo."

59 For Bembo's influence on the "questione della lingua" see especially: Mazzacurati, *La questione della lingua dal Bembo all'accademia Fiorentina*; Sabattino, *L'idioma volgare*; Sansone, *Da Bembo a Galiani*.

60 The bibliography on Petrarchism as a sixteenth-century poetic movement is vast. For book-length studies see especially: Baldacci, *Il Petrarchismo italiano nel Cinquecento*; Forster, *The Icy Fire*; Roland Greene, *Post-Petrarchism* and *Unrequited Conquests*; Thomas Greene, *The Light in Troy*; Kennedy, *Authorizing Petrarch* and *The Site of Petrarchism*; Navarette, *Orphans of Petrarch*. For Bembo's influence on sixteenth-century Petrarchism see especially McLaughlin, *Literary Imitation in the Italian Renaissance*.

61 Bembo, *Prose e rime*, 566–7. Unless otherwise noted, all English translations of Bembo's poetry are mine.

62 Della Terza, "Imitatio: Theory and Practice," 130.

63 Ariosto uses the same image in *Orlando Furioso* 34.

64 Bembo, *Prose e rime*, 538–9, my translation.

65 Ibid., 548.

66 Dante Alighieri, *Vita nova* I.1.

67 *Carteggio d'amore*, Savorgnan letter 9, 8, and Bembo letter 8, 52–3.

68 Bembo, *Prose e rime*, 520–1.

69 The *Rime* came out the same year as the second edition of the *Asolani*, whose dedication to Borgia was removed. He did not dedicate the *Rime* to anyone, but as Brian Richardson has noted, he benefited from its lack of dedication: "In order to have his poems published as he wanted, Bembo would have had to come to a contractual arrangement with the printers, agreeing to pay at least some share of their costs in return for a share of the copies printed. He chose not to seek any reward by addressing the work to a dedicatee … But Bembo did not use his stock of printed copies solely as a source of income for himself; he also derived another kind of advantage by presenting some of them as gifts to friends. Bembo did not dedicate his *Rime* to a patron" (Richardson, "From Scribal Publication to Print," 693).

70 For Bembo's literary friendship with Colonna and Gambara as a model for others, see Cox, *Women's Writing in Italy*, 100–1.

71 Vittoria Colonna was a patron of the arts in her own right, and was also the subject of visual art, literature, and medallions. See especially Gouwens, "Female Virtue and the Embodiment of Beauty."

Bibliography

Primary Sources

Alighieri, Dante. *De vulgaria eloquentia*. Trans. Steven Botterill. Cambridge: Cambridge UP, 1996.

– *The Divine Comedy of Dante Alighieri. Volume 1: Inferno*. Ed. and trans. Robert M. Durling. Intro. and notes Ronald L. Martinez and Robert M. Durling. New York and Oxford: Oxford UP, 1996.

– *The Divine Comedy of Dante Alighieri. Paradiso*. Trans. Allen Mandelbaum. New York: Bantam, 1984.

– *Vita nova*. Ed. Manuela Colombo. Milan: Feltrinelli, 1999.

Antologia della poesia italiana. Duecento. Ed. Cesare Segre and Carlo Ossola. Turin: Einaudi, 1997.

Bembo, Pietro. *Gli Asolani*. Trans. Rudolf B. Gottfreid. Bloomington: Indiana UP, 1954.

– *Carteggio d'amore (1500–1501)*. Ed. Carlo Dionisotti. Florence: Felice Le Monnier, 1950.

– *Prose e rime*. Ed. Carlo Dionisotti. Turin: UTET, 1966.

Bembo, Pietro, and Lucrezia Borgia. *La grande fiamma*. Ed. Giulia Raboni. Milan: Archinto, 2002.

– *The Prettiest Love Letters in the World: Letters between Lucrezia Borgia and Pietro Bembo, 1503 to 1519*. Trans. Hugh Shankland. London: Collins Harvill, 1987.

Boccaccio, Giovanni. *Decameron*. Ed. Vittore Branca. Turin: UTET, 1960.

– *Famous Women*. Ed. and trans. Virginia Brown. Cambridge, MA: Harvard UP, 2001.

– *Opere in versi. Corbaccio. Tratatello in laude di Dante. Prose latine. Epistole*. Ed. Pier Giorgio Ricci. Milan and Naples: Riccardo Ricciardi, 1965.

Capellanus, Andreas. *The Art of Courtly Love.* Trans. John Jay Parry. New York: Columbia UP, 1960.

Cereta, Laura. *Collected Letters of a Renaissance Feminist.* Ed. and trans. Diana Robin. Chicago: U of Chicago P, 1997.

– *Epistolae. Iam primum e m[anu]s[criptis] in lucem productae a Iacobo Philippo Tomasino, qui eius vitam et notas addidit*. Ed. Giacomo Filippo Tomasini. Padua: Sardi, 1640.

Cicero. *Letters to Friends.* Vols I–III. Ed. and trans. D.R. Shackleton Bailey. Cambridge, MA: Harvard UP, 2001.

– *On Old Age. On Friendship. On Divination.* Trans. William Armistead Falconer. Cambridge, MA: Harvard UP, 1923.

Ciceronian Controversies. Ed. JoAnn DellaNeva. Trans. Brian Duvick. Cambridge, MA, and London: Harvard UP, 2007.

Fedele, Cassandra. *Epistolae & orationes posthumae.* Ed. Giacomo Filippo Tomasini. Padua: Francesco Bolzetta, 1636.

– *Letters and Orations.* Ed. and trans. Diana Robin. Chicago: U of Chicago P, 2000.

– *Orazione ed epistole.* Trans. and ed. Antonino Fedele. Padua: Il Poligrafo, 2010.

Nogarola, Isotta. *Complete Writings: Letterbook, Dialogue on Adam and Eve, Orations.* Ed. and trans. Margaret King and Diana Robin. Chicago: U of Chicago P, 2003.

– *Isotae Nogarolae veronensis opera quae supersunt omnia, accedunt Angela et Zenevrae Nogarolae epistolae et carmina.* 2 vols. Ed. Eugenius Abel. Vienna: apud Gerold et socios, 1886, and Budapest: apud Fridericum Kilan, 1886.

Ovid. *Fasti.* Trans. James G. Frazer. 2nd ed. Cambridge, MA: Harvard UP, 1989.

– *Metamorphoses.* Vols 1–8. Trans. Frank J. Miller. Cambridge, MA: Harvard UP, 1916.

Petrarca, Francesco. *L'Africa.* Ed. Nicholas Festa. Florence: G.C. Sansoni Editore, 1926.

– *L'Afrique/Affrica.* Ed. and trans. with intro. Pierre Laurens. Paris: Belles Lettres, 2006.

– *Canzoniere.* Ed. Marco Santagata. Milan: Mondadori, 2001.

– *Le Familiari.* Ed. Vittorio Rossi. Florence: G.C. Sansoni, 1933.

– *Letters on Familiar Matters (Rerum familiarum libri).* Vol. 3: books XVII–XXIV. Trans. Aldo S. Bernardo. New York: Italica Press, 2005.

– *Petrarch's Africa.* Trans. Thomas Bergin and Alice Wilson. New Haven: Yale UP, 1977.

– *Petrarch's Lyric Poems. The* Rime sparse *and Other Lyrics.*Trans. Robert M. Durling. Cambridge, MA: Harvard UP, 1976.

– *The Revolution of Cola di Rienzo.* Trans. Mario Emilio Cosenza. New York: Italica Press, 1996.

– *Scritti inediti di Francesco Petrarca*. Ed. Attilio Hortis. Trieste: Tipografia del Lloyd Austro-Ungarico, 1874.
– *Triumphi*. Ed. Marco Ariani. Milan: Mursia, 1988.
Plato. *Complete Works*. Ed. with intro. and notes John M. Cooper. Associate ed. D.S. Hutchinson. Indianapolis and Cambridge: Hackett Publishing Company, 1997.
Plutarch. *Lives: Pericles and Fabius Maximus. Nicias and Crassus*. Trans. Bernadotto Perrin. Cambridge, MA: Harvard UP, 1916.
Poliziano, Angelo. *Angeli Politiani liber epigrammatum Graecorum*. Ed. Filippomaria Pontani. Rome: Edizione di storia e letteratura, 2002.
Ronsard, Pierre de. *Les Amours*. Ed. Henri and Catherine Weber. Paris: Classiques Garnier, 1998.
Vergil. *Eclogues. Georgics. Aeneid*, I–VI. Trans. H.R. Fairclough. Cambridge, MA: Harvard UP, 1999.

Secondary Sources

Abulafia, David. *Frederick II: A Medieval Emperor*. London: Allen Lane, Penguin Press, 1988.
Allen, Prudence. *The Concept of Woman. The Early Humanist Reformation, 1250–1550*. 2 vols. Grand Rapids, MI: Wm B. Eerdmans Publishing, 2002.
Anderson, Penelope. "The Absent Female Friend: Recent Studies in Early Modern Women's Friendship." *Literature Compass* 7.4 (April 2010): 243–53.
– *Friendship's Shadows: Women's Friendships and the Politics of Betrayal in England, 1640–1705*. Edinburgh: Edinburgh UP, 2012.
Andreadis, Harriette. "Re-configuring Early Modern Friendship: Katherine Philips and Homoerotic Desire." *Studies in English Literature 1500–1900* 46.3 (2006): 523–42.
Andreani, Veronica. "Gaspara Stampa as Salamander and Phoenix: Reshaping the Tradition of the Abandoned Woman." *Rethinking Gaspara Stampa in the Canon of Renaissance Poetry*. Ed. Unn Falkeid and Aileen A. Feng. Farnham, Surrey: Ashgate, 2015. 171–84
Antoni, Claudio G. "Esperienze stilistiche petrose da Dante e al Petrarca." *Modern Language Studies* 13.2 (Spring 1983): 21–33.
Ascoli, Albert R. *Ariosto's Bitter Harmony: Crisis and Evasion in the Italian Renaissance*. Princeton, NJ: Princeton UP, 1987.
– *A Local Habitation and a Name: Imagining Histories in the Italian Renaissance*. Bronx, NY: Fordham UP, 2011.
Ascoli, Albert R., and Unn Falkeid, eds. *The Cambridge Companion to Petrarch*. Cambridge: Cambridge UP, 2015.

Asmis, Elizabeth. "The Stoics on Women." *Feminism in Ancient Philosophy.* Ed. Julie Ward. New York: Routledge, 1996. 68–94.

Baldacci, Luigi. *Il petrarchismo italiano nel Cinquecento.* 2nd ed. Padua: Livinia, 1974.

Barchiesi, Alessandro. *Speaking Volumes: Narrative and Intertext in Ovid and Other Latin Poets.* London: Duckworth, 2001.

Barkan, Leonard. *The Gods Made Flesh. Metamorphosis and the Pursuit of Paganism.* New Haven, CT: Yale UP, 1986.

Baron, Hans. *The Crisis of the Early Italian Renaissance.* Princeton, NJ: Princeton UP, 1966.

Bellonci, Maria. *Lucrezia Borgia la sua vita e i suoi tempi.* Milan: Mondadori, 1939.

Benedeck, Thomas G. "Belief about Human Sexual Function in the Middle Ages and Renaissance." *Human Sexuality in the Middle Ages and Renaissance.* Ed. Douglas Radcliff-Umstead. Pittsburgh, PA: U of Pittsburgh P, 1978. 97–119.

Benson, Pamela. *The Invention of Renaissance Woman.* University Park: Pennsylvania State UP, 1992.

Benvenuti, Antonia Tissoni. "L'Arrivo di Lucrezia a Ferrara." *Lucrezia Borgia: Storia e mito.* Ed. Michele Bordin and Paolo Trovato. Florence: Leo S. Olschki, 2006. 3–22.

Bernardo, Aldo S. *Petrarch, Scipio, and the Africa: The Birth of Humanism's Dream.* Baltimore, MD: Johns Hopkins UP, 1962.

Bianconi, Giuseppina La Face, and Antonio Rossi. "Sulla diffusione del repertorio strambottistico di fine Quattro- inizio Cinquecento: Premesse e bibliografia." *Schifanoia* X (1990): 129–60.

Billanovich, Giuseppe. "Petrarca e il Ventoso." *Italia medioevale e umanistica* 9 (1966): 389–401.

Biow, Douglas. *Mirabile Dictu: Representations of the Marvelous in Medieval and Renaissance Epic.* Ann Arbor: U of Michigan P, 1996.

Bolzoni, Lina. *Il cuore di cristallo: Ragionamenti d'amore, poesia e ritratto nel Rinascimento.* Saggi 914. Turin: Einaudi, 2010.

Braden, Gordon. "Love and Fame: The Petrarchan Career." *Pragmatism's Freud: The Moral Disposition of Psychoanalysis.* Psychiatry and the Humanities 9. Ed. Joseph H. Smith and William Kerrigan. Baltimore, MD: Johns Hopkins UP, 1986. 126–58.

Branca, Vittore, ed. *Lauro Quirini umanista: Testi e studi a cura di Konrad Krautter, Paul Oskar Kristeller, Agostino Pertusi, Giorgio Ravegnani, Helmut Roob e Carlo Seno.* Florence: Leo S. Olschki, 1977.

Butler, Judith. *Gender Trouble: Feminism and the Subversion of Identity.* 2nd ed. New York: Routledge, 2006.

Casas, Rafel Domínguez. "The Artistic Patronage of Isabel the Catholic: Medieval or Modern?" Trans. Matthew V. Desing. *Queen Isabel I of Castile: Power, Patronage, Persona*. Ed. Barbara F. Weissberger. Woodbridge, Suffolk: Tamesis, 2008. 123–48.

Cassell, Anthony K. *Dante's Fearful Art of Justice*. Toronto: U of Toronto P, 1984.

Catalano, Michele. *Lucrezia Borgia Duchessa di Ferrara*. Ferrara: Taddei, 1920.

Celenza, Christopher. *The Lost Italian Renaissance: Humanists, Historians, and Latin's Legacy*. Baltimore, MD: Johns Hopkins UP, 2004.

Cesarini, Remo. "'Petrarca': Il nome come auto-reinvenzione poetica." *Quaderni Petrarcheschi* 4 (1987): 121–37.

Cestaro, Gary. *Dante and the Grammar of the Nursing Body*. Notre Dame, IN: U of Notre Dame P, 2003.

Chiappelli, Carolyn. "The Motif of Confession in Petrarch's 'Mt. Ventoux.'" *Modern Language Notes* 93.1 (January 1978): 131–6.

Chiodo, Domenico. "Un petrarchismo negletto: L'arengo politico nella lirica cinquecentesca." *Il petrarchismo: Un modello do poesia per l'Europa*. Ed. Loredana Chines. 2 vols. Rome: Bulzoni Editore, 2006. Vol. 2: 293–303.

Churchill, Laurie J., Phyllis R. Brown, and Jane E. Jeffrey, eds. *Women Writing Latin: From Roman Antiquity to Early Modern Europe*, 3 vols. Vol. 3, *Early Modern Women Writing Latin*. New York: Routledge, 2002.

Clough, Cecil H. "Pietro Bembo's *Gli Asolani* of 1505." *Modern Language Notes* 84 (1969): 16–45.

– "The Printing of the First Edition of Pietro Bembo's *Gli Asolani*." *Modern Language Notes* 87 (1972): 134–9.

– "The Problem of Pietro Bembo's *Rime*." *Italica* 41.3 (September 1964): 318–22.

Colilli, Paul. *Petrarch's Allegories of Writing*. Naples: de Dominicis, 1988.

Cornish, Alison. *Vernacular Translation in Dante's Italy: Illiterate Literature*. Cambridge: Cambridge UP, 2011.

Cox, Virginia. "Leonardo Bruni on Women and Rhetoric: *De studiis et litteris* Revisited." *Rhetorica* 27.1 (2009): 47–75.

– *Women's Writing in Italy, 1400–1650*. Baltimore, MD: Johns Hopkins UP, 2008.

Cox, Virginia, and Chiara Ferrari, eds. *Verso una storia di genere della letteratura italiana*. Bologna: Il Mulino, 2012.

Cremonini, Stefano. "Una topica petrarchesca: I versi in morte di amici, colleghi e mecenati." *Il petrarchismo: Un modello di poesia per l'Europa*. Ed. Loredano Chines. 2 vols. Rome: Bulzoni Editore, 2006. Vol. 2: 329–47.

Cretoni, Antonio. "Il Petrarca e i Colonna." *Studi Romani* 8.2 (1 March 1960): 140–54.

Curti, Elisa. "'Le sue lacrime con le mie mescolando': Lacrima amorose tra Boccaccio e Bembo." *Heliotropia* 11.1–2 (2014): 105–19.

D'Amico, John. "Paolo Cortesi's Rehabilitation of Giovanni Pico della Mirandola." *Bibliothèque d'Humanisme et Renaissance* 44 (1982): 37–51.

D'Ascia, Luca. *Erasmo e l'umanesimo romano*. Florence: Olschki, 1991.

De Lauretis, Teresa. *Alice Doesn't. Feminism, Semiotics, Cinema.* Bloomington: Indiana UP, 1984.

De Stefano, Antonino. *La cultura alla corte di Federico II imperatore.* Bologna: Zanichelli, 1950.

DellaNeva, JoAnn. "Poetry, Metamorphosis, and the Laurel: Ovid, Petrarch, and Scève." *French Forum* 7.3 (September 1982): 197–209.

– "Reflecting Lesser Lights: The Imitation of Minor Writers in the Renaissance." *Renaissance Quarterly* 42.3 (Autumn 1989): 449–79.

Della Terza, Dante. "Imitatio: Theory and Practice. The Example of Bembo the Poet." *Yearbook of Italian Studies.* Florence: Casalini Libri, 1971. 1: 119–41.

Dilemmi, Giorgio. "'Andrem di pari': Maria Savorgnan e *Gli Asolani* del Bembo." *Quaderni del Dipartimento di Lingue e Letterature neolatine* 4 (1988–9): 49–72.

Durling, Robert M. "The Ascent of Mt. Ventoux and the Crisis of Allegory." *Italian Quarterly* 18.69 (Summer 1974): 7–28.

– "'Io son venuto': Seneca, Plato, and the Microcosm." *Dante Studies* 93 (1975): 95–129.

– "Petrarch's 'Giovene donna sotto un verde lauro.'" *Modern Language Notes* 86.1 (1971): 1–20.

Durling, Robert M., and Ronald Martinez. *Time and the Crystal: Studies in Dante's Rime petrose.* Berkeley: U of California P, 1990.

Dutschke, Dennis. "The Anniversary Poems in Petrarch's *Canzoniere.*" *Italiaca* 58.2 (Summer 1981): 83–101.

Eisenbichler, Konrad. *The Sword and the Pen: Women, Politics, and Poetry in Sixteenth-Century Siena.* Notre Dame, IN: Indiana UP, 2012.

Enterline, Lynn. "Embodied Voices: Petrarch Reading (Himself Reading) Ovid." *Desire in the Renaissance: Psychoanalysis and Literature*. Ed. Valeria Finucci and Regina Schwartz. Princeton, NJ: Princeton UP, 1994. 120–46.

Feliciangeli, Bernardino. "Notizie sulla vita e sugli scritti di Costanza Varano-Sforza (1426–1447)." *Giornale storico della letteratura italiana* 23 (1894): 1–75.

Feng, Aileen A. "In Laura's Shadow: Casting Female Humanists as Petrarchan Beloveds in Quattrocento Letters." *The Inner Life of Women in Medieval Romance Literature: Grief, Guilt, and Hypocrisy*. Ed. Jeff Rider and Jamie Friedman. New Middle Ages Series. New York: Palgrave MacMillan, 2011. 223–47.

– "'Volto di Medusa': Monumentalizing the Self in Petrarch's *Rerum Vulgarium Fragmenta,*" *Forum Italicum* 47.3 (November 2013): 497–521.

Fenzi, Enrico. "Dall'*Africa* al *Secretum*: Il sogno di Scipione e la composizione del poema." *Saggi Petrarcheschi*. Fiesole: Cadmo, 2003. 305–64.
– "Le rime per la donna Pietra." *Miscellanea di studi danteschi*. Ed. Vincenzo Pernicone. Genoa: Bozzi, 1966. 229–309.
– *Saggi petrarcheschi*. Florence: Cadmo, 2003.
– "Tra Isabella e Lucrezia: Niccolò da Corregio." *Lucrezia Borgia: Storia e mito*. Ed. Michele Bordin and Paolo Trovato. Florence: Leo S. Olschki, 2006. 43–74.
Feo, Michele. "Le 'due redazioni' della *Collatio laureationis*." *Quaderni petrarcheschi* 7 (1990): 186–203.
Fera, Vincenzo. *La revisione petrarchesca dell'Africa*. Messina: Centro di Studi Umanistici, 1984.
Ferrante, Joan. *The Political Vision of the 'Divine Comedy.'* Princeton, NJ: Princeton UP, 1984.
Festa, Nicholas. *Saggio sull'Africa del Petrarca*. Palermo: Sandron, 1926.
Fionotti, Fabio. Review of Carol Kidwell, *Pietro Bembo: Lover, Linguist, Cardinal*. *Renaissance Quarterly* 58.4 (Winter 2005): 1294–6.
Forster, Leonard. *The Icy Fire: Five Studies in European Petrarchism*. Cambridge: Cambridge UP, 1969.
Fortini, Laura. "Itinerari di scrittura: Pietro Bembo e *Gli Asolani*." *La Rassegna della Letteratura Italiana* 88 (1984): 389–98.
Foster, Kenelm. "*Beatrice* or *Medusa*: The Penitential Element in Petrarch's *Canzoniere*." *Italian Studies Presented to E.R. Vincent*. Ed. C.P. Brand, K. Foster, and U. Limentani. Cambridge: W. Heffer and Sons, Ltd, 1962. 41–56.
Freccero, Carla. "Ovidian Subjectivities in Early Modern Lyric: Identification and Desire in Petrarch's *Rime sparse*." *Ovid and the Renaissance Body*. Ed. Boran Stanivukovic. Toronto: U of Toronto P, 2001. 21–37.
Freccero, John. "Dante's Medusa: Allegory and Autobiography." *By Things Seen: Reference and Recognition in Medieval Thought*. Ed. David Jeffrey. Ottawa: U of Ottawa P, 1979. 33–46.
– "Medusa: The Letter and the Spirit." *The Medusa Reader*. Ed. Marjorie Garber and Nancy J. Vickers. New York and London: Routledge, 2003. 109–21.
Galli, Paola Vecchi. "Strambotti anonimi quattrocenteschi da un codice della Colombina di Siviglia." *Studi in onore di Raffaele Spongano*. Bologna: Boni, 1980. 173–93.
Garin, Eugenio. *Italian Humanism: Philosophy and Civic Life in the Renaissance*. Trans. Peter Munz. New York: Harper and Row, 1965.
– *L'educazione in Europa, 1400–1600; Problemi e programmi*. Bari: Laterza, 1966.
Gaylard, Susan. "*De mulieribus claris* and the Disappearance of Women from Illustrated Print Biographies." *I Tatti Studies in the Italian Renaissance* 18.2 (2015): 287–318.

Ghirardo, Diane Yvonne. "Lucrezia Borgia as Entrepreneur." *Renaissance Quarterly* 31.1 (Spring 2008): 53–91.

Gilbert, Sandra M., and Susan Gubar. *The Madwoman in the Attic: The Woman Writer and the Nineteenth-Century Literary Imagination*. New Haven, CT: Yale UP, 1979.

Gill, Amyrose. "Fraught Relations in the Letters of Laura Cereta: Marriage, Friendship, and Humanist Epistolarity." *Renaissance Quarterly* 62.4 (Winter 2009): 1098–1129.

Gilman, Donald. "Petrarch's Sophonisba: Seduction, Sacrifice, and Patriarchal Politics." *Sex and Gender in Medieval and Renaissance Texts. The Latin Tradition.* Ed. Barbara K. Gold, Paul Allen Miller, and Charles Platter. Albany: State U of New York P, 1997. 111–38.

Gothein, Percy. "L'Amicizia fra Lodovico Foscarini e l'Umanista Isotta Nogarola." *La Rinascita* 6 (1943): 394–413.

Gouwens, Kenneth. "Female Virtue and the Embodiment of Beauty: Vittoria Colonna in Paolo Giovio's *Notable Men and Women*." *Renaisance Quarterly* 68.1 (Spring 2015): 33–97.

Grafton, Anthony. *Joseph Scaliger: A Study in the History of Classical Scholarship.* Oxford: Oxford UP, 1983.

Grafton, Anthony, and Lisa Jardine. *From Humanism to the Humanities. Education and the Liberal Arts in Fifteenth- and Sixteenth-Century Europe.* Cambridge, MA: Harvard UP, 1986.

Grayson, Cecil. *A Renaissance Controversy: Latin or Italian?* Oxford: Clarendon Press, 1960.

Grebe, Sabine. "Marriage and Exile: Cicero's Letters to Terentia." *Helios* 30.2 (Fall 2003): 127–46.

Greene, Roland. *Post-Petrarchism.* Princeton, NJ: Princeton UP, 1991.

– *Unrequited Conquests. Love and Empire in the Colonial Americas.* Chicago: U of Chicago P, 1999.

Greene, Thomas. "The Flexibility of the Self in Renaissance Literature." *The Disciplines of Criticism*. Ed. Peter Demetz, Thomas Greene, and Lowry Nelson, Jr. New Haven, CT: Yale UP, 1968. 241–64.

– *The Light in Troy: Imitation and Discovery in Renaissance Poetry.* New Haven, CT: Yale UP, 1982.

Grendler, Paul. *Schooling in the Renaissance. Schooling in Renaissance Italy: Literacy and Learning, 1300–1600.* Baltimore, MD: Johns Hopkins UP, 1991.

Hankins, James. "The 'Baron Thesis' after Forty Years and some Recent Studies of Leonardo Bruni." *Journal of the History of Ideas* 56 (1995): 309–38.

Hardie, Philip. "Ovid into Laura: Absent Presences in the *Metamorphoses* and Petrarch's *Rime sparse*." *Ovidian Transformations: Essays on Ovid's*

Metamorphoses and Its Reception. Ed. Philip Hardie, Alessandro Barchiesi, and Stephen Hinds. Cambridge: Cambridge Philological Society, 1999. 254–70.

Harley, Marta Powell. "Narcissus, Hermaphroditus, and Attis: Ovidian Lovers at the Fontaine d'Amors in Guillaume de Lorris's Roman de la Rose." *PMLA* 101 (1986): 324–37.

Haskins, Charles H. "Latin Literature under Frederick II." *Speculum* 3.2 (1928): 129–51.

Heslin, Peter. *The Transvestite Achilles: Gender and Genre in the Achilleid of Statius*. Cambridge: Cambridge UP, 2005.

Hillman, Larry H. "Another Look into the Mirror Perilous: The Role of the Crystals in the *Roman de la Rose*." *Romania* 101 (1980): 225–38.

Hinds, Stephen. "Medea in Ovid: Scenes from the Life of an Intertextual Heroine." *Materiali e discussione per l'analisi dei testi classici* 30 (1993): 9–47.

Hult, David. "The Allegorical Fountain: Narcissus in the *Roman de la Rose*." *Romance Review* 72 (1981): 125–48.

Humfrey, Peter. "The Portrait in Fifteenth-Century Venice." *The Renaissance Portrait: From Donatello to Bellini*. New York: Metropolitan Museum of Art, 2011. 48–63.

Izora, Scott. *Controversies over the Imitation of Cicero*. New York: Columbia U Teachers' College, 1910; Davis, CA: Hermagoras, 1991.

Jardine, Lisa. "'O decus Italiae virgo', or the Myth of the Learned Lady in the Renaissance." *The Historical Journal* 28.4 (1985): 799–819.

Jones, Ann Rosalind. *The Currency of Eros: Women's Love Lyric in Europe, 1540–1620*. Bloomington: Indiana UP, 1990.

Jones, Ann Rosalind, and Peter Stallybrass. *Renaissance Clothing and the Materials of Memory*. Cambridge: Cambridge UP, 2001.

Jordan, Constance. *Renaissance Feminism. Literary Texts and Political Models*. Ithaca, NY: Cornell UP, 1990.

Kallendorf, Craig. *In Praise of Aeneas: Vergil and Epideictic Rhetoric in the Early Italian Renaissance*. Cambridge, MA: Harvard UP, 1989.

Kelly, Joan. *Women, History, and Theory. The Essays of Joan Kelly*. Chicago: U of Chicago P, 1984.

Kelly, Samantha. *The New Solomon. Robert of Naples (1309–1343) and Fourteenth-Century Kingship*. Leiden: Brill, 2003.

Kennedy, William J. *Authorizing Petrarch*. Ithaca, NY: Cornell UP, 1994.

– "Public Poems, Private Expenditures: Petrarch as Homo Economicus." *Mediaevalia* 32 (2011): 99–121.

– *The Site of Petrarchism: Early Modern National Sentiment in Italy, France, and England*. Baltimore, MD: Johns Hopkins UP, 2003.

Kidwell, Carol. *Pietro Bembo: Lover, Linguist, Cardinal*. Montreal and Kingston: McGill-Queen's UP, 2004.

King, Margaret. "Book-lined Cells: Women and Humanism in the Early Italian Renaissance." *Beyond Their Sex: Learned Women of the European Past*. Ed. Patricia Labalme. New York: New York UP, 1980. 66–90.

– "The Religious Retreat of Isotta Nogarola (1418-1466): Sexism and Its Consequences in the Fifteenth Century." *Signs* 3 (1978): 807–22.

– *Renaissance Humanism: An Anthology of Sources*. Indianapolis: Hackett Publishing Company, 2014.

– *Venetian Humanism in an Age of Patrician Dominance*. Princeton, NJ: Princeton UP, 1986.

– *Women of the Renaissance*. Chicago: U of Chicago P, 1991.

King, Margaret, and Albert Rabil, eds. *Her Immaculate Hand: Selected Works by and about the Women Humanists of Quattrocento Italy*. Binghamton, NY: Center for Medieval and Renaissance Studies, 1982.

Kinoshita, Sharon, and Peggy McCracken. *Marie de France: A Critical Companion*. Woodbridge, Suffolk: Boydell & Brewer, 2012.

Kirkham, Victoria. "Petrarch the Courtier: Five Public Speeches." *Petrarch. A Critical Guide to the Complete Works*. Ed. Victoria Kirkham and Armando Maggi. Chicago: U of Chicago P, 2009. 141–50.

Kirkham, Victoria, and Armando Maggi, eds. *Petrarch. A Critical Guide to the Complete Works*. Chicago: U of Chicago P, 2009.

Klapisch-Zuber, Christiane. *Women, Family, and Ritual in Renaissance Italy*. Trans. L.G. Cochrane. Chicago: U of Chicago P, 1985.

Kolsky, Stephen. *The Ghost of Boccaccio: Writings on Famous Women in Renaissance Italy*. Turnhout: Brepols, 2005.

Lakoff, Robin. *Language and Woman's Place*. New York: Harper and Row, 1975.

Laqueur, Thomas. *Making Sex: Body and Gender from the Greeks to Freud*. Cambridge, MA: Harvard UP, 1990.

Larson, Katherine R. *Early Modern Women in Conversation*. Basingstoke, Hants: Palgrave Macmillan, 2011.

Lehfeldt, Elizabeth. "Ruling Sexuality: The Political Legitimacy of Isabel of Castile." *Renaissance Quarterly* 53.1 (Spring 2000): 31–56.

Looney, Dennis. "The Beginning of Humanistic Oratory: Petrarch's *Coronation Oration* (*Collatio laureationis*)." *Petrarch. A Critical Guide to the Complete Works*. Ed. Victoria Kirkham and Armando Maggi. Chicago: U of Chicago P, 2009. 131–40.

Lord, Mary Louise. "Petrarch and Vergil's First Eclogue: The Codex Ambrosianus." *Harvard Studies in Classical Philology* 86 (1982): 253–76.

McLaughlin, Martin L. *Literary Imitation in the Italian Renaissance: The Theory and Practice of Literary Imitation from Dante to Bembo*. Oxford: Clarendon P, 1995.

Maclean, Ian. *The Renaissance Notion of Woman*. Cambridge: Cambridge UP, 1980.

Mallette, Karla. *The Kingdom of Sicily, 1100–1250: A Literary History*. Philadelphia: U of Pennsylvania P, 2005.

Marchese, Simone. "Petrarch's Philological Epic. *Africa*." *Petrarch. A Critical Guide to the Complete Works*. Ed. Victoria Kirkham and Armando Maggi. Chicago: U of Chicago P, 2009. 113–30.

Martinez, Ronald L. "The Latin Hexameter Works: *Epystole, Bucolicum carmen, Africa*." *The Cambridge Companion to Petrarch*. Ed. Albert R. Ascoli and Unn Falkeid. Cambridge: Cambridge UP, 2015. 87–99.

Marzocco, Angelo. *Linguistic Theories in Dante and the Humanists. Studies of Language and Intellectual History in Late Medieval and Early Renaissance Italy*. Leiden: Brill, 1993.

Mazzacurati, Giancarlo. *La questione della lingua dal Bembo all'Accademia Fiorentina*. Naples: Liguori, 1965.

Mazzotta, Giuseppe. *Dante, Poet of the Desert: History and Allegory in the 'Divine Comedy.'* Princeton, NJ: Princeton UP, 1979.

– *The Worlds of Petrarch*. Durham and London: Duke UP, 1993.

Migraine-George, Thérèse. "Specular Desires: Orpheus and Pygmalion as Aesthetic Paradigms in Petrarch's *Rime sparse*." *Comparative Literature Studies* 36.3 (1999): 226–46.

Murphy, James J. *Renaissance Eloquence: Studies in the Theory and Practice of Renaissance Rhetoric*. Berkeley: U of California P, 1983.

Navarette, Ignacio. *Orphans of Petrarch: Poetry and Theory in the Spanish Renaissance*. Berkeley, CA: U of California P, 1994.

Nolhac, Pierre de. *Pétrarque et l'humanisme*. 2 vols. Paris: Champion, 1907.

Olschki, Leonardo. "Dante and Petrus de Vinea." *Romanic Review* 31 (1940): 105–11.

Osborne, John. "A Possible Colonna Family 'Stemma' in the Church of Santa Prassede, Rome." *A Wider Trecento: Studies in 13th- and 14th-century European Art Presented to Julian Gardner*. Ed. Louise Bourdua and Robert Gibbs. Leiden: Brill, 2012. 21–30.

Paris, Gaston. "Études sur les romans de la Table Ronde: Lancelot du Lac." *Romania* 12 (1883): 459–534.

Parker, Holt. "Angela Nogarola (ca. 1400) and Isotta Nogarola (1418-1466): Thieves of Language." *Women Writing Latin: From Roman Antiquity to Early*

Modern Europe. Vol. 3: *Early Modern Women Writing Latin.* Ed. Laurie J. Churchill, Phyllis R. Brown, and Jane E. Jeffrey. New York: Routledge, 2002. 11–30.

– "Costanza Varano (1426–1447): Latin as an Instrument of the State." *Women Writing Latin: From Roman Antiquity to Early Modern Europe.* Vol. 3: *Early Modern Women Writing Latin.* Ed. Laurie J. Churchill, Phyllis R. Brown, and Jane E. Jeffrey. New York: Routledge, 2002. 31–53.

– "Latin and Greek Poetry by Five Renaissance Italian Women Humanists." *Sex and Gender in Medieval and Renaissance Texts.* Ed. Barbara K. Gold, Paul Allen Miller, and Charles Platter. Albany: State U of New York P, 1997. 247–85.

– "Women and Humanism: Nine Factors for the Woman Learning." *Viator* 35 (2004): 581–616.

Patterson, Annabel. *Pastoral and Ideology: Vergil to Valéry.* Berkeley: U of California P, 1987.

Pesenti, Giovanni. "Alessandra Scala: Una figurina della rinascenza fiorentina." *Giornale Storico della Letteratura Italiana* 85 (1925): 241–67.

– "Lettere inedite del Poliziano." *Athenaeum* 3 (1915): 284–304.

Pigman, George W. "Imitation and the Renaissance Sense of the Past: The Reception of Erasmus' *Ciceronianus.*" *Journal of Medieval and Renaissance Studies* 9 (1979): 155–77.

– "Versions of Imitation in the Renaissance." *Renaissance Quarterly* 33 (1980): 1–32.

Pomilio, Mario. "Una fonte italiana del *Ciceronianus* di Erasmo." *Giornale italiano di filologia* 8 (1955): 193–207.

Pozzi, Mario. "Andrem di pari all'amorosa face: Appunti sulle lettere di Maria Savorgnan." *Les femmes écrivains en Italie au Moyen Âge et à la Renaissance. Acte du colloque international, Aix-en-Provence, 12–14 novembre 1992.* Aix-en-Provence: Publications de l'Université de Provence, 1994. 87–101.

Prizer, William F. "Isabella d'Este and Lucrezia Borgia as Patrons of Music: The Frottola at Mantua and Ferrara." *Journal of the American Musicological Society* 38.1 (Spring 1985): 1–33.

Quaglio, Antonio Enzo. "Intorno a Maria Savorgnan. I. Per una riedizione delle lettere." *Quaderni Utinensi* 5–6 (1985): 103–18.

– "Intorno a Maria Savorgnan. II. Un 'sidio' d'amore." *Quaderni Utinensi* 7–8 (1986): 77– 101.

Quaintance, Courtney. *Textual Masculinity and the Exchange of Women in Renaissance Venice.* Toronto: U of Toronto P, 2015.

Quilligan, Maureen. *The Allegory of Female Authority. Christine de Pizan's Cité des Dames.* Ithaca, NY: Cornell UP, 1991.

Rabil, Albert, Jr. "The Significance of 'Civic Humanism' in the Interpretation of the Italian Renaissance." *Renaissance Humanism: Foundations, Forms, and Legacy*. Ed. Albert Rabil, Jr. Philadelphia: U of Pennsylvania P, 1988. 1: 141–74.

Rabin, Lisa. "Speaking to Silent Ladies: Images of Beauty and Politics in Poetic Portraits of Women from Petrarch to Sor Juana Inés de la Cruz." *Modern Language Notes* 112.2 (March 1997): 147–65.

Rajna, Pio. "I versi spagnoli di mano di Pietro Bembo e di Lucrezia Borgia serbati da un codice ambrosiano." *Homenaje Ofrecido a Menéndez Pidal: Miscelánea de estudios lingüísticos, literarios e históricos*. Madrid: Hernando, 1925. 2: 299–321.

Ratti, Achille. "Ancora del celebre codice manoscritto della opera di Vergilio già di Francesco Petrarca ed ora alla Biblioteca Ambrosiana." *Francesco Petrarca e la Lombardia*. Ed. Società Storica Lombarda. Milan: Hoepli, 1904. 217-42.

Ray, Meredith K. *Writing Gender in Women's Letters Collections of the Italian Renaissance*. Toronto: U of Toronto P, 2009.

Richardson, Brian. "From Scribal Publication to Print Publication: Pietro Bembo's *Rime*, 1529–1535." *Modern Language Review* 95.3 (July 2000): 684–95.

Richter, George Martin. "A Portrait of a Lady by Giovanni Bellini." *The Burlington Magazine for Connoisseurs* 69.400 (July 1936): 2–5.

Robin, Diana. "Cassandra Fedele's *Epistolae* (1488-1521): Biography as Effacement." *The Rhetoric of Life-Writing in the Renaissance*. Ed. Thomas Mayer and Tom Woolf. Ann Arbor: U of Michigan P, 1994. 187–203.

– *Publishing Women: Salons, the Presses, and the Counter-Reformation in Sixteenth-Century Italy*. Chicago: U of Chicago P, 2007.

– "Space, Woman, and Renaissance Discourse." *Sex and Gender in Medieval and Renaissance Texts: The Latin Tradition*. Ed. Barbara K. Gold, Paul Allen Miller, and Charles Platter. Albany: State U of New York P, 1997. 165–88.

Ross, Sarah G. *The Birth of Feminism: Woman as Intellect in Renaissance Italy and England*. Cambridge, MA: Harvard UP, 2009.

Rowlands, John. "Simone Martini and Petrarch: A Vergilian Episode." *Apollo* 81 (1965): 264–9.

Rubenstein, Nicolai. *Lucrezia Borgia*. Rome: Istituto della Enciclopedia Italiana, 1971.

Russo, Mauda Bregoli. *Letterati a corte: Ferrara, Firenze, Mantova*. Naples: Loffredo, 2004.

Sabbadini, Remigio. *Storia del Ciceronianismo e di altre questioni letterarie dell'età della Rinascenza*. Turin: Loescher, 1885.

Sabattino, Pasquale. *L'idioma volgare: Il dibattito sulla lingua letteraria nel Rinascimento*. Rome: Bulzoni, 1995.

Sanson, Helena. *Women, Language and Grammar: Italy 1500–1900*. Oxford and London: Oxford UP for the British Academy, 2011.

Sansone, Mario, and Francesco Tateo. *Da Bembo a Galiani. Il dibattito sulla lingua in Italia.* Bari: Adriatica, 1999.

Santagata, Marco. *I frammenti nell'anima. Storia e racconto nel* Canzoniere *di Petrarca.* Bologna: Il Mulino, 2011.

Scaglione, Aldo. "Classical Heritage and Petrarchan Self-Consciousness in the Literary Emergence of the Interior 'I.'" *Petrarch*. Ed. Harold Bloom. New York and Philadelphia: Chelsea House Publishers, 1989. 125–37.

Scarpa, Emanuela. "Qualche proposta (e qualche ipotesi) per i primi *Asolani*." *Studi di Filologia Italiana* 52 (1994): 93–109.

Schibanoff, Susan. "Botticelli's *Madonna del Magnificat:* Constructing the Woman Writer in Early Humanist Italy." *PMLA* 109 (1994): 190–206.

Segarizzi, Arnaldo. "Niccolò Barbo patrizio veneziano del sec. XV e le accuse contro Isotta Nogarola." *Giornale storico della letteratura italiana* 43 (1904): 39–54.

Seifert, Lewis C., and Rebecca M.Wilkin. *Men and Women Making Friends in Early Modern France.* Farnham, Surrey, and Burlington, VT: Ashgate, 2015.

Seigel, Jerrold E. "'Civic Humanism' or Ciceronian Rhetoric? The Culture of Petrarch and Bruni." *Past and Present* 34 (1966): 3–48.

Shafer, Keith A. "The Eclectic Style in Theory and Practice in Angelo Poliziano's Ep. VIII.16." *In Laudem Caroli: Renaissance and Reformation Studies for Charles G. Naurert*. Ed. James V. Mehl. *Sixteenth Century Essays and Studies* 49. Kirksville, MO: Thomas Jefferson UP, 1998. 23–33.

Shemek, Deanna. *Ladies Errant: Wayward Women and Social Order in Early Modern Italy.* Durham, NC: Duke UP, 1998.

Signorini, Stefania. "Da Maria a Lucrezia. Su due rime giovanili di Pietro Bembo." *Italique* 6 (2003): 55–76.

Simonetta, Marcello. *Rinascimento segreto: Il mondo del segretario da Petrarca a Machiavelli.* Milan: Franco Angeli, 2004.

Skinner, Quentin. *The Foundations of Modern Political Thought.* Vol. 1. Cambridge: Cambridge UP, 1978.

Smarr, Janet L. *Joining the Conversation: Dialogues by Renaissance Women.* Ann Arbor: U of Michigan P, 2005.

Spitzer, Leo. "Speech and Language in *Inferno* XIII." *Italica* 19.3 (1942): 81–104.

Stephany, William A. "Pier della Vigna's Self-Fulfilling Prophecies: The 'Eulogy' of Frederick II and *Inferno* 13." *Traditio* 38 (1982–3): 193–212.

Stevenson, Jane. *Women Latin Poets: Language, Gender, and Authority from Antiquity to the Eighteenth Century.* New York: Oxford UP, 2005.

Stroup, Sarah Culpepper. *Catullus, Cicero, and a Society of Patrons: The Generation of the Text*. Cambridge: Cambridge UP, 2010.

Sturm-Maddox, Sara. "'La pianta più gradita in cielo': Petrarch's Laurel and Jove." *Dante, Petrarch, and Boccaccio: Studies in the Italian Trecento in Honor of Charles S. Singleton*. Ed. Aldo Barnardo and Anthony Pellegrini. Medieval and Renaissance Texts and Studies, vol. 22. Binghamton, NY: State U of New York P, 1983. 255–71.

– *Petrarch's Laurels*. University Park: Pennsylvania State UP, 1992.

Trinkaus, Charles E. *In Our Image and Likeness: Humanity and Divinity in Italian Humanist Thought*. Chicago: U of Chicago P, 1970.

Tylus, Jane. *Writing and Vulnerability in the Late Renaissance*. Stanford, CA: Stanford UP, 1993.

Velli, Giuseppe. "Il proemio dell'*Africa*." *Italia medioevale e umanistica* 8 (1965): 323–32.

Vickers, Nancy. "Diana Described: Scattered Woman and Scattered Rhyme." *Critical Inquiry* 8.2 (Winter 1981): 265–79.

Vitale, Maurizio. *La questione della lingua*. Palermo: Palumbo, 1984.

Vollendorf, Lisa. "The Value of Female Friendship in Seventeenth-Century Spain." *Texas Studies in Literature and Language* (issue on The Culture of Early Modern Friendship) 47.4 (Winter 2005): 425–45.

Wallace, David. *Chaucerian Polity: Absolutist Lineages and Associational Forms in England and Italy*. Stanford, CA: Stanford UP, 1997.

Westwater, Lynn Lara. "The Uncollected Poet (*Lettere disperse*)." *Petrarch. A Critical Guide to the Complete Works*. Ed. Victoria Kirkham and Armando Maggi. Chicago: U of Chicago P, 2009. 301–8.

Whittington, Leah. *Renaissance Suppliants. Poetry, Antiquity, Reconciliation*. Oxford: Oxford UP, 2016.

Wider, Kathleen. "Women Philosophers in the Ancient Greek World: Donning the Mantle." *Hypatia* 1.1 (Spring 1986): 21–62.

Wiesner-Hanks, Merry. *Women and Gender in Early Modern Europe*. 3rd ed. Cambridge: Cambridge UP, 2008.

Wilkins, Ernst Hatch. *Life of Petrarch*. Chicago: U of Chicago P, 1963.

– *Petrarch's Eight Years in Milan*. Cambridge, MA: The Mediaeval Academy of America, 1958.

– *Studies in the Life and Works of Petrarch*. Cambridge, MA: The Mediaeval Academy of America, 1955.

Witt, Ronald. *In the Footsteps of Ancients: The Origins of Humanism from Lovato to Bruni*. Leiden: Brill, 2000.

Wojciehowski, Hannah (Dolora). *Old Masters, New Subjects: Early Modern and Poststructuralist Theories of Will*. Stanford, CA: Stanford UP, 1995.

Woodford, William Harrison. *Vittorino da Feltro and Other Humanist Educators.* Cambridge: Cambridge UP, 1897.

Zak, Gur. *Petrarch's Humanism and the Care of the Self.* Cambridge: Cambridge UP, 2010.

Zanato, Tiziano. "Indagini sulle rime di Pietro Bembo." *Studi di Filologia Italiana* 60 (2002): 141–216.

Zancan, Marina. "L'intellettualità femminile nel primo Cinquecento: Maria Savorgnan e Gaspara Stampa." *Annali d'Italianistica* 7 (1989):42–65.

Zappi, Roberto. "Chi era Maria Savorgnan?" *Studi veneziani* 49 (2005): 281–3.

Index

www.ingramcontent.com/pod-product-compliance
Lightning Source LLC
LaVergne TN
LVHW090154080826
844660LV00013B/804/J

* 9 7 8 1 4 8 7 5 0 0 7 7 1 *